The U.S. Health Workforce

Power, Politics, and Policy

Marian Osterweis
Christopher J. McLaughlin
Henri R. Manasse, Jr.
Cornelius L. Hopper
Editors

*with introductory papers by
economist Uwe E. Reinhardt
and
ethicist Dan W. Brock*

AHC
ASSOCIATION OF
ACADEMIC
HEALTH
CENTERS

The Association of Academic Health Centers (AHC) is a national, nonprofit organization comprising more than 100 institutional members in the United States and Canada that are the health complexes of the major universities of these nations. Academic health centers consist of an allopathic or osteopathic school of medicine, at least one other health professions school or program, and one or more teaching hospitals. These institutions are the primary resources for education in the health professions, biomedical and health services research, and many aspects of patient care services.

The AHC seeks to influence public dialogue on significant health and science policy issues, to advance education for health professionals, to promote biomedical and health services research, and to enhance patient care.

The views expressed in this book are those of its authors and do not necessarily represent the views of the Board of Directors of the Association of Academic Health Centers or the membership at large.

Library of Congress Cataloging-in-Publication Data

The U.S. health workforce : power, politics, and policy / Marian
    Osterweis . . . [et al.], editors.
        p.   cm.
    Includes bibliographical references.
    ISBN 1-879694-11-5
    1. Medical personnel—United States. 2. Medical personnel—United
States—Forecasting. 3. Medical personnel—United States—Supply
and demand. 4. Medical policy—United States. 5. Medical
personnel—Education—United States.   I. Osterweis, Marian.
RA410.7.U2   1996
331.11'913621'0973—dc20   95-51479
                                                        CIP

Copies of this book may be obtained from:
Association of Academic Health Centers
1400 Sixteenth Street, NW
Suite 720
Washington, DC 20036
202-265-9600   Fax: 202-265-7514

Price: $25.00

Design and production by Fletcher Design, Washington, DC

Cover photos by (clockwise, from top): Custom Medical Stock Photo; Uniphoto Picture Agency, Uniphoto Picture Agency, Uniphoto Picture Agency, Michael Fisher/Custom Medical Stock Photo, Uniphoto Picture Agency, Jose L. Pelaez/The Stock Market.

Preface

The papers in this book were commissioned by the Association of Academic Health Centers (AHC) during 1994 and 1995 for the AHC/Josiah Macy, Jr. Foundation Health Workforce Policy Project and the 1995 Annual Meeting of the AHC. Making up a unique contribution to the workforce policy literature, the collection is the only publication available that examines all levels of policy making and all of the health professions that make up the health workforce. The editors have made every effort to preserve each author's unique style.

The AHC is a national, nonprofit association of more than 100 of the health professions education, research, and clinical service complexes within the universities of the United States and Canada. For the past twenty-five years, one of its primary interests has been the education of the entire health workforce. This interest reflects the broad scope of educational responsibility embodied in these institutions and the concerns of the chief executive officers who are the representatives to the association.

Health workforce policies are formulated by many players: the Federal government, the states, the health care marketplace, the health professions, and educational institutions. These policies are put in place to influence the size, character, and distribution of the health workforce, either directly or indirectly. They range from health services reimbursement to student assistance, from incentives to increase the size of educational programs to incentives to change professional curricula, from state regulation and licensure of the professions to the self-determination of professional roles, from lobbying efforts by professional organizations to staffing decisions by provider organizations.

In the absence of comprehensive national reform, the years immediately ahead are likely to bring continued rapid change in the organization and financing of health care—a reform, driven in large part by a cost-conscious, competitive health care market. Reform driven by market forces is often unpredictable, chaotic, and painful for those producers and users of goods and services unable to adapt in time. Everyone involved in some way with the health workforce and the services it produces faces uncertainty as the health care system undergoes these changes. Concerned groups include the health professionals themselves and the patients they serve, legislators and other policy makers who influence workforce composition, health professions educators and their students, health care delivery organizations, and the government and foundations who help fund health professions education.

No one knows what the future holds, but broad, market-based trends in the health workforce make it clear that, before long, the *status quo ante* will be only a fond memory for many of the health professions. Furthermore, as large-scale aggregation of health care delivery arrangements continues, a major workforce policy question arises: Will the market or will professional standards determine the future roles of the health professions and the resulting demand for their services?

The market view of health care is dominated by economic theory. Thus, price and informed choice by the patient are major factors in determining demand for health services. Competition among health plans and among substitutable providers considers price, too, and also pays attention to objective data on care outcomes and patient satisfaction. Decentralized decision making about health care arrangements, resources, and the roles of the various health professionals, is encouraged.

The professional view of health care emphasizes the importance of proper preparation for professional practice and the acquisition of expert knowledge. Rather than demand for services, the information provided by epidemiological data is the major factor for determining the need for health services. National norms greatly influence standards for individual professional practice, while health professions education instills in students a commitment to autonomous decisions and each profession emphasizes its ability to define its own role in the care process. The large number of health professions, in turn, produces opportunities for professional conflict over roles, especially when the roles overlap; these "turf battles" can create barriers to reconfiguration of health care processes in the interest of efficiency and effectiveness.

Resolving the conflict between the market and professional views is not likely to be a stark "either-or" choice. As reflected in many of the papers in this book, both views are so powerful that continuing controversy is almost certain. Its resolution will be critical to the development of the health workforce, for it is unclear if meaningful workforce policy making can be attempted as long as the clash of views remains unresolved.

This book is divided into eight sections. The two papers in the introductory section set the stage for thinking about the issues. The contributors to the next half-dozen sections in the collection identify both the roles and responsibilities of the parties involved with health care policymaking in the United States. The paper in the final section develops an analytical framework for examining the processes of health workforce policymaking and recommends ways to improve and coordinate these processes.

The editors thank the authors for their fine contributions, particularly Dr. Reinhardt for his excitement about the papers as they were being developed for publication and his interest in preparing an introductory piece. We also thank Joan Durgin for her service in preparing the manuscripts, Richard Fletcher for his design and production expertise, and Shirley Sirota Rosenberg and her staff at SSR, Incorporated, for tremendous assistance in the entire editing process. The members of the AHC Task Force on Human Resources for Health also deserve thanks for their enthusiastic participation and insightful comments during the three workshops of the workforce policy project where these issues were analyzed and debated.

This book is also the result of the generosity of many sources: The Josiah Macy, Jr. Foundation, the U.S. Health Resources and Services Administration of the Public Health Service, The FHP Foundation, and the Kaludis Consulting Group. We are particularly indebted to Thomas H. Meikle, Jr., M.D., president of The Josiah Macy, Jr. Foundation for his support of the AHC workforce policy project. Dr. Meikle is retiring from the Foundation in the summer of 1996 and we dedicate this book to him in recognition of his steadfast support of AHC initiatives over the past eight years.

M.O.
C.J.M.
H.R.M.
C.L.H.

Contents

Roles of the Market

Contributors

Michael Ashley-Miller, MD, is the secretary of The Nuffield Provincial Hospitals Trust in London.

Harvey Barkun, MD, is a consultant and a former executive director of the Association of Canadian Medical Colleges in Ottawa.

Geraldine D. Bednash, PhD, RN, FAAN, is executive director of the American Association of Colleges of Nursing in Washington, DC.

Dan W. Brock, PhD, is professor of philosophy at Brown University in Providence, Rhode Island.

Eli Capilouto, DMD, ScD, is interim dean and associate professor of the School of Public Health of the University of Alabama at Birmingham.

James F. Cawley, MPH, PA-C, is associate professor of health care sciences at The George Washington University Medical Center in Washington, DC.

C. Donald Combs, PhD, is vice president for planning and program development at Eastern Virginia Medical School in Norfolk, Virginia.

Kathleen Cooney, RN, MBA, is vice president for clinic operations of HealthPartners, Inc. in Minneapolis.

Jerry Cromwell, PhD, is president of Health Economics Research, Inc., in Waltham, Massachusetts.

Richard J. Davidson, EdD, is president of the American Hospital Association in Washington, DC.

Catherine Dower, JD, is health law and policy analyst at the Center for Health Professions at the University of California, San Francisco.

Leonard Finocchio, MPH, is associate director at the Center for the Health Professions at the University of California, San Francisco.

Daniel M. Fox, PhD, is president of the Milbank Memorial Fund in New York City.

Vincent A. Fulginiti, MD, is chancellor of the University of Colorado Health Sciences Center in Denver.

Sandy Gamliel is deputy chief of the Workforce Analysis and Research Branch in the Bureau of Health Professions, Health Resources and Services Administration, U.S. Department of Health and Human Services in Rockville, Maryland.

Ruth S. Hanft, PhD, is a health policy consultant in Alexandria, Virginia.

Cornelius L. Hopper, MD, is vice president for health affairs of the University of California in Oakland.

Stephen A. Horan, PhD, is senior health policy analyst at the Joint Commission of Health Care of the Commonwealth of Virginia in Richmond.

Judy C. Kany, MPA, is project director for health professions regulation of Medical Care Development in Augusta, Maine.

David A. Kindig, MD, PhD, is director of the health policy program in the School of Medicine at the University of Wisconsin-Madison.

Henri R. Manasse Jr., PhD, is vice president for health sciences of The University of Iowa in Iowa City.

Bernard J. Mansheim, MD, is president and chief executive officer of HealthSpring, Inc., and senior vice president of MetraHealth in Reston, Virginia.

David G. Marker, PhD, is president of the University of Osteopathic Medicine and Health Sciences in Des Moines, Iowa.

Christopher J. McLaughlin is program associate of the Association of Academic Health Centers in Washington, DC.

R. Michael Morse, MD, is director of the Virginia Center for the Advancement of Generalist Medicine in Charlottesville.

Robert Ohsfeldt, PhD, is associate professor in the School of Public Health of the University of Alabama at Birmingham.

Edward H. O'Neil, PhD, is associate professor and executive director of the Center for the Health Professions at the University of California, San Francisco.

Marian Osterweis, PhD, is senior vice president of the Association of Academic Health Centers in Washington, DC.

Uwe E. Reinhardt, PhD, is the James Madison Professor of Political Economy at the Woodrow Wilson School of Public and International Affairs of Princeton University in Princeton, New Jersey.

Leonard L. Ross, PhD, is provost of the Medical College of Pennsylvania and Hahnemann University in Philadelphia.

Neal A. Vanselow, MD, is professor of medicine and adjunct professor of health systems management at Tulane University Medical Center in New Orleans.

C. Edwin Webb, PharmD, MPH, is director of government affairs and health policy at the American Association of Colleges of Pharmacy in Alexandria, Virginia.

Jonathan P. Weiner, DrPH, is professor of health policy and management in the School of Hygiene and Public Health at the Johns Hopkins University in Baltimore.

Carol S. Weissert, PhD, is associate professor of political science at Michigan State University in East Lansing.

Karl D. Yordy is study director at the Institute of Medicine and visiting professor at the University of Arizona in Tucson.

Setting the Stage

Workforce policies determine the number, character, and distribution of the health professionals who tend to the nation's health. Two introductory papers provide different perspectives on such policy decisions from the points of view of economics and ethics. Together, they illustrate the importance of health workforce policy to the quality of life of all Americans.

The Economic and Moral Case for Letting the Market Determine the Health Workforce

UWE E. REINHARDT

The invitation to write an introductory paper for this book is a privilege, albeit daunting. It is a privilege to deposit one's two cents worth on health-workforce policy ahead of the accomplished group of authors who follow. The question is what further insights might be added to this far-ranging set of essays.

Perhaps it can be useful to step back from these thoughtful papers to revisit two overarching questions intrinsic to many of the papers in this book. First, precisely how ought we to define a *surplus* or a *deficit* of a particular type of health professional at the conceptual level? Second, to what extent and how should the coercive power of government be enlisted to address perceived imbalances in the health workforce and to assure the quality of that workforce?

I ruminate on these questions, which I feel have a moral character, hoping that the discussion will echo in readers' minds as they work through the book. In a nutshell, I argue that traditional notions of *surpluses* and *shortages* of particular health professionals are seriously misguided, as are the workforce policies that have emanated from them. Furthermore, the case for an interventionist public policy on the health workforce strikes me as weaker than seems widely supposed. It is time to entrust much of that policy to the free play of market forces.

Defining a Surplus or Deficit of Health Professionals

On the surface, ascertaining whether there will be a surplus or deficit of a particular type of health professional at some time seems deceptively simple.

First, one projects the sociodemographic composition of a population to be served. Second, clinical experts are engaged to predict the morbidity likely to be prevalent among that projected population. Third, an attempt is made to quantify the set of medical interventions deemed appropriate for the projected morbidity pattern. Fourth, the projected set of "needed" interventions is translated into a corresponding set of "needed" health professionals, typically on the assumption that there exists an ideal fixed ratio between the two.

All of these steps appear purely objective—scientific, even. The famous, some would say "infamous" (Reinhardt 1981), report of the Graduate Medical Education National Advisory Committee (1980) is the classical example of this "scientific" approach. Osterweis and McLaughlin in this book wisely warn the reader against this simplistic approach. They do so in two important recommendations, as follows:

1. Because the [health] workforce issues of supply, demand, and professional roles are so intertwined, the policy formulation process should explicitly consider those interactions.
2. [Health workforce] policies should take into account the substitutable and complementary roles of multiple professions to make the best and most efficient use of the available workforce and to simultaneously promote cost control, quality, and access.

Discussions on health workforce policy in the past have abstracted unduly from these two injunctions, which may explain the rather checkered history of that policy.*

Economic Perspectives

First, empirical research in health economics has shown consistently that the producers of health care have considerable latitude in the composition of the input mix used to produce given types of health services. This is true for both inpatient and ambulatory care. The various tasks going into the response to particular illnesses can be flexibly assigned to a variety of different health care facilities and to different types of health professionals within each facility.

Furthermore, modern technology constantly opens up new possibilities to substitute capital inputs for human labor (e.g., superior diagnostic equip-

---

* In a review and critique of this policy, see the Fox paper in this book and Reinhardt (1991, pp. 234–83).

ment of computer-based monitoring systems). Under these circumstances, one would be hard put to identify the *ideal* physician or nurse to population ratio for this country, even for the current year, let alone for a period five to ten years hence, as so many workforce models attempt to do.

Second, because there is considerable flexibility in the assignment of tasks to the various health professions, it is reasonable to assume that the particular staffing patterns employed by health facilities are sensitive to the relative costliness of particular types of health professionals. For example, if the cost of physician time rises relative to the time of physician assistants, an efficient health-care facility will delegate tasks that traditionally have been performed by physicians to physician assistants. On the other hand, if the cost of physician time falls relative to that of physician assistants, then it may be efficient to move toward more physician-intensive treatment methods.

It is reasonable to assume that the future American health system will be dominated by integrated delivery systems that receive their revenue up front in the form of competitively bid, annual capitation payments. These health systems must act like giant cost centers whose net income depends on their ability to operate efficiently. In their quest for efficiency, these systems are likely to be quite sensitive to the relative cost of different types of health professionals in determining their staffing patterns.

It is not surprising that, at this time, these staffing patterns still vary so much across systems and across regions within the United States. For one, the quest for efficiency in American health care is as yet quite novel. Considerable experimentation with alternative staffing patterns will occur before the systems have groped their way towards the economically most efficient and clinically effective staffing pattern. Second, the relative incomes of various health professionals do vary across regions, so that even in the long run we should expect some variance in staffing patterns across regions.

It follows from the preceding observations that, for any type of health professional, there must exist a traditional, downward sloping demand curve according to which the number of those professionals "needed" or "demanded" by society varies inversely with the annual income paid those professionals. In that respect, even educated human labor really does not differ all that much from apples and bagels. Those who find this philistine thought offensive might look to the newly emerging integrated health systems that understand this fundamental Law of Demand only too well and are actively teaching it now to the nation's physicians.

The preceding discussion also leads one to wonder how anyone can possibly purport to project a future shortage or surplus for a particular type of health professional without assuming something explicitly about the relative future incomes of the various health professionals that can act as substitutes for one another. Indeed, this question leads to the following bold proposition, namely: *Anyone who asserts that there now is a surplus of a particular type of health professional is also asserting implicitly that these professionals are being overpaid relative to the incomes they would have to be paid to assure society of an adequate supply of these professionals.*

The Market Model

Figure 1 is the simple demand-and-supply framework that is the staple of freshman economics. Suppose the line labeled DD in the diagram represents the aggregate national demand for full-time employed (FTE) physicians at alternative levels of physician income. The shape of that curve represents the previously offered hypothesis that the demand for physicians by capitated health plans will be likely to be quite sensitive to the incomes they need to pay physicians. Next, suppose the curve labeled SS represents the number of FTE physicians willing to be active in patient care at alternative levels of physician income. It is surely not offensive to assume that this curve slopes upward to the right. Incorporated into this diagram is the idea that there must exist a level of physician income that clears the market, leaving neither a physician surplus nor a shortage. Alas, at this time it is anyone's guess just what that level of income might be.

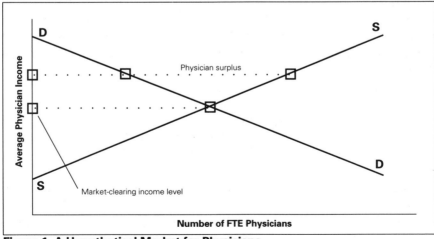

Figure 1. A Hypothetical Market for Physicians

Figure 1 makes graphic the previously stated proposition that to assert the existence of a physician surplus is tantamount to asserting that physician incomes are higher than they need be to attract an adequate number of physicians into practice. Figure 1 also illustrates that anyone who proposes to eliminate an existing or projected physician surplus through artificial limits of entry into the medical profession is *ipso facto* advocating that average physician incomes be shored up artificially, above the market-clearing level needed to attract the "right" number of physicians into medical practice. The proposition seems on par with the posture routinely adopted by unions of law enforcement officers or firefighters who bestow relatively high wages on those lucky enough to find entry into these activities but who, in the process, also create long queues of hopeful applicants for these activities.

DEVIATIONS FROM THE MARKET MODEL

Are there persuasive reasons peculiar to the medical profession for shoring up physician incomes in this way? Perhaps there are. It might be argued, for example, that the education and training of physicians pushes many young physicians deeply into debt and that they "need" ample incomes to amortize that debt. The argument has surface appeal, although no more so here than it would in the case of lawyers or, indeed, of anyone making debt-financed investments in their education or business.

It might further be argued, however, that severely depressed physician incomes might trigger depressive reactions among physicians, or at least lower their morale sufficiently to impair the quality of their services. Others might hold that such low incomes might jeopardize the trust patients can have in their physicians. On this point one might cite none other than Adam Smith, the father of modern economics, who remarked in *The Wealth of Nations*:

> We trust our health to the physician; our fortune and sometimes our life to the reputation of the lawyer and attorney. Such confidence could not safely be reposed in people of a very mean or low condition. Their reward must be such, therefore, as may give them that rank in society which so important a trust requires (Smith 1937, p. 105).

Evidently, Adam Smith would set aside the normative prescription emerging from figure 1—that is, to let raw market forces drive the incomes of physicians to whatever level clears the market in favor of the medieval Doctrine of Just Price, according to which highly educated persons, such as physicians and lawyers (perhaps even economists) ought to be compensated in accordance with their high status in society. It is a doctrine with much currency among educated people. Alas, it does not invariably have equal currency among politicians or people in the business world.

THE MORAL QUESTION

Whatever one may think about these rival propositions—the case for the free-market and that for the Doctrine of Just Price—the interplay between surpluses or deficits of particular types of health professionals, on the one hand, and their level of compensation, on the other, ought not to be swept delicately under the rug in discussions on health workforce policy. Those who propose to put artificial limits on the supply of particular health professionals must be challenged to present both an *economic* and a *moral* rationale for that strategy.

To make this case, for example, one might imagine the thousands of qualified and highly motivated American youngsters who have vainly sought entry into medical school and who quite probably would have been willing to practice medicine at incomes much below those now customary in the profession. An advocate for artificial limits on entry into the profession ought to be able to explain to such youngsters why their rejection serves the nation's best interest and that, moreover, it obeys prevailing notions of distributive justice. It is not an easy case to make; but it must be made forthrightly, lest such proposals be greeted with utter cynicism.

Traditional Rationales for Government Intervention

Much of the literature on the health workforce is premised on the notion that government has a legitimate role in regulating the size and geographic distribution of that workforce, along with the competence and the job description of each type of health professional. Is there a defensible basis for this premise?

Professional Quality

Let us first of all dispose of one rationale that is too transparently self-serving to warrant much discussion: the perennial quest by particular types of health professionals—most prominently physicians—for government mandated occupational licensure and for government regulation of the professions' job content through professional practice acts. (See, for example, the bottom row of Osterweis and McLaughlin's table 1, Health Workforce

Policy Matrix.) Health professionals who enlist the coercive power of government in this way usually appeal to "quality" and the "protection of patients" as rationales for their pleas. As health-economist Paul Feldstein (1988) has argued in his marvelously sardonic piece on The Political Economy of Health Care [Regulation], more often than not, the true but hidden motive for supplier-induced government regulation is the mere protection of economic turf. This argument had been made even more forcefully by Nobel Laureate economist Milton Friedman (1962) in his classic *Capitalism and Freedom.** As a general rule, economists respect pleas for such interventions only when they emanate from consumers or from other disinterested parties.

Supplier-induced government regulation aside, what other rationale is there for government to regulate the size, composition, and geographic distribution of the health workforce? Two justifications are traditionally advanced.

Support of Education
Government has traditionally financed a large fraction of the education of health professionals mainly, of course, to provide greater equity in access to the economic opportunities provided by that education. Therefore, it is argued, government not only has the right but also the duty to influence what is "bought" with the taxpayer's money. Although the argument has appeal, it seems rarely to be applied with equal vigor to other forms of government-subsidized education—be it higher education in general, or advanced training in law, business, or engineering in our public universities. The case for a highly interventionist policy on the health workforce would be more compelling if it was more equally applied to all publicly subsidized professional education.

Perverse Demand in the Health Care Market
A much more compelling reason for regulating the size and composition specifically of the health workforce lies in the traditional lack of countervailing power on the demand side of the health care market. Until about the mid-1980s, the patient's freedom to choose among doctors and hospitals *at the time of illness* was sacrosanct in the United States. Government, employers, and private insurance carriers encroached upon that freedom only at the

---

* Friedman proposes to replace mandatory licensure. Under the latter, a health professional may use a particular label (MD, RN, etc.) only after having passed an officially recognized set of academic and professional requirements.

risk of vehement opposition from the general public and from the providers of health care. Furthermore, until about the mid-1980s, fee-for-service payment for health care was widely accepted as the *sine qua non* of high-quality health care, certainly among physicians and hospitals, but also among their conservative allies in the Congress. In tandem, the principle of free choice and fee-for-service compensation served to splinter the demand side of the health system so effectively that neither government nor private insurance carriers had the leverage to control the use of health services. Although government did have the power to fix the prices of the health services it purchased on behalf of patients, private insurance carriers were forced to cede extraordinary discretion to physicians and hospitals even over the prices these carriers paid for health care.

In such an open-ended market, virtually any mix of health care professionals and health-care facilities somehow managed to find adequate economic sustenance. Consequently, there was no need to tailor the mix of health professionals produced by our academic health centers to some perceived "need" for them by society. Ultimately, society's "need" for health care and for health professionals always adapted itself passively to the income "needs" of whatever workforce the nation's academic health centers saw fit to train. (In this connection, for example, see Ebert and Ginzberg 1988.)

In such an environment, the logic of using the size and the composition of the health workforce as a leverage for cost-control grew increasingly compelling. Through their decisions, physicians control, on average, about three-quarters of total national health spending. It was therefore believed that every additional physician effectively committed the nation to underwrite a thirty- to forty-year annuity equal to a multiple of the physician's own, sizable gross income. It was known that this annuity was much larger for medical specialists than it was for primary care physicians.

Geographic Maldistribution

Finally, because newly trained physicians found it relatively easy to earn handsome incomes even in patently overdoctored areas, there was little prospect of pushing physicians into traditionally underdoctored areas simply by raising the overall size of the physician workforce. It was therefore natural to conclude that the problem of ever-rising health care costs and the chronic geographic maldistribution of physicians could be addressed most effectively by limiting the overall size of the physician supply, changing its specialty composition drastically in favor of primary care physicians, and enticing physicians into underdoctored areas through powerful, government-funded financial incentives. Thus arose the case for a highly interventionist workforce policy whose central premises survive in the literature to this day.

The Withering Case for Government Intervention

For better or for worse, these (truly) golden days of American health care are over. As noted, it is safe to assume that future medical graduates in this country will increasingly adopt the status of other health professionals: employees in an integrated health system or quasiemployees subject to a cancelable contract with such a system. Gone are the days when the physicians could somehow, collectively, push out the demand for their services within remarkably broad limits.*

In the newly emerging market environment, power has shifted to the demand side of the health-care market. Henceforth society no longer will passively adapt its utilization of health care to the income needs of whatever mix of health professionals happens to have been trained by academic health centers. The adaptation will be the other way around: The employment opportunities and the incomes of health professionals will be dictated by society's demand for efficiently produced medical treatments. It is a causal flow that will reverberate all the way into the board rooms of academic health centers whose decisions, too, will henceforth be adaptations to the demand side of the health-care market.

The question can be asked—as I asked it explicitly in an earlier paper on health workforce policy—whether the new American market for health care really needs as interventionist a public policy on the health workforce as is still being proposed in the literature (Reinhardt 1994). In the new market environment, the risk of a potential oversupply of a particular type of health professional is no longer borne by the users of health care. It is borne by the professionals themselves, as it now is borne by young professionals in law, in business, in engineering, and in economics. Therefore, it would seem safe to leave the overall size and the composition of the health workforce to the hand of the market place, concentrating the thrust of public policy on only three distinct areas.

---

* Economists have debated endlessly whether individual physicians can or cannot induce demand for their services in defense of their income. The debate has bordered on the metaphysical and remained largely inconclusive. Be that as it may. Evidently physicians as a group have been able to push the demand for their services far beyond what the capitated managed-care now tells us is necessary.

First, if the nation wishes to make careers in the health professions accessible to all qualified members of society, regardless of parental income, there surely will have to be a government-run or government-supervised system of financial support aimed at the offspring in low-income households. Part of this support will have to be outright subsidies, lest the economically disadvantaged be frightened away by the prospect of huge debts. But part of it could also take the form of loans to be amortized out of the professionals' future earnings. An important *desideratum*, however, would be to hang this financial support directly around the neck of the students or residents, rather than to funnel it to them indirectly in the form of institutional grants to academic health centers (Reinhardt 1994).

Second, there will always have to be a credentialing mechanism capable of assuring that health professionals claiming a particular label (e.g., MD or RN or LPN) possess the minimum set of qualifications generally thought to be conveyed by these labels. That accreditation need not be government certification. Indeed, direct government intrusion into this sphere has always invited the political manipulation of credentialing purely to protect economic turf, just as the archaic work rules now governing the construction trades in many states exist solely to protect the economic turf of particular unions through deliberate, government-induced inefficiency.* Even so, given the authority vested in some health professionals, notably physicians, at least some government supervision of any credentialing process probably will always be required.

Third, in the novel and highly dynamic market environment of the future, government will have a crucial and as yet unexercised role to play in providing all relevant decision makers with up-to-date information on the markets for health professionals. By its very nature such information is a *public good*,† which implies that its production ought to be publicly subsidized. In the present context, for example, the Federal government might produce and disseminate, or contract with private parties to produce and disseminate, an ongoing series on current and projected conditions in the markets for distinct types of health professionals. That information should be easily and freely made available to college students who contemplate

---

* In health care as elsewhere, one person's inefficiency is another's income.
† A public good is one whose consumption by one person (or institution) does not preclude the consumption of the same good by another person (or institution). The fruits of basic research and almost all information fall into this category. Because the bulk of the benefits from public goods tends to accrue to others than those who produce it, a free private market will always underproduce public goods. The efficient production of public goods therefore always requires intervention by government. At the least, government must subsidize the production of such goods.

careers in health care, so that they can make fully informed decisions about investing their time and money in particular careers. Such an information system might be the chief task assigned to the new "national policy board" that Osterweis and McLaughlin call for in their paper.

Works Cited

Ebert, R.H. and E. Ginzberg. 1988. The reform of medical education. *Health Aff.* 7 (2) Supplement.

Feldstein, P.J. 1988. *Healthcare Economics.* Third edition. *New York: Wiley.*

Friedman, M. 1962. *Capitalism and Freedom.* Chicago: University of Chicago Press.

Graduate Medical Education National Advisory Committee (GMENAC). 1980. *Summary Report.* Vol. 1. GPO Publications No. 1980-0-721-748/266. Washington: Government Printing Office.

Reinhardt, U.E. 1981. The GMENAC forecast: An alternative view. *Am. J. Public Health,* 71(10).

———. 1991. Health manpower forecasting: The case of physician supply. 1991. In *Health Services Research: Key to Health Policy,* Eli Ginzberg, ed. Cambridge, MA: Harvard University Press.

———. 1994. Planning the nation's health workforce: Let the market in. *Inquiry* 31 (fall).

Smith, A. *1937. An Inquiry into the Nature and Causes of the Wealth of Nations.* New York: Modern Library.

Ethical Responsibilities of Academic Health Centers in the New Health Care Market

Dan W. Brock

The marketplace often brings dramatic changes in many sectors of the economy without generating either economic or ethical concerns. Why, then, do we consider health care different from any other goods? Why can't we let the market determine what gets produced, who can purchase what, and what the cost will be? Several major events and trends in the health care sector during the last decade or so have set the context for today's thinking about the ethical responsibilities of academic health centers.

Effects of the Recent Past

The first event is the dramatic and, in my view, unfortunate, or even tragic, failure of national health care reform recently. It is an ethical tragedy if you believe along with me that only comprehensive reform has any realistic hope of making progress with the single most important ethical deficiency of our health care system—the 40 million Americans who are without health insurance. This situation is a national disgrace in an advanced country as rich as ours. Opportunities for national health reform do not occur often— one has to go back to the early 1970s to find a previous attempt at comprehensive national health care reform and that effort, too, resulted in failure. As a result, we are unlikely to have any coordinated, comprehensive workforce policy in the health care sector. Instead, we will witness a variety of not-always-consistent responses to powerful market forces. Thus, in the near future, the changes in the health care system will not come from national health care reform.

The second circumstance has been the growth of for-profit enterprises in the health care system. In the 1980s, this growth took the form of large for-profit hospital chains. There has been considerable debate about how differently from their nonprofit brethren the for-profit institutions actually operate and behave in such areas as providing unreimbursed care (Gray 1986). More recently, the rapid growth of large, integrated managed care organizations, often for-profit and in some cases owned by large insurance companies, has extended the for-profit penetration of the health care sector. This rapid growth gives every sign of continuing (Iglehart 1992), and has important implications for the ethical responsibilities of academic health centers and health professionals in shaping the new health care workforce.

The third development is the ongoing change, visible in managed care, in the practice setting of the typical physician. Two changes in particular are important for workforce policy and training. One is that fewer physicians are practicing in fee-for-service settings with incentives—financial, professional, and moral—to provide more care to patients, but instead are necessarily in capitated reimbursement systems in which the financial incentives are to provide less care (Iglehart 1994; Hillman 1987). The second is that fewer and fewer physicians are self-employed, autonomous professionals, but instead have joined other health care workers, like nurses, in becoming salaried employees of large health care delivery organizations.

The fourth concern is the ever-intensifying pressure to control the growth in health care costs. This pressure has come from the government, concerned with reducing the growth of public health care programs like Medicare and Medicaid and lowering budget deficits; from employers, who want to control the rapidly rising cost of doing business in an increasingly intense international competition; and from the public, who are often faced with overwhelming out-of-pocket health care costs from serious illness even when apparently well insured.

Thus, as a great many commentators have noted, even in the absence of national health reform, market forces are bringing dramatic changes to the health care system. New graduates of medical school or residency training face a system dramatically different from that faced by their counterparts one or two decades ago. Typically, they can expect to practice in a system that fails to provide access to health care to a growing proportion of the country's citizens. They will also probably work as employees of a large, for-profit managed care organization, with capitation reimbursement systems and other measures driving them to be ever more cost-effective and cost-conscious at the behest of third-party payers and stockholders.

The Dilemma of the Health Marketplace

Economists remind us of various forms of market failure in the health care sector (Arrow 1963). Sellers (usually physicians) are commonly considered to control most health care utilization decisions: the consumers (i.e., patients) are usually in a poor position to determine their needs, engage in prudent comparison shopping for the care they need, or even judge if the care has been competently rendered. Moreover, because individual needs for health care vary substantially in largely unpredictable ways and are often costly to satisfy, it is difficult for consumers to budget for health care. Goods with similar features are often provided through some form of public or private insurance. However, providing these goods through insurance brings further market failures when the ones insured have some control over their use of insured goods.

Why is there an ethical problem in leaving the allocation of health care to the market, which could, in turn, give the ethical responsibilities to the producers of inputs (i.e., health care professionals)? The fundamental reason is the often profound effect that health care has on people's well-being and opportunities (President's Commission for the Study of Ethical Problems in Medicine 1983). Health care is a moral good or, more carefully put, is a moral matter, a requirement of justice. Therefore, it is imperative that the allocation of health care not be left solely to the market.

Health care can prevent serious loss of function and disability or it can restore lost function, prevent or ameliorate pain and suffering, prevent premature loss of life, and give us the information we need to plan our lives in the face of changes in our health status. Our political culture professes a moral commitment to equality of opportunity, and because access to health care has at least as great an effect on opportunities as education, justice requires that all people have access to at least basic health care services (Daniels 1985). Just as we have a social and ethical responsibility to ensure that no member of our society suffer without adequate food or shelter, so we should make certain that none suffer serious loss of well-being from lack of health care.

Workforce Responsibilities of the Academic Health Center

The most obvious concern of the academic health center are the categories and proportions of different health care professionals produced by health professions schools. For example, there seems to be widespread agreement in health policy circles that we need to increase the proportion of primary care physicians in relation to specialists (COGME 1992).

Balance Primary Care and Specialization

Primary care practitioners are in greatest demand in managed care organizations, which use them as gatekeepers to limit access to more expensive specialists and often emphasize health promotion and preventive services. Conversely, managed care organizations, both the more tightly controlled staff-model HMOs and the more loosely controlled preferred-provider organizations, typically limit the number of specialists who can join the organization as well as how often and under what conditions patients have access to the services of specialists. This two-pronged approach may sometimes be a result of different philosophies of health care, such as a greater concern with the continuity of care possible from primary care providers. But surely, it often stems equally, if not more, from the higher costs of specialist services (Schroeder and Sandy 1993). International comparisons with other countries, most of whom have been more successful in controlling the growth of health care costs, also show a higher proportion of primary care providers, often roughly a 50:50 balance between primary care and specialist physicians. There is, of course, controversy over just what the correct balance is, but we are so far from a 50:50 balance in both numbers and time, that there is much room for increasing primary care providers before one gets into the range of controversy.

Reduce Physician Maldistribution

It is also widely agreed that there is an undersupply of physicians, often both primary care and specialists, in undesirable practice locations such as rural and poor urban areas, resulting in limited access to care even for people with health insurance. People who are members of public insurance programs, like Medicaid, commonly have two strikes against them: inadequate provider reimbursement from the government programs, which makes providers reluctant to treat them; and residence in areas considered relatively undesirable by physicians. Here, too, there may be disagreement about the degree of underservice, but there is room for much improvement before the issue becomes seriously controversial.

Reduce Physician Supply

Many health policy makers and analysts believe there is, or soon will be, an overall oversupply of physicians in general (COGME 1992). One reason is the expected continued rapid growth of managed care and the proportionately lower physicians per capita that such organizations support. Here too, of course, there is disagreement about the magnitude of the problem.

Grow More Allied Health Care Professionals

Finally, many believe there is a need to increase the numbers and proportions of some allied health professionals, in particular nurse practitioners and physician assistants (see the Bednash and Cawley discussions in this book). Still unclear is the extent to which these professionals largely substitute for physicians: whether they threaten physicians, especially in the context of an impending physician oversupply; and if they complement physicians by providing services that physicians do not supply or make physicians more efficient.

In an increasingly competitive health care marketplace, especially one in which competition is largely in terms of price or cost, one can expect demand for these and other health care professionals to increase. The expected growth in demand for nonphysician health care professionals, however, is not uniform across the spectrum of care. In particular, the large, national oversupply of hospital beds, the shift of services from the hospital to the ambulatory setting, and the pressures from managed care plans to reduce the lengths of hospital stay suggest a possible oversupply of nurses. Approximately 85 percent work in hospitals (see the Yordy discussion in this book).

Ethical Challenges Facing the Academic Health Center

I believe that effecting the necessary workforce changes falls largely to academic health centers, not just because it is in their economic interest or the self-interest of the professionals they produce. It is also their ethical responsibility. Assuming that I am correct, it bears noting that intervention depends on what others are doing to effect such changes. If, for example, the market fails to produce a workforce that meets effective demand for health care professionals, or if we have moral or other reasons for producing a workforce different in some respects from what a well-functioning competitive market will produce, then there are reasons for intervention. But how best to intervene to bring about specific changes is a separate question. So is whether specific interventions, and the ethical responsibility to take them, rests with academic health centers, with others, or with both.

I believe it is almost certainly the case that academic health centers are not the best ones to bring about workforce changes on their own. In some cases, the Federal government may be best placed, for example, through funding residency training programs or retraining specialists, to take on primary care roles. In other cases, joint efforts between state governments and academic health centers may be more effective than academic health centers acting alone. A case in point is the joint program to effect physician supply in the state of Virginia (the Morse, Horan, and Combs discussions in this book). I also believe it is part of the academic health centers' ethical responsibility (and usually in their self-interest), to take the initiative in developing such joint efforts.

The ideal division of labor and responsibility to effect large-scale and complex changes rarely exists or can be produced by the best efforts of educational leadership. One important reason the Clinton administration sought comprehensive health care reform is that only comprehensive reform is likely to be effective, or optimally effective, in producing a number of ethically needed changes in the system. With the recent failure of such reform, part of the ethical responsibility to effect needed changes in the health care system falls on academic health centers; they have some ability to effect those changes, even if they can do so less effectively and less fully than efforts coordinated by the Federal government. It is a frustrating, but nevertheless pervasive, part of our lives that ethical responsibilities, which ideally fall on others, instead fall on leaders of educational institutions. It often results in an unfair distribution of the burden (e.g., caring for the uninsured because of the Federal government's clear failure to meet its responsibilities). It also means that ethical responsibilities often fall on individuals or institutions with only a limited ability to handle them. I believe this is exactly the case with academic health centers and workforce changes.

Improve Access to Care

It is not difficult to see how academic health centers will have economic motivations to meet the changes in the demand and supply of different health care professionals. But why should we assume that helping to bring about these changes is a specifically ethical responsibility? There are two different, though related, answers. The first is that these changes may each have some positive effect on individual access to health care. Just increasing the presence of physicians and other health care providers in underserved rural and inner city areas, for example, will have a significant, direct effect. It is probably the most difficult workforce change for academic health centers to directly effect of the four I cited above.

Increase System Capacity

The second reason is that workforce changes can increase the health care system's capacity to meet individual health care needs. For example, if nurse practitioners and physician assistants provide services that physicians do not, they increase the system's overall ability to meet the full array of patient needs. Increasing the proportion of primary care physicians not only might reduce health care costs, but also improve continuity of care and increase attention to healthy behavior and illness prevention. Even controlling the oversupply of physicians could lessen the overutilization of services and procedures driven by an oversupply of physicians and their consequent response to maintain income. Unnecessary services and procedures not only waste money and thereby produce fewer health benefits for a given level of health care expenditures, but can harm patients as well.

Each of the four workforce changes discussed above thus has some potential to increase the ability of our health care system. I have not spelled out all of the ways this could happen. Similarly, we should not assume that all such changes will be positive for the patient. On balance, however, the effects are likely to be good.

More important, I have not elaborated any theoretical account of health care needs, but simply assumed enough common-sense understanding of these needs to make the relevant claims of the effects on meeting them plausible. A few points are in order here. The first is that although the effects of disease on function are largely biologically determined, the relative importance of different health care needs is in part an ethical, or value, judgment about the relative importance of the area of function affected by a disease and its treatment. The second point, argued briefly earlier, is that the distribution of health care is a matter of ethics and justice because it affects well-being and opportunity. Powerful economic forces may sometimes make it difficult to focus in this way but, in the final analysis, it is for reasons of ethics that institutions are in the business of training health care professionals.

Develop the Ethical Character of Health Professionals

I turn now to another broad responsibility of academic health centers, namely, the moral and ethical character in the professionals they produce. It is an ethical responsibility ultimately of considerably greater importance than any other discussed in this paper. Although I use physicians as my example in the discussion to follow, the same applies largely to other health care professionals as well.

Most physicians (quite rightly, I believe) resist the idea that medicine is just a business producing and selling a product, and like any other business, it should be ruled by the marketplace (Kassirer 1995). Instead, medicine is a profession, with the role of the physician substantially defined by ethical commitments special to medicine and not found in other social and commercial relations (Brock 1991; Council on Ethical and Judicial Affairs, AMA 1992; ACP 1992). Unlike a commercial venture, in which profit maximization is accepted as a proper motivation of the provider, the professional ethos of physicians requires that the interests of their patients, first and foremost, guide physician behavior. This commitment, and the concomitant setting aside of the interests of all others, including the physician's own, is perhaps the most striking defining norm of medicine. It is on the basis of this commitment that physicians typically ask for and receive their patients' trust. The ability to trust a physician is important to the patient because of the fear, anxiety, vulnerability, and dependence that often accompany serious illness, and because of the inequalities between typical physician and patient knowledge, experience, and training in health care. The need to gain informed consent to treatment expresses this commitment to the interests of the patient, to serve the patient's health and well-being, and to respect the patient's right to self-determination.

The requirement to be truthful with patients is another ethical commitment that sets the medical profession apart. We don't always expect truthfulness elsewhere, but the medical commitment to truthfulness with patients is relatively strong and prominent. Related to truthfulness is a strong commitment to confidentiality of information provided by the patient or gathered by the physician in the course of the patient's care. Finally, there are ethical and professional norms governing access to health care. Access to basic health care, at the least, should not be determined by the ability to pay, but by medical need.

Of course, all of these ethical norms are far more complex and controversial than the simple formulation above, and not all physicians always live up to these norms. The point, however, is that physicians commonly understand that being a physician entails a commitment to a related and coherent body of ethical standards by which the profession judges itself and its members, and asks others to judge it. These norms give substance to the traditional ethos of the medical profession as a "high calling."

Consider the popular image of the used car salesperson (admittedly extreme and stereotyped). When customers step onto a used car lot, they usually expect the salesperson to pursue his or her economic self-interest by trying to make the deal that will bring in the greatest profit, and not trying to sell only what the customer "needs." Customers do not expect complete truthfulness or confidentiality, and they certainly expect that the ability to pay will govern their "access" to a car on the lot. Any naive customer who puts his or her trust in the used car salesperson will likely be sorely disappointed and quickly learn the meaning of "caveat emptor." Of course, not all used-car salespeople are unethical but the comparison points to real, albeit subtle, differences in the norms that govern medicine as contrasted with "arms length" commercial relationships. Patients expect and want something quite different from their physicians than they want from others who try to sell them goods and services.

Powerful forces in health care are putting great pressure on maintaining this ethical conception of the profession. Physicians are increasingly no longer self-employed professionals, but are now often employees of large for-profit corporate entities. These entities have legal responsibilities to shareholders to maximize their profitability; they will suffer the disciplines of the marketplace and the securities markets if they fail to do so.

They use a variety of means to discipline participating physicians so they can keep operations and costs competitive and profitable (Emanuel and Dubler 1995). The most prominent in managed care plans are various capitation systems in which a fixed premium is paid independent of patient use of services; physicians, in turn, have a variety of incentives to limit their provision of services. Continuing employment depends on the profitability of the employer. The practice is typically monitored to ensure prudent use of resources.

In nonstaff model managed-care plans, participating physicians are often subject to the withholding of a part of their fee, with later payment dependent on the plan's profitability (Hillman, Pauly, and Kerstein 1989). Treatment guidelines and protocols, as well as various requirements for approval before invasive procedures, surgery, and hospitalization, are common to limit the use of "unnecessary" services. Physicians whose practice fails to conform to the plan's guidelines and expectations can, and do, lose their jobs or their continuing status as participating physicians in the plan.

In specializations with an oversupply of physicians, the latter considerations are powerful incentives to conform one's practice to the plan's expectations. If predictions that we face a broader and greater oversupply of physicians are correct, the incentives will become more powerful still. They are part of a variety of incentives, some blatant and some subtle, for physicians to limit services and place their own and the organization's interests ahead of—or at least in conflict with—those of their patients (Rodwin 1995).

These arrangements are not all bad for patients. They help correct the overutilization of services generally agreed to be common in traditional fee-for-service practice.* It is a mistake to assume that the only harm to patients from overutilization under traditional fee-for-service funding is a waste of economic resources. We lack the data to know whether the harm of underutilization is greater than the harm of overutilization, much less how the two factors will balance out if cost-control pressures continue to increase.

Nevertheless, there are some reasons to be especially concerned about the effects of these incentives on the physician's commitments. We do know, for example, that the effects of withholding beneficial care will often be invisible to patients unless they are informed by their physicians of the care that is not available. It will usually be easier for physicians not to do so, and both conscious and unconscious factors will often lead them in this direction (Council on Ethical and Judicial Affairs, AMA 1990, 1995). Such lack of action will put serious pressures on the norms requiring that physicians be truthful with patients and also secure the patient's informed consent after informing him or her of all significant treatment alternatives. In addition, the incentives to put one's own, or the plan's interests ahead of the patient, will hold down health care costs only if physicians qualify or abandon the patient-centered, ethical approach. Although the traditional fee-for-service setting also created a conflict between the physician's economic interests and the patient's health interests, professional and ethical standards told the physician that the patient's interests came first even if, in fact, the physician did not always do so. Moreover, the conflict of interest was probably substantially modulated by the broader context in which fee-for-service medicine was practiced; it allowed physicians to secure high incomes without applying unnecessary or useless treatments to their patients. Thus, the vast majority of physicians could "do well by doing good" (Brock and Buchanan 1987).

More generally, medicine is threatened with fundamental changes if physicians come to view themselves not as independent professionals guided

---

* For example, excess hospitalization increases risks of hospital-acquired infections. Unnecessary surgery, such as coronary artery bypass grafts, increases morbidity and mortality. Even overuse of everyday diagnostic procedures like X-rays carries the risk of cancer and other risks.

first and foremost by a commitment to the well-being of their patients, but as employees of a profit-oriented business selling a commodity or service. Since they often, in fact, will be employees of that kind of a business, this shift will be difficult to resist fully. The language and operation of hospitals, hospital chains, and large managed care organizations, and of the people who run them (whether or not they are for profit or nonprofit) already have become those of business and the business schools. Serving patient needs is being replaced by strategic planning to capture profitable market segments and shed unprofitable operations. With the dramatic rush to consolidation and merger in the health care industry over the last couple of years, a trend to greater concentration of economic power is likely to continue, and the professional autonomy of physicians employed by these large complex organizations will continue to erode.

With national health care reform supplanted by health care reform by the marketplace, the commercialization and de-professionalization of medicine will be extremely difficult to resist. Some changes, such as more efficient and cost-effective practices and greater attention to developing outcomes data to guide practice, will be beneficial and should be welcomed. But physicians have both professional and ethical obligations and, to a significant degree, self-interest as well, to resist many aspects of this transformation of medicine from an ethically guided profession to profit-guided commerce. And all of us, as patients, have strong reasons to join in resisting this transformation.

Conclusion

If the ethical norms by which the health professions have traditionally defined themselves are to continue to guide and shape practice, and not become mere window-dressing, the professional norms must be instilled in physicians and o`her health care professionals during their formative years in undergraduate and postgraduate training. It must also come from examples set by teachers and mentors and by those who run the training institutions.* The new climate of the health care marketplace will make these tasks more difficult, but also more important.

---

* Academic health centers must also develop institutional responses to the market forces now driving changes in health care that will protect the ethical commitments of the profession.

Works Cited

ACP (American College of Physicians). 1992. Ethics manual, 3d ed. *Annals of Internal Medicine* 117.

Arrow, K. 1963. Uncertainty and the welfare economics of medical care. *American Economic Review* 53.

Brock, D.W. 1991. The ideal of shared decision making between physicians and patients. *Kennedy Institute Journal of Ethics* 1.

—— and A.E. Buchanan. 1987. The profit motive in medicine. *J. Med. Philos.* 12.

Council on Ethical and Judicial Affairs, AMA. 1990. Financial incentives to limit care: Financial implications for HMOs and IPAs. In vol. 1 of *Code of Medical Ethics: Reports of the Council on Ethical and Judicial Affairs of the American Medical Association.* Chicago: AMA.

——. 1992. *Code of Medical Ethics: Current Opinions.* Chicago: AMA.

——. 1995. Ethical issues in managed care. *JAMA* 273.

COGME (Council on Graduate Medical Education). 1992. *Third Report: Improving Access to Health Care Through Physician Workforce Reform: Directions for the 21st Century.* Washington: U.S. Department of Health and Human Services.

Daniels, N. 1985. *Just Health Care.* Cambridge: Cambridge University Press.

Emanuel, E.J. and N.N. Dubler. 1995. Preserving the physician-patient relationship in the era of managed care. *JAMA* 273.

Gray B., ed. 1986. *For-Profit Enterprise in Health Care.* Washington: National Academy Press.

Hillman, A.L. 1987. Financial incentives for physicians in HMOs: Is there a conflict of interest? *N. Engl. J. Med.* 317.

——. M.V. Pauly, and J.J. Kerstein. 1989. How do financial incentives affect physicians' clinical decisions and the financial performance of health maintenance organizations? *N. Engl. J. Med.* 321.

Iglehart, J.K. 1992. The American health care system: Managed care. *N. Engl. J. Med.* 327.

——. 1994. Physicians and the growth of managed care. *N. Engl. J. Med.* 331.

Kassirer, J.P. 1995. Managed care and the morality of the marketplace. *N. Engl. J. Med.* 333.

President's Commission for the Study of Ethical Problems in Medicine. 1983. *Securing Access to Health Care.* Washington: Government Printing Office.

Rodwin, M.A. 1995. Conflicts in managed care. *N. Engl. J. Med.* 332.

Schroeder, S.A. and L.G. Sandy. 1993. Specialty distribution of U.S. physicians–the invisible driver of health care costs. *N. Engl. J. Med.* 328.

Federal Roles

Since the Second World War, the Federal government has implemented a variety of policies that educate and reimburse health professionals, and advance new diagnostic and therapeutic technologies. The first two papers in this section explore the history, politics, and current status of some of these Federal policies. The final two papers describe health workforce policies in the United Kingdom and Canada.

The Political History of Health Workforce Policy

DANIEL M. FOX

Policy to subsidize the preparation of health professionals in the United States has become contentious and uncertain. With alliterative oversimplicity, the justification for this policy could be described as changing during the past half century from piety to platitudes to pork.

Many highly regarded policies have a similar history. Antagonists usually outnumber advocates when new policy is proposed. Events, opinions, and hard political work then create a consensus that a particular policy is in the public interest. The policy is endorsed, often for decades, by leaders of the Federal government, the states, and interest groups. Editorials in the general and professional press praise the policy. Its critics are marginalized. The policy seems proper and permanent.

After some years, critics describe the policy as expensive and contradictory to other desirable public goals. Nevertheless, the interest groups that prosper as a result of the policy succeed in preserving their subsidies, although they reluctantly accept more intrusive regulation. Leading social scientists eventually maintain that the assumptions underlying the policy are tenuous and its coalitions fragile. Their analysis is summarized by authors of textbooks and media commentaries and thus informs the opinions of politicians, leaders of business and the professions, and the general public. Yet much of the policy and its subsidies persist.

This, briefly, is the story, of several policies during the past half-century (to name but a few): expansion of higher education, the Federal highway construction program, agricultural price supports, veterans' benefits, aid to families with dependent children, and defense against international Communism. Persisting policies with similar histories during the nineteenth and early twentieth centuries include manifest destiny, the sale of public lands, open immigration, and civil service reform.

Each of these policies was once perceived as self-evident, a matter of civic piety. As consensus eroded, proponents continued to assert that the policy yielded benefits for the public; hence the policy entered the stage of platitudes. Finally, each of these policies came to be regarded by many, especially people who ran for office and met payrolls, as serving particular rather than general interests: thus, pork.

Policy to increase the supply of health professionals may be following this pattern. The political history that follows assesses this possibility.

The Stakeholders

Health workforce policy has helped to attract, educate, and pay an enormous number of professionals to apply the diagnostic and therapeutic technologies of the late twentieth century. The only comparably successful labor policy in our history is the GI Bill of Rights.

Health workforce and veteran policies are more closely connected than published histories tell us. In June 1945, talking to the director of the Federal budget, President Harry Truman worried about health care in the "communities of this country, saying that "I think [the shortage of physicians] must be solved." He continued: "We will have a million or so veterans coming back . . . and we have an inadequate supply of doctors to take care of them" (Smith 1945).

Policies that awarded subsidies mainly to institutions eventually remedied the shortage of health professionals that concerned Harry Truman. Under the GI Bill, in contrast, it was individuals who received direct subsidy for education and housing. Yet both policies achieved their goals. Their success had other sources than the policy technology (i.e., to whom money flows or the mix of direct appropriations and tax expenditures) that experts debate.

Advocates of both the GI Bill and health workforce policy overcame initial opposition. Conservative business leaders feared that GI benefits would be political and financial fuel for a postwar revival of New Deal politics. They wanted to thwart a broad welfare state. Similarly, organized medicine, which had successfully restricted access to the profession since the beginning of the century, worried that public subsidy for education would lead to more government intrusion in medical practice.

Economic incentives and Americans' aspirations for a better life overwhelmed this opposition. The GI Bill augmented consumer purchasing power and thus helped to sustain postwar prosperity in ways that individuals could readily appreciate. Public investment in the education of health professions produced tangible benefits for many people: for example, income, status and access to health care.

Higher Education

Both the GI Bill and policy to enlarge the professional workforce for health care fueled the growth of higher education. From the 1940s to the 1980s, expenditures for higher education increased about tenfold in dollars adjusted for inflation. Public appropriations increased in one generation from less than one-half to two-thirds of total spending for higher education. The Federal share of public higher education doubled from the 1950s to the 1980s. The states' share increased almost three times. By the 1980s, states were appropriating about 10 percent of their tax revenues to higher education (Millett 1982).

Surging general demand for higher education benefitted the health professions. When the number of applicants for each place in the entering classes of medical and dental schools did not increase during the 1950s, leaders of the academic sector within these professions insisted that the absence of subsidy impeded effective demand. The expansion of higher education, moreover, encouraged the aspirations of leaders of the allied health professions and nursing to exchange what they defined as subjugation in hospital-based training programs for higher status and greater autonomy within liberal arts colleges and universities.

Health Professions Education

Beginning in the 1950s, education for the health professions grew more rapidly than for general higher education. Spending for medical education alone, adjusted for inflation, increased more than thirtyfold in the first four decades after World War II (Rothstein 1987). Forty new allopathic medical schools opened after 1960, compared to a mere sixteen in the previous half-century (Schofield 1984).

Expenditures for education in other health professions also increased, but they were obscured in general budgets for higher education. The number of allied health and nursing programs in colleges and universities increased at least fivefold from the 1950s to the 1980s (National Commission on Allied Health Education 1980).

Educators of health professionals said that the additional cost of training for clinical practice justified more generous subsidies than was due any other sector of higher education. They insisted that officials of universities and state governments accept recommendations about staffing—and, therefore, funding levels—from the organizations that accredited education for each health profession.

Such advocacy for separate and higher funding was often successful, although it created persistent resentment among university administrators and state budget officials. Most government officials believed that subsidies for higher professions education would soon be transformed into greater access to health care. Most Americans agreed there was a shortage of health professionals, especially of physicians. There seemed to be evidence that young professionals would choose to practice in their home states if they received their education there.

By the early 1980s, state appropriations per student in academic health centers were five times greater than for students in other programs in research universities, and more than ten times than for baccalaureate institutions (Millett 1982). These higher appropriations were mainly a response to the arguments of medical and dental educators, but students preparing for every health profession enjoyed larger subsidies than those in other programs.

Federal subsidies to educate health professionals both followed and leveraged state appropriations. More important, federal policy created what Fitzhugh Mullan (1994) recently described as the unanticipated "medicalization of workforce policy." Mullan, until recently Assistant Surgeon General and Director of the Bureau of Health Professions, argues that between 1961 and the mid-1970s, Federal policy aimed to meet the demand for health professionals in a variety of disciplines through "various iterations of the Health Professions Education Assistance Act." Since the early 1970s, however, Medicare has become overwhelmingly the largest source of funds for health professions education. The program spent about $6.5 billion for graduate medical education by 1994 and only about $300 million in what Mullan calls a "mindless fashion on other health professions, largely diploma nurses."

Health professions education was also a significant beneficiary of tax appropriations for capital to finance both education and health care, especially by states. Between 1960 and 1980, for example, state governments provided almost two-thirds of the capital for multipurpose buildings and equipment of medical schools, despite the availability of generous Federal construction grants (Schofield 1984).

Public spending for medical research flowed mainly to institutions that educated and trained health professionals. In 1949, the National Institutes of Health funded half of only $22 million in Federal grants to medical schools for research (Axt 1952). By 1993, total research spending by medical schools, adjusted for inflation, had grown almost fifty times. The Federal share, most of it from NIH, was now about 75 percent (Ganem, Krakower, and Beran 1994).

Institutions that prepared the health workforce were major beneficiaries of growth in overall health care spending. Federal, state, and local government funds built and equipped most teaching hospitals, through either direct or tax appropriations. Cost-reimbursement policies initiated by Blue Cross plans in the late 1940s, and federalized after 1965 by Medicare and Medicaid, helped pay the salaries and educational costs of graduate medical education. As a result of public spending for patient care, medical schools began to record some of the clinical income of their faculty members in the mid-1960s.

In the 1940s, university presidents often complained about the burdensome deficits of their medical schools. In a reversal, deans of medicine and vice presidents for health affairs have devised elaborate tactics to protect their budgets against presidential raids since the 1960s.

State Economies
The financial stakes in preparing the health care workforce became enormous. Financing the health sector became, proportionally, an ever-larger object of public expenditure. Defense spending, for example, was 52 percent of the Federal budget in 1960; by 1993 it had fallen to 20 percent. Moreover, defense has fallen from 9.5 percent to 5.5 percent of the gross national product in the past three decades (Bureau of the Census 1993). During the same time, Medicaid became what a Governor of Oregon has called the "monster that ate the states." But the monster brought Federal matching funds and created many jobs. By the 1990s, when health care was one-seventh of the national economy, every American was likely to be, or know well, someone whose income and career prospects depended on somebody else being hurt by cost-containment policies.

Spending for higher education and health care in combination became an increasingly productive expenditure for state governments. In 1940, each dollar of economic activity generated in the region surrounding a public medical school cost the state about 35 cents in appropriations.* By 1994,

---

* For this calculation, I assumed a regional multiplier of 1.5 (a conservative estimate according to many econometricians). Then I applied the multiplier, using data about state appropriations for medical education for 1940 (Rothstein 1987) and 1993 (Ganem, Krakower, and Beran 1994) as a percentage of total medical school spending. Note that I initially made this calculation in 1988

states spent about 15 cents for each dollar of regional economic activity generated by their medical schools. As a result, state officials were torn between the conflicting goals of reducing overall spending for health care and encouraging the expansion of research and patient care at academic institutions.

By the end of the 1960s, the health professions had a special place in the politics of higher education. Health professionals in academic settings had responsibility for patients, unlike engineering faculties, which did not take responsibility for the safety of bridges, or law schools, which were not administering appellate courts.

The closest parallel to health professional education was agriculture, where academics had been providing direct services and demonstrations of best-practice to each state's farmers since the nineteenth century. But the parallel was small comfort for the health professions. By the 1970s, it seemed unlikely that the privileges of agriculture in higher education would survive the submergence of Jeffersonian idealism in agribusiness.

The Stakes

Interest groups within and outside the health sector transformed into workforce policy a consensus that more subsidies to higher education would improve professional opportunities for individuals and, eventually, the health of Americans. The consensus became policy for four closely linked reasons.

Public and private policy to finance health services increased demand for additional professionals and encouraged institutions that provided education and training to provide direct services. Public policy for medical research paid a substantial portion of the overhead and many direct costs of institutions that educated health professionals.

Many interest groups within and outside the health sector benefitted substantially from workforce policy.

Public officials were pleased to make decisions that pleased so many powerful interests, promised more accessible services and, at the same time, met the demand from voters and their children for educational opportunity.

---

using a multiplier of 1.75 and expenditure data for a particular institution (State University of New York at Stony Brook), including its teaching hospital. I also factored in leakage, that is, funds returned to state government by income and sales taxes. The result was an estimate that this academic health center was costing state taxpayers 5 cents for each dollar of state appropriations.

Funding

By financing policy, the most important of these reasons, I mean the many decisions since the 1940s that created four payment streams for health services.

- Social insurance financed by payroll taxes and federal subsidy.
- Federal and state tax appropriations.
- Direct public subsidies.
- Payments by consumers.

These streams are more commonly known as Medicare, employee benefits, Medicaid and its predecessors, and direct consumer spending.

For a generation, policy makers for each of these streams agreed that the workforce should grow larger and its division of labor more complex, specialization should be more highly rewarded than generalism in every profession, and direct service dollars should pay for graduate medical education and for some of the training costs of other professionals (Fox 1995).

By the 1970s, the leaders of every organization of health professionals or institutions understood that it was in their members' interests to sustain each of the financing streams. These streams flowed together to create jobs, raise incomes, and expand opportunities for senior professionals to enjoy the satisfactions of teaching their juniors.

The existence of four sources of financing, each with different politics, prevented the centralization of health policy. As a result, exhortations to contain costs or reduce the size of the workforce were unlikely to damage the interests of groups with the largest stakes in the status quo.

Tax expenditure policy guaranteed that aggregate decisions about the workforce would continue to be based on the consensus that had gathered adherents since the 1940s. For reasons of principle and practicality, the members of Congress and Treasury officials who made Federal income tax policy refused to consider the cost and substance of health care.

State tax expenditures complemented Federal and private sector financing policy, providing subsidized capital to build and equip hospitals and facilities for higher education. Nonprofit institutions and states serviced their health care debt with revenue from patient care and student tuition. The reliability of this revenue enhanced support for the consensus workforce policy among interest groups in construction and investment banking, organized labor, real estate, and retail sales.

Some interest groups had more incentives than others to support higher education to enlarge the health care workforce. For example, the interests of physicians in the regions surrounding academic health centers were only partially congruent with academic interests. Local and academic physicians increasingly competed with each other for patients and the funds that financed their health care. Academic institutions wanted to command an ever-larger share of expenditures in their regions for sophisticated health services financed by payroll taxes, tax expenditures, and direct subsidy. Beginning in the late 1960s, they hired more faculty at higher salaries to generate income and share it with the institution. As the cost-containment policies of public and private payers became more intrusive in the 1980s and 1990s, the gains made by the academic physician became the community practitioner's loss.

Life Styles

Funding for biomedical research inadvertently reduced economic conflict between academic and community physicians. Research funding, primarily from NIH, changed the size, work, and conditions of employment of medical school faculties beginning in the 1950s. Federal research funds also created a new class of academic cosmopolitans who wanted a steady flow of grants, recognition from colleagues around the world, and job mobility to more prestigious institutions. Wherever they held faculty appointments, the cosmopolitans emulated their colleagues at the leading private universities and the handful of state institutions with research traditions.

The cosmopolites leveraged their grants to delegate routine patient care and considerable teaching, especially of medical undergraduates, to house staff and physicians whose interests were mainly local. In Fitzhugh Mullan's words (1994), they have "maintained their academic lifestyle by the use of larger numbers of resident physicians to do most of the patient care and teaching work in academic health centers." They thus contributed to their institutional budgets and their regional economies while relieving competitive pressure on local physicians and hospitals. At the same time, they displayed good academic citizenship by lobbying for education and training subsidies from health care financing streams.

Leaders of general higher education were another unexpected source of support for the groups with the highest stakes in an expanding health care workforce. Jealousy of the health professions, especially of medical school faculties, became endemic in higher education in the 1960s. Faculty members and administrators on liberal arts campuses and employees of the central administrations of public university systems complained that colleagues in the health professions were affluent and arrogant and had privileged access to funds from public budgets for health care and higher education.

Many university officials responsible for general campuses could increase their claim to some of the funding for the health care workforce by administering education for nursing and the allied health professions. Deans and faculty in nursing and allied health education frequently welcomed supervision by general universities as a means to increase the prestige of their professions and escape domination by physicians.

The Costs

As a result of the politics of health care financing, research, and higher education, the actual cost of educating and training the health care workforce has been obscured for four decades. To assess what has been spent for educating and training requires a complicated audit not only of the four health financing streams, but also of the flow of research dollars, tax-exempt capital financing, and general university expenditures.

Deriving net social cost from the results of this audit requires heroic assumptions about offsets. These offsets would include, for example, regional multipliers, tax leakages, lifetime earnings and tax payments, and benefits to health care employers from downward pressure on wages in regional labor markets in which nurses, the most numerous health workers, were cyclically in oversupply. A proper analysis would also examine public expenditures foregone, including spending that might have improved the health status of populations, in order to invest in producing health care.

This cost analysis will almost surely never be conducted, not so much because it is a technical challenge but more because few practical people ever want to know precisely how consensus became complicity. The costs, and therefore the net benefits, of health workforce policy in the second half of the twentieth century are no more likely to be assessed in a sophisticated way than those of the Cold War.

Until the 1990s, the assumptions that guided health workforce policy—like those of foreign and defense policy—seemed self-evident to the people who made policy for spending and taxation. Debates about public financing for health professions education were almost always about *when*, rather than *whether*, it is desirable to increase public spending. Educators of health professionals and their allies had considerably warmer relationships with budget officials and senior legislators than, for example, enthusiasts for public health, services for the mentally ill, or more spending for the poor.

People who ran for office and led public agencies often enjoyed making health care workforce policy. They agreed that improving access to care and increasing opportunities for individuals were in the public interest. They liked to make decisions that were supported by many voters and their children as well as by interest groups that contributed generously to both political parties.

For legislators and senior executive branch officials, making and implementing health workforce policy was easier than almost any other work they did. For instance, they suffered no adverse consequences from pressing interest groups to be accountable for their rhetoric. Thus legislative committees and executive budget offices perfunctorily asked deans of medicine, vice presidents for health affairs, and chancellors to describe how they were achieving their proclaimed commitments to primary care, underserved areas, opportunities for minorities, children with severe disabilities, the elderly and, more recently, to cost containment. In state after state and Washington, D.C., the educators gave the best answers they could and then smiled all the way to the bank.

Most of the people whose political behavior I have described believed most of what they said and were proud of their work. One anecdote must stand here for what I have heard, read and witnessed. During the New York fiscal crisis of the mid-1970s, while I was helping to manage a public academic health center, I received a reassuring telephone call from an official in the higher education unit of the state's budget division. "Don't worry," he said, "the good guys will win."

The Changing Politics

The frustration of aspiring health care reformers in 1994 demonstrates that policies that have ceased to be the subject of civic piety, or even consensus, still have potent constituencies. During the 1980s, assumptions about health care that once appeared self-evident lost moral force and considerable interest group support. Problems that had been familiar for years were now declared to be matters for urgent action. Employers had complained about rising health care costs for a generation. Consumers had been concerned about the coverage, renewability, and portability of their insurance policies for forty years. Shifting costs in order to subsidize other people's welfare had been as acceptable in health policy as it was in agriculture and transportation.

Beginning in the 1970s, events in the general economy converged with doubts about certitudes that drove health policy. As the international competitiveness of American industry declined and job mobility decreased, more people worried that their personal security and standard of living were declining. Individuals and corporations, already anxious about their incomes and prospects, found that the health policy they had once endorsed no longer allayed their anxieties about disease and imminent death at a price they were willing to pay.

Doubts about the certitudes of health policy that arose in the 1970s became open skepticism by the mid-1990s. Most important for workforce policy were doubts about inexorable progress from laboratory research, through teaching hospital services and the education of new professionals, to visible decrease in the burden of dread disease. For almost a century this theory of progress dominated policy to supply health services. Public and philanthropic policy had jointly created an institutional and professional hierarchy in health affairs in every urban region.

From the early 1920s, experts and textbooks depicted this hierarchy as a pyramid. At the top of each regional pyramid stood tertiary services, the research laboratories and teaching hospitals affiliated with medical schools; at the bottom was primary care, described as physician practices and public clinics that were supposed to offer ordinary citizens their first contact with the opportunity to benefit from the progress of medical science (Fox 1986).

Attacks on this theory of progress—for more than half a century merely a subversive tendency within academic medicine and public health practice—eventually became a subject of public discourse in the 1970s. Journalists, polemicists, and social scientists described how behavior, socioeconomic status, race, ethnicity, and gender contributed to the risk of disease in individuals and populations. Advances in biomedical science, it seemed, contributed less than most people had long assumed to the struggle for health (Fox 1995).

Simultaneously, advances in technology and changes in clinical opinion combined with cost-containment policy to encourage declining hospital utilization. New surgical techniques, for example, enabled the most frequently performed procedures to be done less expensively in ambulatory settings. Changing views about the management of chronic diseases reduced hospital stays for complications of such conditions as diabetes, asthma, and arthritis. Technology and Medicare financing policy together stimulated the expansion of the home care industry.

By the 1990s, pressure for cost containment permitted policy to be crafted that combined the attack on biological reductionism as the key to understanding disease with advancing technology that could be implemented in ambulatory settings. Corporate and government payors instituted policies lumped together with the vague phrase "managed care": these policies, for instance, included the negotiation of steep discounts by health maintenance organizations and preferred provider organizations from hospitals, consolidation and downsizing of inpatient services, and use of primary care physicians as gatekeepers and case managers.

Both nationally and in the states, many employers withdrew from the coalitions that linked policy to finance health care with subsidies to increase the supply of professionals, facilities, and equipment. Many of these employers had begun to self-insure for health care in the mid-1970s in order to take advantage of Federal law permitting them to avoid state-mandated benefits and premium taxes. In the 1980s, growing numbers of large and mid-sized employers combined self-insurance with utilization controls under the euphemism of managed care. These employers reduced what they paid hospitals to treat uninsured patients, subsidize graduate medical education, and replace facilities and equipment. Employers now had what a member of the Governor's staff in Minnesota has, in confidence to me, called a "ticket out of town" guaranteed by Federal law.

Employers and state Medicaid programs that adapted the techniques of managed care became increasingly effective in reducing costs. Self-insurance and managed care in combination stimulated the organization of new coalitions of public and private sector leaders who were eager to reduce the supply of acute care facilities and change the division of labor, especially in medicine.

The self-evident theory that had justified the growth of the academic health establishment was in disarray. For the first time in almost half a century, government agencies began to challenge fundamental workforce policies. Medicare subsidies for graduate medical education became targets for cost cutters. States began to accord higher priority to containing the growth of Medicaid costs than to subsidizing public teaching hospitals. In several states, legislators pressed public universities to increase the number of graduates of medical schools who specialized in primary care, often to a specified percentage of each graduating class. This pressure has led to voluntary compliance in some states (e.g., California) and legislative mandates in others (e.g., Washington State).

The politics of 1994 revealed strong support for existing policies for financing health care and its workforce. This situation is hardly unusual. Everyone's local military base, government laboratory, or welfare system is a special case. Most heads of congressional committees run for reelection. It is difficult to disentangle, for example, the beliefs of Senators Edward M.

Kennedy (D-Mass.) and Daniel Patrick Moynihan (D-N.Y.) about the contributions of academic medicine to the public good from the obligation to protect the economic interests of their constituents.

But the politics of 1994 and 1995 also made it plain that health workforce policy is increasingly just another arena for distributional politics. Many people still regard training health professionals as a higher grade of pork than dredging harbors or building Federal offices, but their number is decreasing. A prominent medical educator recently complained to me, "Why can't state legislators understand how little influence medical schools have on specialty choice and graduate education?" Legislators, I replied, target medical schools when they address primary care because they have enough influence on their budgets to attract their attention.

Are There Any Lessons?

A great deal of health financing policy in the twentieth century was justified by the assumption that it was in the public interest to invest in more knowledge about human biology and increase the supply of health professionals and services while encouraging consumers to want more health care. During the past century, health policy subsidized the transformation of advances in medical knowledge into services at a price that most people were willing to pay. The cost of this policy was offset by the economic and social benefits from longer and more productive lives and by the alleviation of considerable pain and suffering.

A decade from now, health workforce policy will surely have changed significantly, but probably not as much as reformers now hope or educators of health professionals now fear. Government is likely to retain major responsibility for financing health professions education or deciding who will do so. States will surely continue to influence workforce policy because of the importance of academic institutions in local and regional economies and because the Federal government is unlikely to replace state subsidies. Moreover, fiscal pressure will encourage states to reexamine the tax exemptions and capital subsidies they provide to nonprofit institutions, including medical schools and hospitals, in a market for health care in which competition and profit-seeking are the norm. It is also likely that individuals aspiring to professional careers and providers of health care will bear more of the costs of education and training, and recover some of the costs in negotiations about prices.

A few people who insist on thinking abstractly about politics will ask whether it is fair for some states or some individuals to bear a greater financial burden than others. Fairness will continue, however, to be a matter for negotiation among interest groups rather than speculation about the public good.

Health workforce policy has become contentious instead of consensual. The politics of workforce policy is now more explicitly about money than about health, opportunity, or access to care. Formulas and set-asides or special funding mechanisms, such as those proposed by academic interest groups and their allies in 1994, will continue to find favor mainly among those who would benefit from them. Such policy fixes are unlikely to be enacted because they are less compelling in the politics of pork than in the politics of piety or platitudes. The assumption that there was a shortage of 50,000 physicians had political significance from the 1940s to the 1970s, even though it was the softest of numbers. Because the assumption was made in an era of policy consensus when solutions could be justified by piety or platitudes, it justified the flow of funds to medical education. The current stance that there should be a 50:50 generalist to specialist mix of physicians, and that the number of residency slots should be limited to 110 percent of U.S. medical school graduates, is likely to have a shorter useful life.

Several readers of drafts of this chapter have pressed me to speculate more precisely about the future of health workforce policy. What, they asked, are the likely results of the convergence in this decade of market forces and fiscal and social conservatism on Federal and state policy and on the efforts of academic health centers to accommodate to their environment?

As I documented three decades ago (Fox 1967), social scientists who extrapolate from history and current events have almost always been wrong. Thus I reluctantly extrapolate, listing five predictions for the convenience of those who may later take note of the ways in which they did not anticipate the future.

1. *The care of persons who lack health care coverage will cease to be an academic responsibility.* The history that began centuries ago with medical charity and was transformed in the 1960s into the harvesting of Medicaid and Medicare payments will continue as risk-contracting, an enterprise that takes no account of academic traditions, missions, and pretensions.

2. *The removal of care for indigent persons from the mission of academic medicine will accelerate the separation of workforce policy from policy to finance health services.* This separation could cause

the drastic reduction of public subsidies for health professions education, including graduate medical education. If demand for such education from prospective students remains as strong as it has recently been, students and their families are likely to bear more of the costs of obtaining undergraduate and first-professional degrees. Employers are likely to pay more of the costs of post-licensure training. Thus education for the health professions is likely to resemble preparation for law, business, and education.

3. *The flattening of the regional pyramids in which health care has been organized since the beginning of the twentieth century will continue.* Flattening will cause shrinkage in the number of hospitals that claim privileged financial status as teaching institutions and lead to the consolidation of hospitals and academic health centers (leading to the elimination, in all but name and symbol, of some venerable medical schools and hospitals).

4. *Medical research will cease to be a calling that is justified by a theory of beneficent progress and instead will resemble research and development in other sectors of the economy.* More of this medical R&D will be proprietary, because it was initially sponsored by private corporations or, more likely, because academics will see the advantages of unconstrained entrepreneurialism over tenure. David Packard and Edward Land in other industries in generations past are some notable examples.

5. *Government, at all levels, will exercise more intrusive oversight of academic health centers.* As the statements of academic institutions that the health care they offer is of higher quality than the products of their competitors become less credible, public scrutiny of their work may increase. Government officials are likely to ask more penetrating questions about the costs and effectiveness of education in clinical settings and about how efficiently research results translate into care and training. Those academics who can document that they offer benefits that the public once accepted on faith may enjoy more security than they now have, if they survive other changes in the health sector.

I hope, however, that readers will accord less attention to these speculations than to the evidence I have arrayed that health workforce policy in the half-century before the 1990s was a signal achievement of American politics. The policy that replaces it will most likely not be so successful and not nearly as satisfying to those who make, implement, and benefit from it.

Works Cited

Axt, R.G. 1952. *The Federal Government and Financing Higher Education.* New York: Columbia University Press.

Bureau of the Census, U.S. Department of Commerce. 1993. *Statistical Abstracts of the United States, 1993.* Washington: Government Printing Office.

Fox, D.M. 1967. *The Discovery of Abundance: Simon N. Patten and the Transformation of Social Theory.* Ithaca, NY: Cornell University Press.

———. 1986. *Health Policies, Health Politics: The British and American Experience, 1911–1965.* Princeton: Princeton University Press.

———. 1995 [and 1993]. *Power and Illness: The Failure and Future of American Health Policy.* Berkeley, CA: University of California Press.

Ganem, J.L., J.K. Krakower, and R.L. Beran. 1994. Review of U.S. medical school finances, 1992–93. *JAMA* 272.

Millett, J.D. 1982. *Conflict in Higher Education: State Government Coordination vs. Institutional Independence.* San Francisco: Jossey Bass.

Mullan, F. 1994. Letter to author, December.

National Commission on Allied Health Education. 1980. *The Future of Allied Health Education.* San Francisco: Jossey Bass.

Rothstein, W.G. 1987. *American Medical Schools and the Practice of Medicine.* New York: Oxford University Press.

Schofield, J.R. 1984. *New and Expanded Medical Schools, Mid-Century to the 1980s.* San Francisco: Jossey Bass.

Smith, H.D. 1945. Diary of conference with the President, June 8, 1945. Harold D. Smith Papers, Franklin D. Roosevelt Presidential Library, Hyde Park, NY.

Federal Regulation and Market Forces in Physician Workforce Management

DAVID A. KINDIG

Since 1965, most of the growth in physicians per capita in the United States has been in the specialties, with the number per 100,000 population rising from 56 in 1965 to 123 in 1992 (figure 1). Over the same period, by contrast, the number of generalists per 100,000 population increased only slightly from 59 to 67 even as the proportion of physicians in generalist practice fell from 51 percent to 35 percent (COGME 1995a).

The number of residents in training has also grown dramatically, especially the international medical graduate (IMG) component. We are train-

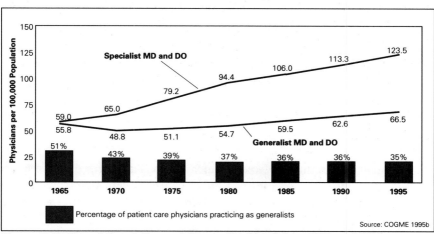

Figure 1. Ratios of Specialist and Generalist Physicians (MD and DO) per 100,000 Population, 1965–95

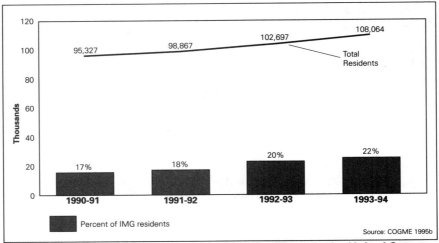

Figure 2. Total Residents and Percent of IMG Residents in the United States, 1990–94

ing 140 percent of the number of American medical graduates in graduate medical education, and this rate has been increasing at a rate of about 4 percent per year over the past seven years (figure 2).

Although there is considerable discussion about whether and to what extent these numbers and trends are on target. The Council of Graduate Medical Education (COGME) concluded in 1994 that the specialist component was considerably in excess of what the country will need or demand in the next several decades (COGME 1994). Since that time, more sophisticated analysis confirms this view (Weiner 1994).

This paper examines the issues of managing the physician workforce, with particular attention to the balance between market forces and regulation in the current environment. It also looks at integrated workforce requirements across various professional groups, particularly in primary care.*

COGME's Physician Workforce Goals

The Council on Graduate Medical Education was authorized by Congress in 1986 to provide an ongoing assessment of physician workforce trends and to recommend appropriate Federal and private sector policy efforts to

---

* Many of the views derive from my role as chair of the COGME, and some are my opinions based on my policy research.

address physician workforce concerns. COGME's charge is to provide advice and make recommendations to Congress and the Secretary of the U.S. Department of Health and Human Services on the following physician workforce issues:

- The supply and distribution of physicians in the United States.
- Current and future shortages or surpluses in the medical and surgical specialties.
- The status of foreign medical school graduates in the United States.
- The quality of existing data bases measuring the supply and distribution of physicians.

COGME also proposes appropriate goals for policy in the physician workforce arena. These goals may result in Federal or private sector policy actions to change the financing and structure of graduate medical education and encourage hospitals, schools of medicine (allopathic and osteopathic), and accrediting bodies to address physician workforce issues.

The goals laid out by COGME in its third report on physician workforce reform (1992) are still relevant and accurate. They are as follows:

1. Decrease the number of physicians, and particularly the number of specialists.
2. Increase the number of generalists.
3. Improve physician geographic distribution.
4. Increase minority representation in medicine.

Since then, much of the discussion on workforce policy has focused on the first two goals.

Projecting Workforce Requirements

Figures 3 and 4 show how the current output of residents with four different generalist to specialist ratios will relate to future physician workforce requirements in a delivery system of fee-for-service and managed care. For generalists, the requirement assumptions indicate a range of 60 to 80 physicians required per 100,000 population; Figure 3 shows that intermediate generalist to specialist production ratios generally approach this range.

For specialists, several managed care requirement scenarios indicate a range of from 85 to 105 physicians required per 100,000 population; only fee-for-service models show higher requirements. None of the four generalist to specialist ratios at the current physician output of 140 percent—the current GME output—of American graduates brings specialist supply into the range of managed care requirements.

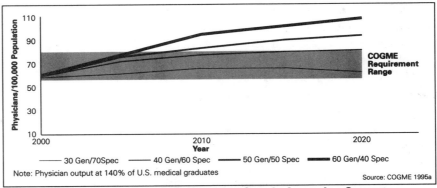

Figure 3. Generalist Patient Care Physician Supply Assuming Current Physician Output Under Various Specialty Mix Scenarios, 2000–20

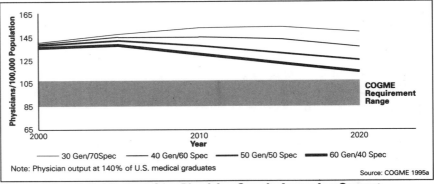

Figure 4. Specialist Patient Care Physician Supply Assuming Current Physician Output Under Various Specialty Mix Scenarios, 2000–20

Figures 5 and 6 show similar projections for generalists and specialists if total GME output is reduced to 110 percent of American medical graduates at various specialty mixes; only when 50 to 60 percent of residents opt for generalist GME training does specialist supply (and, therefore, total physician supply) approach the requirement range under managed care conditions.

The Roles of Market Forces and Regulations

When viewing these data, the manager and politician must decide if policy intervention is necessary. Those who favor no action may challenge the validity of the supply or requirements figures; they may hold that managed care will continue to expand and, therefore, the excess will not materialize. Or they may believe that the differences will resolve themselves through natural or market forces.

In its third report, COGME determined that the potential excess was so great, the gap would not limit itself naturally. COGME, therefore, developed a policy that would lead to a reduction of total resident output to 110 percent of U.S. medical graduates, with a 50:50 generalist to specialist output. In addition, COGME felt that the influence of Medicare GME funding in driving the growth in the number of residents, particularly international medical graduates, was counter to national goals (COGME 1992).

In its fourth report, COGME (1994) proposed a regulatory approach to

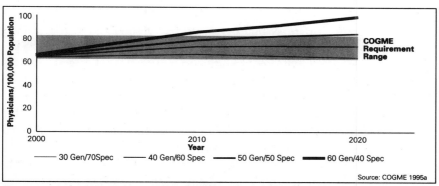

Figure 5. Generalist Patient Care Physician Supply Under Alternative Specialty Mix Scenarios When Physician Output Reduced to 110% of U.S. Medical Graduates, 2000–20

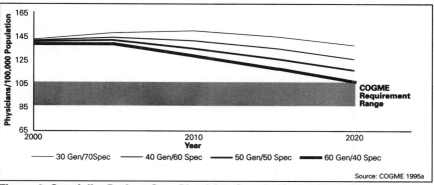

Figure 6. Specialist Patient Care Physician Supply Under Alternative Specialty Mix Scenarios When Physician Output Reduced to 110% of U.S. Medical Graduates, 2000–20

this problem. The approach was characterized by decentralization of decision making and limited Federal micromanagement. The 110 percent/50:50 graduate medical education strategy implemented through consortia and supported by funds from all payors was seriously considered as a part of President Clinton's unsuccessful general health reform plan.

Since that time, many analysts have speculated that market forces are bidding up generalist salaries and reducing salaries for a number of specialties in some markets. COGME recently reviewed these trends and concluded that Medicare incentives are still strong, particularly in light of the other financial pressures that teaching hospitals now face. In addition, although market forces are working in the generalist direction, the academic underpinnings of ambulatory graduate medical education remain fragile (COGME 1995a).

In the current climate, regulatory or all payor funding approaches are not politically possible. COGME recently recommended (COGME 1995b) that Medicare incentives be used to influence national workforce goals. It is likely that, to reduce the Federal deficit, Medicare GME funding will be significantly reduced. COGME has recommended, therefore, that funding for IMGs be gradually reduced, and upweighted payments be made for GME in all ambulatory settings (e.g., clinics, health centers, and managed care plans). This strategy would not prohibit programs from hiring more residents from non-Medicare funds; nevertheless, it is expected that growth will cease and reductions will be gradually made. Transition strategies for programs dependent on IMGs for critical service provision will need to accompany such provisions. Given the distributional effect of IMG positions, it is possible that such a proposal will attract more support than previously from teaching hospitals facing possible deep, across-the-board cuts in Medicare indirect medical education payments.

A step in the right direction, and one that would be less controversial, would simply be capping the number of residents that Medicare pays for. Adopting this approach depends on how the politics of this issue, and Medicare funding, in general, play out. Whatever the result, it will be essential to continue to track the workforce composition carefully, as well as the effect of such composition on cost, quality, and access.

However, it is difficult for the traditional data collection and research methods to track movement and trends in the physician workforce accurately. It is critical, therefore, to develop mechanisms, perhaps local "listening posts," to track both trends and anecdotal data as accurately and quickly as possible.

Estimating Integrated Requirements for Primary Care

All of the above discussion deals solely with physicians, implicitly assuming a continued constant role for nonphysician providers in physician work. But there is also renewed interest in the interrelationships, mainly fostered by the generalist and nurse-practitioner emphasis in the Clinton health reform debate. Even though no legislation was passed, the "bully pulpit" effect on generalism created an environment in which moderate to extreme expansion of primary care residencies and nurse practitioner and physician assistant programs was planned in addition to the expansion planned for osteopathic medicine at the undergraduate level.

The evidence to date indicates only a modest national need for generalists (Weiner 1994). Some leaders in medicine and nursing, therefore, are looking at integrated requirements in a quasi zero-sum context. Because there has been some recent acrimonious discussion between medicine and nursing in the previous year over turf issues, COGME and the National Advisory Committee on Nursing Education and Practice established a joint work group in 1995 to model appropriate interprofessional relationships.

One reason for some of the recent professional acrimony was the wide dissemination of research findings on a project mainly carried out in the late 1970s in Kaiser Permanente managed care settings (GMENAC 1981). The findings showed that mid-level providers could do 80 percent of the work of primary care physicians. However, although this work suggests that a majority of primary care tasks can theoretically be, or have actually been, handled by nonphysician providers, the data do not translate into direct substitution calculations at the job level. Roles are not simply made up of visits that can be substituted and are also seriously complicated by visit complexity, supervision, and nonsubstituting essential tasks.

Another way to look at the substitution issue is to think of productivity increasing when a nonphysician provider is added to a generalist physician practice; it is the way it is often conceived in managed care organizations. The literature indicates that the number of patients that could be served increases from 20 percent to 60 percent depending on a variety of organizational factors. In one mature health maintenance organization, for example, the patient panel for a generalist physician increases from 1,800 to 2,700 when a nurse practitioner or physician assistant is added (Kindig and Kaufman 1995).

Figure 7 illustrates these relationships. The vertical axis is the number of patient care generalist physicians in the country; the number 182,000 is the

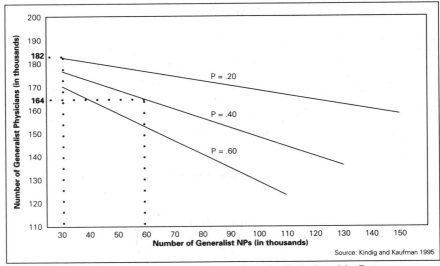

Figure 7. A Substitution Model for Estimating the Relationship Between Generalist MDs and Generalist NPs, 1992

figure for the entire United States in 1992. The horizontal axis represents the number of nurse practitioners in generalist practice; the axis begins at 30,000 which is the approximate number in generalist roles in 1992. The three sloping lines represent productivity increases in additional patients that could be cared for (20%, 40%, 60%) when one nurse practitioner is added to a generalist physician's practice. This approach allows estimates to be made of the combination of generalist physicians and nurse practitioners needed to create the same amount of generalist capacity at a given productivity level.

The dotted line reflects only one of many possible combinations; in this case, doubling the number of nurse practitioners to 60,000 at 40 percent productivity permits the number of generalist physicians to be reduced to 164,000. Thinking about integrated requirements in this way will allow a much more informed policy discussion than has been possible in the past.

It is important that such models also be developed for specialist work. The relative cost-effectiveness considerations should allow for a wider range of possibilities than suggested in the generalist case. An ultimate model might include all workforce members at a community or population level, with the potential to indicate cost implications of an array of integrated workforce combinations.

Conclusion

Interest in health workforce issues seems to wax and wane. Nevertheless, the critical role the workforce plays in terms of access, cost, quality, academic health center organization, and academic health center finance will keep the issues discussed above under scrutiny for quite awhile. In a health economy characterized by market forces and regulation, society will continue to debate the appropriate balance of such forces. At the least, there is a national responsibility to undertake data collection and analysis so that markets and public policy are informed by accurate information. And, given the pace of change in the system, new mechanisms need to be developed to accurately track trends.

In my opinion, market forces will be somewhat effective in the short run in increasing generalist supply, although continued public support for generalist education programs will be an important factor in generating this increase; they should also have some effectiveness in encouraging nonphysician substitution. I doubt, however, that these forces will reduce the number of specialists being produced nor deal effectively with the issues of geographic distribution (in the absence of universal coverage) and minority representation. To deal with these matters, Federal and state intervention will continue to be needed for some time.

Works Cited

COGME (Council on Graduate Medical Education). 1992. *Third Report: Improving Access to Health Care Through Physician Workforce Reform Directions for the 21st Century.* Rockville, MD: COGME, U.S. Department of Health and Human Services.

————. 1994. *Fourth Report. Recommendations to Improve Access to Health Care Through Physician Workforce Reform.* Rockville, MD: COGME, U.S. Department of Health and Human Services.

————. 1995a. *Sixth Report. Managed Health Care: Implications for the Physician Workforce and Medical Education.* Rockville, MD: COGME, U.S. Department of Health and Human Services.

————. 1995b. *Seventh Report. COGME 1995 Physician Workforce Funding Recommendations for Department of Health and Human Services Programs.* Rockville, MD: COGME, U.S. Department of Health and Human Services.

GMENAC (Graduate Medical Education National Advisory Committee). 1981. *Nonphysician Health Care Provider Technical Panel.* Vol. 6. Washington: U.S. Department of Health and Human Services.

Kindig, D.A. and N.J. Kaufman. 1995. How Much Physician Work Can Nurse Practitioners and Physician Assistants Do? Unpublished paper.

Weiner, J.P. 1994. Forecasting the effects of health reform on U.S. physician workforce requirement: Evidence from HMO staffing patterns. *JAMA* 272.

Health Workforce Policy Lessons From Britain

MICHAEL ASHLEY-MILLER

Both the United States and the United Kingdom are undergoing the most significant changes in health care in several decades and face a number of common problems. Although the different cultures and systems in the two countries do not allow for common solutions, there are potential lessons that policy makers in the United States can learn from the United Kingdom. Not dissimilar changes are also occurring in many European countries at this time (Defever 1994).

As in the United States, (1) the large array of concerned players and interested and influential bodies, and (2) the impossibility of maintaining a status quo for a sufficient length of time have made it impossible to examine fully the basic issues of "Where are we now?"; "Where do we want to be in a specific time?"; "How do we get there?" This inability to examine the total situation has resulted in a next-best approach. The approach is not without its wide scans but always falls short of full appreciation of complex interrelationships and fails to anticipate the sometimes significant knock-on effects of imposed changes.

In this paper I briefly describe the salient features of the health care system in the two countries at present, discuss the circumstances and pressures imposed on them both internally and externally, and offer some conclusions and recommendations for the United States.

The Drive for Efficiency in the National Health Service

The prime driving force for the recent changes in the United Kingdom (Secretary of State for Health 1989) has been a wish by government to control the escalating costs of health care provided through the National Health Service (NHS). The original concept of controlling or even reducing costs was to be met by introducing the principles of competition and establishing a "market." However, it soon became apparent to the government that the goal of a free market could not be accomplished. Instead, competitive principles would have to be introduced in a controlled or contrived market situation. For example, using market freedom, one purchasing health authority placed a contract for cheaper services with another hospital rather than with the major teaching hospital they usually use in London. The latter hospital immediately became financially nonviable. Because of a predetermined hospital strategy for London, the government could not allow this failure, and stepped in to cover the shortfall.

The United Kingdom, therefore, is now moving toward savings through increased efficiency (although there is little scope for much further savings), a drive for evidence-based medicine, and strict budgeting within a contrived market. Budgetary control is increasingly resulting in temporary suspensions or even abolition of certain hospital and community services. The result is increasing media concern over such maneuvers and an occasional testing of their legality in the courts.

In the United Kingdom, the need for important cost and budgeting information within this contrived market has also resulted in a considerable increase in information technology costs (both capital and recurrent). The drive for better management of resources has also brought about a near-threefold increase in managerial staff, far greater than expected. As yet, there is no evidence that this expenditure and drive have led to improvements in patient care and outcomes. Even information about readmissions following early discharge from the hospital is not yet available. A determined (and proper) attempt to reduce the "two years and over" hospital waiting lists was successful, but with a concomitant rise in the one-year waiting list. Once the latter was reduced, there was an increase in the length of time between referral by the primary care physician to the patient's being seen by a specialist and then put on another waiting list. "The construction of NHS waiting lists is a peculiar art form!" remarks Klein (1995).

Unequal Access to Care

The introduction of fund-holding, or budget-holding,* into the well-established system of general practices has resulted in a two-tier NHS system in

---

* A system introduced in the 1990 reforms in which large general practices are allocated a fund or budget to purchase health care for patients registered with the practice. The incentive for efficiency is that any unexpended portions of the budget may be used to improve or expand practice services.

certain areas. When hospitals exceed their budgets for the financial year, they can afford to offer nonemergency treatment only to patients referred from fund-holding practices; in these cases, the practices can pay for treatment. Patients in nonfund-holding practices are forced to wait for treatment until the new year's centrally determined financial allocations allow full hospital activity to be resumed. Urgent action to correct such unexpected developments may create further unanticipated effects.

NHS care of long-term, chronically ill, and elderly patients is shrinking; one example is the wholesale closure of long-stay institutions for psychiatric patients. Following implementation of the Community Care Act in 1993, local authorities have the responsibility for purchasing continuing care for citizens in their community, but this care is now more likely to be provided by private nursing homes, relatives, or, in some cases, no one. Unfortunately, it appears that community care is proving too expensive for local authorities to fund adequately; it is also poorly managed.

Although the latest major reorganization to the NHS that took place in 1990 occurred with a "big bang," consequent changes have taken a considerable amount of time. The NHS has only a single paymaster, the government. The private sector offers little competition; its services are mainly restricted to elective surgery. In some areas, there is active public and private collaboration, with purchasers buying services the NHS doesn't provide.

The one area where the private sector has expanded considerably is in providing community and nursing home care, services that have been specifically encouraged through fiscal direction by government. However, the private sector does cause concern by creaming off qualified medical, nursing, and other staff for whom they have not made any contribution toward training costs.

In general, the NHS in the United Kingdom now has:

- An internal, controlled market financed solely by central government.
- An expanding but noncomprehensive private sector, mainly in the hospital domain, that does not at present pose particular competitive threats to the NHS.
- A well-established primary health care system staffed by trained medical, nursing, and managerial staff mainly working in groups of four or more doctors.
- Established procedures for assessing medical workforce needs through the Medical Workforce Standing Advisory Committee.*

---

* These have been criticized for paying insufficient attention to the requirements for all health care staff and the issues of skill mix and incentives that could lead to further doctor surpluses.

- Strict control of overall medical student numbers and of entry into hospital specialties and general practice.
- Rudimentary machinery to assess the future nurse workforce requirement.

Morale Concerns of the Workforce

Following major reorganization of the NHS in 1990, one could have expected the system to have shaken down and now be progressing fairly smoothly toward the objectives set by government. Unfortunately, achievement of a considerable number of objectives has been at huge cost, both in financial terms and, more important, in personnel terms. There has been a severe loss of morale in virtually all sections of the service.

For the first time, both the Royal College of Nursing and the Royal College of Midwives and Health Visitors have passed resolutions to abandon their "no strike" agreement. Moreover, nurses feel marginalized, with their problems compounded by the new market culture. They wonder whether "altruism, compassion, and social justice have any place in the new world of balance sheets and short-term contracts" (Salvage 1995). There has also been progressive unrest over pay in the largest health worker union.

There is also disillusionment and stress among junior doctors, particularly residents (Firth-Cozens 1987). A recent survey of hospital consultants, general practitioners, and senior hospital managers indicated that this level of stress is high (Caplan 1994). This finding has been confirmed for all doctors (Holland in press). In fact, doctors in the United Kingdom have a threefold higher incidence of suicide than the general population. Applications for early retirement from senior doctors has risen, and the British Medical Association recently claimed a loss of some 20 percent of doctors within three years of their qualifying. Increased workload, both clinical and managerial, is certainly a significant factor. Not surprisingly, applications from students to enter medical school has fallen, although applicants still well exceed the number of places.

Unfortunately, there is still a widespread climate of hostility and distrust between doctors and managers and between health authorities and the social services department of local authorities. In brief, NHS has experienced

- A large proportion of all workforce sectors dissatisfied with working conditions.
- A small but significant shortfall in hospital doctors in senior and specialist grades.

- A recent significant fall-off in people wishing to enter training for general practice.
- A rise in stress-related ill health among doctors.
- A fall in nurse recruitment (and possibly retention).
- A distortion of equity in access due to the introduction of fund-holding into general practice.
- Additional pressures on providers—over and above those from purchasing health authorities—to reduce their costs and improve their services, thereby adding to their difficulties in planning future investment and provision.
- A serious, widespread failure in effective and coordinated community care due to serious underfunding, cost-shifting between local authorities and health authorities, and poor management.

The Pressures Ahead

Clearly, all is far from well with the NHS. In a recent blistering attack on the reforms, Sir Douglas Black (1995), past president of the Royal College of Physicians, offered his personal view of the situation.

> I have argued at some length elsewhere that the basis of a health service should be altruistic cooperation and not commercial competition; and that the reforms have enhanced the role of line-management and correspondingly devalued clinical judgment, to the detriment both of patients and of society which bears the cost. The reforms have done nothing to narrow the gap in health between rich and poor and they have produced an extravaganza of finance-driven contractual bureaucracy, for which the Health Authorities Act will bring no greater amelioration than any of the previous reorganizations from 1974 onwards.
>
> For the immediate future, the priority can only be damaged limitation in the interest of patients. For the longer term, the choice is between more and more managerial devices, in the attempt to wring some clinical and social good out of a witless market; or a frank admission that as a potential regulatory of health care the market has proved inadequate or worse, and must be excised, together with the whole overblown apparatus of purchasers, providers and contracts (p. 188).

The United States

Most health care in the United States is privately funded and provided. Three key issues have serious implications for the future role of the American physician, and each is underpinned by the desire for a "free" market in health care. First, Bulger (1994) points out, competition between providers and health maintenance organizations has led to managed care being delivered by all health care providers.

> [T]he combination of managed care, competition, and for-profit health care organizations has led to serious concerns about purchasing equity for the patient; medical education of the student; and clinical autonomy of doctors. Secondly, there is a lack of definition between the generalist and specialist roles of physicians, since many specialty physicians consider themselves as the primary contact physician. Thirdly, a lack of manpower planning has led to an excess of specialist physicians and undersupply of generalist physicians (p. 1).

These are also the problems of discontinuity of care and huge, increasing and unacceptable costs to Federal and state governments, employers, and the public. The paradox the nation now faces is the wish for low-cost, comprehensive, high-quality health care while retaining the freedom to purchase such care when and where wanted, the justifiable pride in the best technical medicine in the world, and the desire to extend access to this care.

The Move to Managed Care

Despite a genuine rise in concern about health care for the large population of uninsured persons, Federal and state budgetary difficulties, particularly with regard to funding public hospitals, are having perverse effects. In anticipation of the health reform promised by the Clinton administration in 1992, many health insurance companies, HMOs, and business corporations saw financial profit from an expansion of managed care and moved to anticipate the likely changes. Almost overnight, a dynamic competitive market developed in the purchase and provision of health care. This change occurred at an almost bewildering speed, even to the business community, let alone people trained to manage or work in the health field.

Rampant managed care poses a particular threat to teaching institutions because it makes health care a price-sensitive commodity. Service provision becomes the most important function of the hospital, and previous government and third-party payor cross-subsidization of infrastructures for education and research and training time for doctors becomes unsustainable. Education of students is, therefore, in danger of being equated solely with accounting costs rather than being seen as an investment in an organization's or the health system's future standing.

The unacceptable cost of health care is compounded by the awareness of continued inadequate access to care and the uneven distribution of doctors. This state of affairs has led to public disenchantment with its investment in medical education schools. This government frustration has led to specific plans to change the way money is paid to medical schools and teaching hospitals for education. In some cases, it has resulted in laws mandating the percentage of graduating physicians who must go into primary care (Curtis 1995).

Workforce Concerns

In the United States today, in general,

- Medical schools are providing many doctors with skills inappropriate to managed care market needs.
- There is a climate of medical student debt—estimated to average $80,000—upon graduation which has led to excess entrance into specialist training.
- Doctors are becoming more resistant to both nurse substitution and the training of foreign students and graduates.
- There is no well-established primary health care system or an organized and uniformly distributed community-based ambulatory service. Managed care is a strong force for the development of such a system with the greater involvement of nurses, nurse practitioners, and physician assistants in its operations.
- The current increased demand for primary health care staff (doctors, physician assistants, and nurse practitioners) seems to be driven more by financial considerations than by an assessed health care need.
- Pressure for savings has also reduced the length of stay in hospitals. Thus, although there is a need for a more intensive hospital workforce overall, there are too many trained hospital nurses. In addition, little redeployment has yet taken place into the potentially expanding area of community care. (Again, there is understandable resentment and resistance to substitution by nurse assistants.)
- As yet, the United States does not appear to be providing widespread services for an increasingly large number of mentally ill, elderly, infirm, and physically disabled people who will require care in the community.

The United Kingdom experience shows the value of properly and specially trained primary health care physicians. In the United States, as Vanselow points out in this book, many primary care physicians require extensive retraining. Managed care organizations complain about lack of experience and knowledge in the following areas: ambulatory care and common office problems and procedures in gynecology, orthopedics and dermatology; patient communications skills; multidisciplinary team patient care; public health principles of health promotion and disease prevention; referral skills; and information systems. Some managed care organizations have established residency programs to address these concerns, and one has considered opening its own medical school.

So far, most of the limited research undertaken by managed care to demonstrate effectiveness and safety of substitution appears to concentrate on studies of process rather than outcome.

The major force driving personnel substitution is the need to control costs in an increasingly competitive health care marketplace. As emphasized by Schwartz (1994), however, "the marketplace is rapidly implementing new forms of health care workforce substitution without any formal or rigorous evaluation of the safety or effectiveness of such interventions."

Substitution represents both an opportunity and a challenge for academic health centers. The systematic collection of widespread, sound data and the undertaking of quality research appears to be an urgent priority.

The Pressures Ahead
In brief, in the United States,

- The market has far more capacity than is needed for "driven" managed care with increasing enrollment.
- There are too many hospital beds.
- "Health care consumers, especially those from ethnic and culturally diverse communities, are disconnected from the health care system. There is little opportunity to help shape local health care systems and health care education systems to meet their needs." (California State University Institute and The FHP Foundation 1994).
- There are too many hospital-trained and hospital-based nurses.
- The safety of cost-cutting and substitution is inadequately assessed.
- The threat of unemployment is allowing managed care to dictate clinical health care standards to the detriment of traditional professional beliefs, and there seems little way in which the tide can be stemmed in the present circumstances. Once lost, these standards will be very difficult to regain.

Conclusion and Recommendations for the United States

The United Kingdom experience, based on a belief that the U.S. model of competition could lower costs—albeit implemented with a controlled internal market—has produced serious consequences with, on the one hand, no evidence of improved patient care outcomes and, on the other hand, a considerable increase in NHS administration costs. Poor morale and stress-related illness among health care staff, whether it results in permanent illness or a search for alternative employment, is likely to lead to increased dependence on foreign-trained personnel. A possible lesson to be learned by the United States from the UK experience is that the excess of 150,000 doctors predicted in the United States by the turn of the century may be an overestimate due to workforce attrition resulting from dissatisfaction, retraining, and reduced educational opportunities in the health professions.

In the United States, the introduction of managed care in a free market has apparently driven down costs. Increasingly, however, this "saving" is diverted into profit to those who run the organizations and their stockholders rather than improved health care.

Furthermore, there is a danger that the current wave of entrepreneurs may take a short-term view of health care and not invest in a future workforce. At present they can hire a ready-made educated and trained workforce (excepting primary care). They may, for example, decide to sell the enterprise as soon as profits are squeezed to a smaller percentage. Succeeding investors, who will have lower profits, may be equally unwilling to invest in training a balanced workforce. The likelihood is that a number of medical education establishments will be forced to close.

The United States must assess future health demands, needs, and the integrated workforce skills needed to meet these needs. Such assessments are notoriously difficult to make and also need to be repeated at regular, frequent intervals.

Here are some specific recommendations to my colleagues in the United States.

1. Consult widely with providers and the public about the services they want.
2. Deploy specialists to work on a part-time basis supplementing primary care teams in the community.
3. Set up courses to train specialists for primary care work in a primary care setting.
4. Create more course opportunities for appropriately selected medical

and nursing students wishing to work in primary care.

5. Promote joint training, when appropriate, among students in medicine, nursing, and other health professions.

6. Because of the danger of losing professional and ethical standards as the market takes over health care delivery, introduce ethics into all courses for health care staff.

7. Make data collection an immediate priority.

In the long-term, many consumers may refuse to put up with diminishing standards (e.g., limitations upon care, waiting lists), and turn back to buying—probably at increased cost—what they see as the better care they once received on a fee-for-service basis (Light 1995). Alternatively, U.S. health care might become a business and cease to be a profession.

Like an audience watching Houdini, I am filled with apprehension for the future of U.S. medical care. Everyone knew the resilience and strength of the man who would survive death-defying acts unscathed, but it should be remembered that he was killed by an unanticipated blow below the belt.

Works Cited

Black, D. 1995. Equity or Equality. *J. R. Coll. Phys. (London)* 29(3).

Bulger, R. 1994. Overview of the United States Health Workforce. Unpublished paper.

Caplan, R.P. 1994. Stress, anxiety and depression in hospital consultants, general practitioners and senior health service managers. *BMJ* 309(6964).

Curtis, P. 1995. Primary care and the maelstrom of health care reform in the USA. *Brit. J. Gen. Pract.* 45 (August).

California State University Institute and The FHP Foundation. 1994. *A Blueprint for Change: Health Care Education Reform.* Long Beach, CA: The FHP Foundation.

Defever, M. 1994. The politics of health care benefits. *Health Pol.* 28(3).

Firth-Cozens, J. 1987. Emotional stress in junior house officers. *BMJ* 295.

Holland, W. W. In press. London: Nuffield Provincial Hospitals Trust.

Klein, R. 1995. Big bang health reform—Does it work? The case of Britain's National Health Service reforms. *Milbank Q.* 73(3).

Light, D. 1995. Homo economicus: Escaping the traps of managed competition. *Eur. J. Public Health.* 5(3).

Salvage, J. 1995. What's happening to nursing? *BMJ* 311(29).

Schwartz, J.S. 1994. Restructuring and deploying the American health care workforce: Matching needs more appropriately to skills and training. *LDI Health Policy & Research Quarterly*. 2(4).

Secretary of State for Health. 1989. *Working for Patients* (Cmmd 555). London: Her Majesty's Stationery Office.

Physician Workforce Policy in Canada

HARVEY BARKUN

Although a number of projects in Canada currently deal with the effect of nurse practitioners, midwives, and other health workers on health care delivery, health workforce policy at both the Federal and provincial levels is oriented almost exclusively to addressing the number of medical students in the country's sixteen medical schools, the number of residents in postgraduate programs (called graduate medical education in the United States), and the distribution of physicians by discipline and by geography. This is because the education, training, and proper distribution of physicians has been essential to the success of the universal, publicly funded health system of Canada.

The Advent of Universal Coverage

Before 1970, the United States and Canada were indistinguishable in the production of physicians and in physician practice patterns. Universal coverage of hospital costs, implemented in Canada in 1960 (Hospital Insurance and Diagnostic Services Act 1957), was the only real difference between the two. Between 1965 and 1970, however, three major decisions were made that have altered the health care system, the medical education process, and the practice of medicine in Canada. These decisions have inextricably linked physician workforce policy, medical education, and the health care system.

First, the Hall Commission in 1965 recommended increasing the number of physicians in Canada to meet the needs of a population growing steadily, mainly through immigration.

Second, the Commission recommended the installation of the current insurance system, called Medicare, that guarantees reasonable access to all medically necessary services for all permanent residents of Canada.

The third decision was to place all postgraduate medical education under the aegis of the sixteen universities with faculties of medicine.

Financing the Canadian Health Care System

In Canada, provincial governments finance basic medical and institutional care and medical education through revenues derived from general taxation and Federal contributions. Physicians are paid mostly on a fee-for-service basis by provincial health plans, and hospitals are funded through global budgets by provincial ministries of health. In 1994, provincial governments in Canada financed 73 percent of all health care costs. The bulk of the remaining health care costs were for nonessential services (e.g., cosmetic surgery) and pharmaceuticals.

The Federal government has diminished its contributions to provincial health care systems over the years. It now provides between 30 and 35 percent of provincial health care budgets and has announced further decreases for the next several years. These cutbacks are necessary because of the large Federal deficit and heavy debt.*

Federal transfers to the provinces for postsecondary education today have also diminished. All university education today is fundamentally financed by provincial ministries of education, not tuition fees. Current annual medical school tuition ranges from about $2,000 to $4,000 (Canadian dollars) for Canadian students (ACMC 1995). In comparison, for the 1993–94 academic year in the United States, median annual tuition and fees ranged from $8,161 to $17,459 (in American dollars) for public medical schools, depending on residency status of the student, and were $22,272 for private schools (Jolly and Hudley 1995).

Limiting the Number of Practicing Physicians

The largest portion of health expenditures derives from physician remuneration, especially from investigative and therapeutic decisions by physicians. Caps on remuneration are built into the agreements signed by the provincial medical associations with physicians. Consequently, the only mechanisms for cost-control, which has become a major issue in view of the decreased funding, is to limit the number of doctors entering practice and

---

* Some provinces have balanced budgets, although the largest provinces, Ontario and Quebec, with over 58 percent of the total population of Canada, are struggling with large deficits and a heavy debt load.

encourage those in active practice to retire. (The current physician to population ratio in Canada is 1:534, compared with 1:420 in the United States.)

Two strategies are used to limit the number of doctors who will eventually practice medicine in Canada. The first is for provincial ministries of education to limit the number of students admitted to Canadian medical schools. The second is the strict physician workforce planning process that is followed by provincial ministries of health.

Reducing Undergraduate Medical Education

There is little to distinguish undergraduate medical education in Canada from that in the United States. All sixteen schools are accredited by the Liaison Committee on Medical Education (LCME). As in the United States, some schools have moved to problem-based learning, curriculum development is in constant evolution, and each graduating class in Canada has a number of students who match to U.S. residency training programs.

In 1991–92, total first-year enrollments for Canada was 1,775. A gradual 10 percent decrease in admissions has been implemented since then. The actual admissions numbers are negotiated school by school, province by province. Quebec had already begun such a reduction a few years earlier; in Ontario, the faculty of medicine at the University of Toronto reduced its first-year class from 252 in 1990–92 to 177. The effect of these decreases will be felt when the first smaller classes complete their undergraduate and postgraduate training and are eligible for licensing. Today, requests for entry into medical school remains high, with more than five applications for each available position.

Physician Workforce Provincial Planning

Since the late 1970s, provincial ministries of health have placed a limit on the number of physicians who will eventually practice in Canada, and their geographical distribution by instituting a consortium planning structure. This approach was arrived at through discussion and agreement by a number of stakeholders: health ministries, medical schools that train both undergraduate and postgraduate students, student and resident associations, and provincial medical associations. District health councils representing regional health needs have also been involved.

TABLE DE CONCERTATION

The first such planning structure, known as the Table de Concertation, was set up in Quebec in the late 1970s, and similar tables are now in place in all provinces. The table provided a rational planning framework for the physician workforce, and also has been instrumental in correcting disproportions between specialists and primary care physicians, and filling demonstrated needs both in geography and by discipline.

At one of its first meetings, the Table de Concertation in Quebec confronted the problem of too many specialists and too few family physicians. (The ratio was 55:45.) The four medical schools in Quebec agreed that, to correct the problem, 60 percent of the postgraduate positions available to the 600 students graduating in medicine would be reserved for programs in family medicine.

Because these family physicians were needed in the nonurban areas of the province, concurrent measures reduced physician remuneration for the first three years of practice in an urban area, and increased remuneration for practice in rural and other nonurban areas. Within five years, the ratio had evened to 50:50, and family physicians were practicing throughout the province.

The distribution of residents in the thirty-five postgraduate programs in Quebec (thirty-four specialties and family medicine) is reviewed regularly at the Table de Concertation. Once the ratio of specialty to family medicine had been corrected, a number of studies identified a shortage of some specialties and a surplus of others. As a result, the Table de Concertation agreed that some residency positions should be transferred from family medicine to the specialties of general internal medicine, general surgery, and anesthesiology, and training positions available in dermatology and plastic surgery were reduced markedly.

IMG POLICY

One complication that initially skewed the workforce planning process in Quebec was the extensive presence of international medical graduates (IMG) in postgraduate programs. However, as the number of funded residency positions became fixed on a triennial basis at the Table de Concertation, the four faculties of medicine in Quebec began to gradually decrease the number of IMGs admitted to their programs by establishing criteria that gave priority to graduates of medical schools accredited by the Liaison Committee on Medical Education in Quebec, Canada, and the United States. The ministry also placed a limit of ten IMGs per year on admission to these programs after competitive examination and a preresident training period.

Similar programs to address the IMG supply problem have been initiated throughout Canada. National enrollment by IMGs is at an all-time low of 3.5 percent (58 out of 1,652) at the first postgraduate year and 9.7 percent (662 out of 6,831) of the total number of residents (ACMC 1995).

This policy has not been without its problems. IMGs with landed immigrant status have mounted human rights challenges, as yet to no avail. Canadian immigration authorities abroad discourage foreign-trained physicians from applying to immigrate as physicians, and those who do apply (as physicians) must sign a declaration stating that they realize they may never practice in Canada. The number of IMGs arriving in Canada has decreased, but a certain number enter as refugees, spouses of applicants, or with a different declared profession.

In addition, the Canadian Resident Matching Service is now run in two iterations. Since postgraduate training is required for a license to practice, priority in the first iteration is reserved for graduates of Canadian medical schools with no previous clinical postgraduate education. The second iteration is open to all other applicants. Of the 1,300 graduates matched in 1995, 29 were IMGs.

Effect of Postgraduate Medical Education Reform

The success of workforce planning was possible only in the context of a universal, publicly administered, single-payor system of health care with postgraduate medical education under the university.

The decision to place postgraduate medical education under university jurisdiction in Canada has had far-reaching positive outcomes for education, financing, and influencing the distribution of physicians by discipline and by geography.

Some of the outcomes include
- Emphasis on education rather than service for the postgraduate trainee.
- Implementation of important curriculum changes.
- Improvement in evaluation of programs and residents.
- Rapid development of criteria to evaluate clinical competencies.
- Rational physician workforce planning.
- Increased dialogue between funders and trainers.
- Separation of accrediting bodies from those responsible for programs.
- Increased training outside traditional tertiary care sites.
- Creation of policy levers necessary to implement decisions based on population needs.

Postgraduate medical training in Canada is an educational experience in which service constitutes only one pedagogical mode of training. Although program directors would dearly love to have as many residents as possible in their programs in order to enhance prestige and lighten the service load on faculty, the number of residents in any given institution has no effect whatsoever on the budget. This practice is in direct contrast with that in the United States where direct and indirect Medicare graduate medical education costs are tied to numbers of residents.

Once a resident is registered as a postgraduate student in a university-based accredited training program in Canada, the resident is paid regardless of the location of the training site. This policy has permitted programs to extend the educational experience outside the traditional teaching hospital wherever appropriate. Rotations to community hospitals, ambulatory clinics, and rural practices are all possible and are encouraged by the two colleges, the Royal College of Physicians and Surgeons and the College of Family Physicians, that constitute Canada's postgraduate accrediting bodies. The direct costs of resident training have been included in institutional global budgets for many years.

Specialty Medicine

In 1970, the accrediting and certifying body of the Royal College of Physicians and Surgeons of Canada decreed that only university-based programs would be accredited for residency training of specialists, and only those candidates who satisfactorily completed such a training program would be eligible to sit for the certifying (board) examinations. Although major university teaching hospitals initially paid only lip service to this new structure, the threat of withdrawal of accreditation eventually prompted implementation of this policy in all specialty programs at all medical schools.

Programs and curricula are planned by the university. Faculty interview applicants and hire, teach, and evaluate residents. All residents register as postgraduate students at the university, pay modest tuition fees ranging from several hundred dollars to $2,500 (Canadian dollars), and receive remuneration from the province, with either the university or the affiliated hospital acting as paymaster.

When this system was put in place, interns and residents organized through provincial professional associations. These provincial associations negotiate both salaries and conditions of work. Salaries in most provinces ranged from about $30,500 for interns to about $45,000 for residents in 1995 in Canadian dollars.* In Ontario and British Columbia, salaries were

---

* The exchange rate in November 1995 was $1.25 (Canadian) to $1.00 (U.S.).

higher, ranging from close to $38,000 to $55,600 and $36,700, to $51,700, respectively. By comparison, in the 1995–96 academic year, U.S. salary percentiles for first-year residents range from $29,838 to $32,881, and for fifth-year residents they range from $34,793 to $40,275, all in American dollars (Philibert 1995).

Family Medicine

The accrediting and certifying body for family medicine is the College of Family Physicians of Canada. Until 1996, the route to certification in family medicine was through practice eligibility. As academic departments of family medicine were created in the medical schools, the alternative became graduation from a university-based training program in family medicine. The second route has become virtually the only way to become a certified family physician. Of the almost 900 candidates who sat for certification examinations in 1995, only 50 came through the practice-eligible route, which is in the process of being phased out.

Specialty-Family Medicine Mix

Another major contrast between the United States and Canadian systems is the marked difference in the ratio of specialists and primary care physicians.* Currently, the split upon entry into postgraduate medical education is approximately 60:40. Since the goal is to maintain 50:50 at the practice levels, family medicine is a two-year training program compared to five years for most specialties.

Let me suggest why family medicine has attracted almost half the graduates of Canadian medical schools. First and foremost, family physicians are not gatekeepers. They are treating physicians, close to the community and dealing with concepts only rarely considered by specialists—health promotion, disease prevention, life style, and other determinants of health. They can practice among the poor, the indigent, the homeless, and know that in the universal comprehensive health care system, they will be paid. Medical students in Canada are motivated to consider family medicine because it is such a satisfying discipline.

Although student debt is rising in Canada, it is nowhere near the levels in the United States. And although there is an income gap between most specialties and family medicine, it is not in the same proportion as that in

---

* Primary care in Canada means family medicine. General internists and general pediatricians are specialists and, as such, fulfill the role of consultants. Canada no longer trains "general practitioners."

the United States. Moreover, because training in family medicine in Canada is two years, while the average training period in a specialty is five years, family medicine graduates earn a living for three years before their specialist colleagues enter the marketplace.

Every medical school in Canada has an established full academic department of family medicine. The academic image of family medicine was not created overnight. But with the advent of certification in family medicine as a self-standing discipline, resources slowly became available to meet educational and scholarly objectives. Acceptance by academic colleagues was slow and grudging in some cases, but it has been overcome by the primary care physician's performance in areas of education, service, and research.

National Workforce Data Collection

Workforce planning requires a credible data base. In 1987, at the instigation of the Association of Canadian Medical Colleges (ACMC), the Canadian Post-M.D. Education Registry (CAPER) was set up to register every resident and fellow in every postgraduate training program in Canada. CAPER's board comprises ACMC, representing the medical schools; the Canadian Association of Interns and Residents representing the residents and fellows; the two accrediting and certifying colleges; the Federal and provincial ministries of health; and the Canadian Medical Association.

The information gathered by CAPER is confidential and released only as aggregate numbers. But a mine of information is available on resident programs, their distribution, and their numbers in the programs; resident data by citizenship, gender, school of origin, funding sources, and so forth. In addition, it is possible to track trainees into practice. These kind of data are essential for any planning exercise, and can only be gathered when such programs are under a single jurisdiction.

Caveat

In describing Canada's experience dealing with health workforce policy and relating it to the United States, I have dealt only with the physician workforce. This is because actions undertaken by the Canadian Federal and provincial governments have bound physician workforce planning very tightly to medical education and the overall health care system.

Works Cited

ACMC (Association of Canadian Medical Colleges). 1995. *Canadian Post-M.D. Education Registry Database*. Ottawa: ACMC.

Health Insurance and Diagnostic Services Act. April 12, 1957. Statutes of Canada, 1956–57; Chapter 28.

Jolly, P. and D.M. Hudley, eds. 1995. *AAMC Data Book: Statistical Information Related to Medical Education*. Washington: Association of American Medical Colleges.

Philibert, I. 1995. *Council of Teaching Hospitals Survey of House Staff Stipends, Benefits, and Funding, 1995*. Washington: Association of American Medical Colleges.

State Roles

Because states have jurisdiction over both professional regulation and public education, state governments have been making health workforce policies far longer than the Federal government. The first three papers in this section address the highly political regulatory policies that greatly affect health care delivery at the state level. The final three papers offer different perspectives on one state's attempt to directly influence the nature of its health workforce.

The Political Context of State Regulation of the Health Professions

CAROL S. WEISSERT

There has traditionally been little overlap between the world of health professions and the discipline of political science. This is a big mistake for two reasons. First, regulation of the health professions is a highly political issue. Second, regulation of the health professions is an important factor in health care delivery and thus must change as the delivery system changes. Smart states understand these truths and are looking at new ways of dealing with these old issues.

The Politics of Regulation

I had the opportunity in December 1994 to conduct a health policy workshop for newly elected members of the Michigan House and Senate. The state's legislative service bureau provided nuts-and-bolts training on how to introduce bills, hire staff, and avoid ethical transgressions. My role was to provide an overview—and yes, to challenge the legislators—on health issues they might wish to introduce or understand better if others introduced them.

In preparation, I did all the standard things. I compiled a list of what other states had done, classified the recommendations of various groups, and dusted off some of my own speeches and articles. I also made a phone call to a friend who lobbies the Michigan Senate on health issues for the Governor, to get a sense of what she thought the major health issues facing the new legislators would be.

What a shock. Instead of global budgets, managed competition, increased production of primary care practitioners, small-group insurance reforms, or community rating, she rattled off a list of regulatory issues related to pharmacists, optometrists, nurse practitioners, and other health professionals. These issues relating to scope of practice (particularly independence of practice and prescription rights), professional oversight, reimbursement, and "any willing provider" laws were the ones she dealt with every day and those she knew would face the newly elected legislators.

I have had the same conversation with staffers and legislators in Michigan and other states. Some states—for example, Washington, Minnesota, and Florida—may consider the broader issues I was most intrigued with. But even those states deal with regulatory issues, which are the backbone of health politics in most states. In 1994, at least 135 state laws in some way expanded the scope of practice for nurses, physician assistants, chiropractors, opticians, and allied health professionals (IHPP 1995).

State legislatures are largely reactive bodies and are getting more so. I am currently studying state legislative staff and their role in health policymaking in five states. I am particularly interested in the effect of term limits on staffing and the effects of different models of staffing on both the likelihood of state health legislation and its composition. To avoid getting only a snapshot view of the current system, I have been talking to staffers and members who served a decade or so ago to detect any recent changes in the way issues are approached and considered. Preliminary findings—based on one or two states—are that many state legislative staff are isolated, poorly trained in health issues, not well informed by a broad audience, and willing to accept information provided by lobbyists. Further, their bosses are also happy to limit the search for policy options to those issues that interest groups want.

What does this mean for regulation of the health professions? A lot, since it is in the regulatory arena that the professional interest groups are most active. The staffing arrangement I've described clears the way for these groups to set the agendas and succeed in achieving their desired goals.

Political scientists call most health regulatory policies "client politics." These are policy decisions (such as beneficial regulatory provisions) where benefits concentrate on a few people or groups and where the costs are distributed widely among the population (in higher costs or reduced access to care). Client politics are usually not very salient to the public and are usually conducted behind closed doors. In client politics, the clients usually win. They are out to achieve some usually narrow, but highly profitable, provision in the law without substantial opposition. There are few, if any, opposing voices present in hearings, few letters in opposition, and no newspaper editorials in hometown papers. These votes are often a way to please a few, often well-placed constituents who will likely be generous in upcoming elections. The politics are fairly straightforward.

Client politics are particularly potent if they involve top priority issues of politically strong interest groups. For example, the ability of psychologists to receive Medicaid reimbursement might be the only issue that the psychologist professional association lobbies before the legislature. Pharmacists might rally for the ability to prescribe some common drugs, and nurses fight for the ability to practice independently.

In recent legislative sessions, "any willing provider" laws have galvanized political groups to action. These laws prohibit managed care organizations from excluding health care providers from participating in a health plan if they are willing to accept the plan's operating terms and conditions, schedule of fees, covered expenses, utilization regulation, and quality standards. About twenty-five states have such a law on the books; half were enacted since 1993 (PPRC 1995). Some health maintenance organizations and preferred provider organizations have fought these laws, claiming the laws will hurt their ability to hold down costs. But for provider groups, inclusion in HMOs is a top-priority issue, and they have fought hard for it. And it is not simply the physician groups or the groups that might seem most obvious.

A 1995 Arkansas law, which passed 33–1 in the Senate and 88–1 in the House and was "reluctantly" signed by the Governor, provides one of the nation's broadest any-willing-provider provisions, forbidding managed care organizations from prohibiting or limiting the participation of twenty types of providers, from podiatrists and audiologists to dentists, psychologists, and licensed professional counselors (*State Health Watch* 1995). When a second bill was passed to address some potential technical issues arising from the first, five more provider groups were added, including advanced practice nurses (it is interesting that they had been omitted in the first law), licensed dietitians, and licensed psychological examiners.

The Senate sponsor noted that the bill's success was due to "a good, solid, grass-roots campaign" that went far beyond lobbying by the medical society. The other twenty-four providers covered a broad grass-roots area. My guess is that the lobbying was intense. And it was successful. The name of the law, the Patient Protection Act of 1995, is an example of a clever framing of the issue to make it appear that the bill protects patients—not the livelihoods of the providers themselves. Just try to imagine a newspaper coming out against the Patient Protection Act of 1995, or how the two legislators who voted against the bill will explain their position in the next election.

The Link Between Regulation and the Health Delivery System

The rationale behind regulation of the health professions is simple: to protect the health and welfare of the citizenry. Because of certain failures in the health care market, the public cannot judge the effectiveness of the providers who serve as primary advisers for their health care consumption decisions. It is also important to remember that the demand for regulation of the health professions has traditionally come not from consumers but from the professions that benefit from restrictions on market entry.

History of Licensing

Licensing of health personnel goes back a long way. The first licensing board was for healers in Baghdad in 931 A.D. It wasn't long before the government set standards to meet the licensing requirements, determined a scale of fees, and provided a list of services that could and could not be provided. By 1225 A.D., Frederick II, Holy Roman Emperor, presided over what was probably the first medical practice law. The law forbade the practice of medicine without a license, included an examination by teachers of medicine, and required five years of academic study (three were devoted to the study of logic) and one year of practice under the direction of an experienced physician. It also required physicians to provide free care for the poor and prohibited them from running apothecary shops.

The first licensing law in this country, enacted in 1639 in Virginia, regulated fees charged by physicians (Berry and Brineger 1990). The first legislation requiring medical practitioners to take licensure exams was passed in the 1760s in New York and New Jersey. Over the next few years, most states followed their lead. An 1889 U.S. Supreme Court decision, *Dent* v. *West Virginia*, upheld that state's right to deny practice to a physician without state-approved credentials. The case summarized the rationale for state regulation of health professionals:

The power of the state to provide for the general welfare of its people authorizes it to prescribe all such regulation as in its judgment will secure or tend to secure them against the consequences of ignorance and incapacity as well as of deception and fraud. (Gross 1984).

For several hundred years, regulation of health care was accomplished primarily at the state and local levels, and for the health professions this is still the case. Federal regulation of the delivery of health care has increased in recent decades with provisions in Medicaid, the Employee Retirement and Income Security Act, the Americans With Disabilities Act, and other

Federal laws superseding state law. Several Federal health care reform proposals discussed in 1993 and 1994 would have forced uniformity in state practice laws for some professions and granted more power to a suprastate body to regulate the production of health care providers. But these measures—along with many others contained in the proposals—failed.

Types of Regulation

State regulation of the health professions can be accomplished in one of three ways: licensure, certification, and registration. Licensure is the most severe type of regulation. Under licensure, only those people who meet the requirements of education, training, and experience (and, often, who have passed a clinical examination) are allowed to engage in that occupation in that state.

States also may call for certification of some professions, which recognizes a credential issued by a nongovernmental agency or association. Certification does not restrict the practice of profession.

Registration is the least restrictive form of regulation. Only a handful of states in a handful of areas use registration, which requires practitioners to provide their names, addresses, and information on their training to a state agency.

Every state licenses chiropractors, dentists, dental hygienists, hearing-aid dealers, pharmacists, and registered nurses. A few states certify, rather than license, nurse midwives, and states use all three mechanisms to regulate physician assistants, respiratory therapists, and veterinary technicians (CSG 1992). States also set up procedures for renewing licenses and establish enforcement procedures to discipline practitioners proven incompetent or fraudulent.

Licensure—the dominant approach used to regulate the most popular health professions—is important to those regulated in several ways. It can restrict the number of people entering a profession, making the profession more prestigious, and potentially raising the cost of the services provided. Licensure status is also often a prerequisite to reimbursement by third-party insurers, Medicare, and Medicaid. At least forty-five health occupations are licensed by states ranging from acupuncturists to veterinary technicians (CSG 1992).

Regulation of Nonphysician Providers

Although there are some differences in state requirements for physicians to practice, there are more similarities than differences. The same cannot be said for nurses, especially for advanced practice nurses. Eighteen states certify nurse practitioners; nineteen issue a second license for advanced practice. Thirteen states use some other means of recognition, such as granting a letter of authority (NCSBN 1992). A few states do not regulate nurse practitioners at all.

Recognition of advanced practice nursing is complicated by the range of specializations in the field, many of which are recognized by the states. For example, South Carolina recognizes an acute care nurse practitioner, an advanced, psychiatric-mental health clinical nurse specialist, a certified registered nurse anesthetist, a community health clinical nurse specialist, a family nurse practitioner, a family planning nurse practitioner, an occupational health nurse practitioner, a pediatric nurse practitioner, and a school nurse practitioner, all of which require additional or different requirements from those listed under the generic term "nurse practitioner" (CSG 1986).

But it is the scope of practice, not the number of specializations or method of recognition, that is the most pivotal state regulatory issue affecting the role of nursing, allied health professions, pharmacy, chiropractors, and other health professions. In defining scope-of-practice acts, particularly when specifying what duties can be performed and with what supervision, real battles can ensue among the professions. Scope-of-practice acts for physicians are usually defined very broadly; those for nursing and other professions are not. Legislation regulating advanced practice nursing is particularly confusing, often restrictive, and generally varies considerably from state to state. In particular, the right of advanced nurses to prescribe medication and the expansion of independent practice for nurse practitioners have emerged as hotly contested issues, with medical associations often perceiving such expansion as competing with their authority and established roles.

Again, these battles are often framed in far different rhetoric than that of self-interest. For example, a 1993 report of the American Medical Association that denounced the expanded role of nurses in health care delivery said that such an expansion "raises questions of patient safety." The California Medical Association called broadening the scope of practice for nonphysician groups "dangerous to the public's health" (Priest 1993).

Nevertheless, several states have acted to broaden the scope of nurse practice to allow nurse practitioners to practice independently and to be reimbursed for their efforts. Eighteen states allow nurse practitioners to function independently of physicians, although twelve require some physician collaboration, consultation, or supervision. In only six states—Arkansas, Kentucky, Montana, New Hampshire, Oregon, and Washington—can advanced nurses operate without physician collaboration, consultation, or supervision and without written protocols.

Some states exempt nurse practitioners from physician oversight if they practice in underserved areas such as rural communities and inner city health centers. Twenty-six states have given nurse practitioners authority to prescribe medications, although only a handful have given them truly independent authority to prescribe without formularies, supervision by physicians, or limits on medications.

My colleagues and I looked at four state policies in advanced nurse regulation: whether state boards of nursing had sole oversight over the regulation of advanced nursing, whether nurse practitioners could practice independently, whether they had prescriptive authority, and whether certified nurse midwives could practice independently (Weissert, Knott, and Stieber 1994). Telling was the fact that no state had all four laws; and ten states had none of the four in place. The modal response (sixteen states) was one law. Clearly, the states have not led the way in any concerted effort to level the playing field for nurse practitioners.

Interestingly, laws are often less restrictive for physician assistants. One effort to measure the practice environment for nurse practitioners and physician assistants found that the average state provides 73 percent of the idealized practice environment for physician assistants and only 60 percent for nurse practitioners (Sekscenski et al. 1994). Whereas practice acts in many states provide roughly the same ideal practice environments for the two professions, a number of states have significantly more supportive climates for physician assistants. In Michigan, physician assistants enjoy 89 percent of their ideal practice environment; nurse practitioners practice in an environment that is only 45 percent of their ideal. Since physicians generally find that physician assistants offer less competition than nurse practitioners do, the comparative freedom that state legislation provides the two groups of health professionals may also be a political issue.

Other Regulatory Issues

There is also evidence that the restrictive nature of state practice laws has an effect on the numbers of physician assistants, nurse practitioners, and certified nurse-midwives practicing (Sekscenski et al. 1994). For example, in Michigan there are 10.4 physician assistants for every 100,000 people (above the national mean of 8.7) and only 4.5 nurse practitioners (substantially below the national mean of 12.7).

Reimbursement issues—the services covered under Medicaid or mandated in private plans—are also important state health regulation issues. Any-willing-provider laws directly affect the likelihood of providers who might otherwise be left out of important health delivery systems.

Finally, recent changes in the health care delivery system, notably, the immense popularity of managed care, have led to a rethinking of the mix of health care professionals. What types of providers do we need now and in the future? What role do states have in producing the desired mix? Who should make these choices?

New Ways to Address Old Issues

The time seems to be right for a change in health professions regulation. Some political scientists (Baumgartner and Jones 1993) argue that most issue changes occur during periods of heightened general attention to a policy. Although health issues are no longer highly salient in Washington, they remain important in the states. Further, states that began looking at problems and developing solutions in 1993 and 1994 by designating commissions and task forces are now examining possible changes, many of which will affect health professions regulation.

Client politics can operate only when there is little attention given to an issue and the issue is framed relatively narrowly. This situation can be disturbed in two ways.

First, the traditional stakeholders (in this case, professional groups) have been weakened by the formation of additional groups representing only subsets of their members and which have different interests and strengths. There is some evidence that the one dominant physician lobby, the American Medical Association, has been weakened at the national and state levels by the emergence of strong specialty groups as well as by sharply differing views held by its large membership on important issues such as global budgets and employer mandates (Imershein, Rond, and Mathis 1992). At the state level as well, the dominance of state policymaking by the traditional health care elite has been disrupted in recent years by the fragmentation of these elites. In 1993 reforms in Minnesota and Florida, state medical associations were not major actors, and reforms passed in spite of their opposition—a situation that could not have occurred twenty years ago (Leichter 1993; Brown 1993).

A second challenge to client politics can be mounted by stake challengers. Such a challenge can be initiated by a broadening of the scope of conflict of the debate. Rather than being limited to backroom discussions and "gentlemen's agreements," issues are brought to the public, discussed in public forums and on the legislative floor, and considered in newspaper stories and editorials. Other actors, including legislators, managed care leaders, and community leaders, become involved in the issues that were formerly decided only by professional groups and a few sympathetic leaders.

Although both challenges may apply to regulation of the health professions, it is the second that hits closest to home and is most likely to change the behavior of states. When many states began to look seriously at comprehensive health care reform and contemplate a world of managed care, they realized that health professions regulation had not adjusted to the changing delivery system and needed an overhaul. In Canada, Ontario province became interested in changing professional regulation when the provincial government and other players began to question the rationality of the health regulatory system after the passage of universal medical insurance (Coburn 1993).

States in this country, particularly Maine, are looking at Ontario as a model. Ontario is moving away from licensing broad scopes of practice and focusing instead on licensure of thirteen actions that can cause harm to consumers. Further, the new system allows several professions to perform these potentially hazardous acts. For example, both midwives and physicians are permitted to perform uncomplicated deliveries, both audiologists and physicians can prescribe hearing aids, and both dentists and denturists can dispense dentures (Begun and Lippincott 1993). Such a reduction and refocus of regulation fits well with the popular interest in this country in reducing regulatory burdens and focusing instead on outcome measures. In other words, the approach plays well politically to the public.

Some states have set up boards or commissions to examine the issue and make recommendations to their legislatures. Others have made changes in the focus of regulation, highlighting competency issues and the need to collect good data or workforce personnel in the state. Washington has made changes in state regulation to focus on a team approach, cultural sensitivity, protection of the public, and increasing access through more primary care providers. Colorado plans to improve its licensure system to ensure that the state has information that will allow it to make future workforce decisions. Texas has asked its newly established Health Professions Council to eliminate duplication of services by twenty-nine separate health professions regulated by boards or the department of health. And Virginia's Board of Health Professions has eliminated more than half the regulations pertaining to professional practice, expanded the scope of practice for advanced practice nurses, and established new policies to ensure continued professional competency.

Still other legislatures are examining methods to increase the public's role in the regulatory process, ensure continued competence, adopt outcome and evaluation studies, collect important data on the workforce, recognize the need for public access to practitioner information, and set up effective dispute resolution systems (Wade 1995).

Some observers suggest that changes should be made in the composition of health professional boards, specifically medical boards, to add to their roles such duties as relicensing periodically, restricting the scope of practice, developing different types of licenses, and taking a more active role in issues such as medical education and the distribution of physicians (Meikle 1992).

States will likely continue to address issues such as practice independence, prescription rights, reimbursement, any-willing-provider, and other regulations related to managed care. But there appears to be more going on than simply business as usual.

Conclusion

Regulation of the health professions represents the essence of health politics at the state level, but the traditional client politics it entails may well be changing. Market forces and consumer interest have forced many state leaders to examine the role of licensure, scope of practice, reimbursement, and profession participation in provider systems in ways that have expanded the scope of conflict. In a number of states, the politics of health professions regulation is no longer a quiet, backroom issue that is ignored by newspapers and their readers. Managed care providers and others have called into question the effectiveness of the old regulatory system, and efforts are under way to examine new approaches and, perhaps most important, to include health professions regulation in the broader context of state health care reform. The rules of the political game seem to be changing and, with it, the old dominance of a few groups and reliance on the status quo.

Works Cited

Baumgartner, F. and B. Jones. 1993. *Agendas and Instability in American Politics*. Chicago: University of Chicago Press.

Begun, J.W. and R.C. Lippincott. 1993. *Strategic Adaptation in the Health Professions*. San Francisco: Jossey-Bass.

Berry, F.S. and P. Brineger. 1990. State regulation of occupations and professions. *Book of the States, 1990–91.* Lexington, KY: Council of State Governments.

Brown, L. 1993. Commissions, clubs and consensus: Reform in Florida. *Health Aff.* 12(2).

Coburn, D. 1993. State authority, medical dominance, and trends in the regulation of the health professions: The Ontario case. *Soc. Sci. Med.* 37(2).

CSG (Council of State Governments). 1986. *State Credentialing of the Health Occupations and Professions.* Lexington, KY: CSG.

———. 1992. *Book of the States.* Lexington, KY: CSG.

Gross, S.J. 1984. *Of Foxes and Hen Houses.* Westport, CT: Quorum Books.

IHPP (Intergovernmental Health Policy Project). 1995. *Scope of Practice: An Overview of 1994 State Legislative Activity.* Washington: IHPP.

Imershein, A., P. Rond III, and M. Mathis. 1992. Restructuring patterns of elite dominance and the formation of state policy in health care. *American Journal of Sociology* 97.

Leichter, H.M. 1993. Minnesota: The trip from acrimony to accommodation. *Health Aff.* 12(2).

Meikle, T.H. Jr. 1992. States must act to reform medical education. *J. Amer. Health Policy* 13 (March/April).

NCSBN (National Council of State Boards of Nursing). 1992. Regulation of advanced nursing practice. *Update* 13.

PPRC (Physician Payment Review Commission). 1995. *Annual Report to Congress.* Washington: PPRC.

Priest, D. 1993. Doctors attack efforts to delegate more health care duties to nurses. *Washington Post* (December 7).

Sekscenski, E., S. Sansom, C. Bazell, M. Salmon, and F. Mullan. 1994. State practice environments and the supply of physician assistants, nurse practitioners, and certified nurse-midwives. *N. Engl. J. Med.* 331(19).

State Health Watch. 1995. Arkansas legislature approves one of nation's broadest any willing provider laws. (March).

Wade, B. 1995. Regulating health professions. *NCSL Legisbrief.* 3(9).

Weissert, C.S., J. Knott, and B. Stieber. 1994. Education and the health professions: Explaining policy choices among the states. *J. Health Polit., Policy, and Law* 19(2).

Health Care Market Reforms and Their Effect on Health Professions Regulation

Edward H. O'Neil, Leonard Finocchio,
and Catherine Dower

These are extremely turbulent times for health care. What was until recently a relatively stable set of relationships between institutions, professionals, regulators, purchasers, and payors has degraded into a free fall of leveraged buyouts, mergers, closures, and redefinitions of professional practice, all contributing to a general sense of weightlessness and unease throughout the health care sector.

In this emerging system, workforce change is developing in reaction to more general health system changes. These changes will radically alter how the nation defines health professions, how health professionals are trained, and how health professionals enter practice. Mirroring broader health care reforms, these workforce changes may be likened to shifting from supply-based education and workforce policies and practices driven by educational programs and professional associations to an approach that is increasingly based on the *demands* of a health care system driven by financial and organizational changes. This market demand will drive the movement in workforce policy and education for reengineering, deregulation, downsizing, and upskilling. This paper focuses on how the emerging issues in professional regulation are tied to such changes in the health care market.

Overall Effects of Market-Based Reforms

The dislocation of health care's status quo may seem abrupt and even violent, but the forces at work today making for the move toward dramatically altered arrangements for the organization and financing of health care have been going on for more than two decades.

Increasingly, the policies and programs that shape the health care landscape are being determined primarily by the forces of the health care market. Ironically, these market-driven reforms share many values and perspectives that were the substance of the highly integrated systems for managed competition proposed by the Clinton Health Care Task Force. However, the mechanisms available to the market differ vastly from those that public policy makers use to bring about change.

Market-based reform, like political- and policy-based change, has both strengths and weaknesses. Because it does not require the endorsement of a political process, it can move quickly to react to consumer and supplier demands. The public's input to this system will come through choices made on the basis of cost, consumer satisfaction, and, to a lesser degree, quality of care. Some people will support health care systems with these characteristics; others will certainly abhor them. (It provides little comfort to reflect that the cost of market-based reform is the price for failing to change health care through the political process.)

1. *The health system will be more integrated.* The health system of the past was a marvelous collection of independent hospitals, clinics, solo practitioners, and small professional groups. Each carried out its functions and passed along costs to an enormous variety of private and public insurance companies; they, in turn, essentially passed their costs back to employers, consumers, and the public. Emerging in its place is a system of care integrating the delivery of a core set of services—primary, specialty, and hospital care—into a financing mechanism directed to achieve specific goals relative to three mandates: reduce the cost of health care, enhance patient satisfaction, and maintain or improve quality of care.

2. *To achieve the goals of the integrated system, health care will be more managed.* Past arrangements allowed considerable discretion by professionals and health care organizations as to how they organized and delivered care. Many of these patterns were codified in state and professional regulations and guidelines. Increasingly, the integrated system will demand empirically based accountability.

Early management interventions have been intrusive on professional and organizational practice. As time passes, management intervention will turn from the micromanagement of practice to assessment of the outcomes produced by new approaches. Innovations by professionals, educational institutions, hospitals, and technologies will come to be valued in proportion to the extent they help lower costs, enhance consumer satisfaction, and maintain or improve the outcomes of care. They will be ignored as they fail to respond to these goals.

3. *Making both integration and management possible is the phenomenal growth of information and communications technology over the past decade.* By and large, these technologies have not altered health care to the extent they have transformed other parts of society. However, they promise new ways of organizing, delivering, and monitoring health care that will make many of the established patterns obsolete. A robot filling prescriptions, a diagnosis taking place over a fiber optic network that links patient and physician across 2,000 miles, nurses using expert systems contained in portable computers smaller than compact reference manuals, and patients completing their own diagnoses using knowledge couplers: These are but a few early examples of how technology will change the patterns and boundaries of professional practice and public involvement.

4. *Recognition is growing that the changes in health care delivery will mean a different approach to how health professionals are educated, trained, deployed, and utilized.* The education and workforce issues of particular importance are reengineering, deregulation, downsizing, and upskilling.

(Reengineering here refers to changing the processes by which health care is delivered or, as it is more commonly phrased, "reengineering the health care workplace," in order to make delivery systems more responsive to the demands of cost, patient satisfaction, and quality.) It has created a demand for reregulating the health care workforce by reconsidering the laws that govern entry into health professional practice, define professional scopes of practice, and provide consumer protection. The changes in health workplace design coupled with the general oversupply of many types of health care practitioners are producing pressure to decrease the size of the employed professional workforce in many key areas, especially medicine and nursing. A slackening demand is leading to downward pressure on health care wages. Finally, there is a growing recognition that competitive provider organizations must have a workforce with a different set of skills than those that prevail today.

Professionalism in the U.S. Health Professions

The education, licensing, certification, reeducation, oversight, and governance of health professionals in the United States is a large and complex set of arrangements that has developed over the past century. They reflect a host of concerns and values that include

- Professional autonomy.
- The role of science in the health professions.
- The relationship between compensation and independent practice.
- The private nature of most of the health care system.
- The health profession's relationship to higher education.
- A minimalist attitude toward oversight by state and Federal agencies.
- The economic interests of the professions.
- The importance of protecting the public's health from ill-prepared or incompetent professionals.

The result is a regulatory system dominated by the influence of the professions in the design of education, the accreditation of professional schools, the criteria for entry to professional practice, the definition of the scope of practice, and the oversight systems for professional practice. For the most part, medicine has led the way in the development of self-regulatory mechanisms, but the pattern has been replicated by virtually every other health professional group as it has moved into and up the hierarchy of the health care system.

The emergence of professionalism in the health professions at the end of the nineteenth century in America paralleled many other important cultural, scientific, and social transformations. The Progressive Movement applied the principles and techniques of scientific rationality and technical control to a host of social, political, and economic problems (Wiebe 1967). The emergence of many professions in their modern form occurred as a part of this movement (Bledstein 1976). It was aided by the efficacy of biological empiricism and its attention to natural systems that came out of Germany during the middle of the nineteenth century. These approaches, which were dominating continental medicine, increasingly became the model for American physicians as they pursued education and models for practice (Ludmerer 1985).

Similar changes were also occurring in American higher education. The German research university became the dominant model upon which colleges and universities were organizing themselves. The authority of empirically based physical and social sciences led to the division of academic labor through emergence of scholarly disciplines throughout the 1880s and 1890s (Rudolph 1962). The American universities that were emerging became the center of a new commitment to research that combined the native American taste for the practical application of knowledge to common problems with the experimental and systematic brand of investigation that was emerging from Germany (Vesey 1965). From progressivism to empiricism, and from the efficacy of professional development to the growing status of the research university, the health professions could not have had a better nineteenth century model for becoming a dominant part of American culture in the twentieth century. This philosophical heritage has guided the health professions for much of this century.

The Need for Change in Health Professions Regulation

The system of professional self-regulation in place today has provided valuable public benefits by granting licenses to people who are trained and knowledgeable in their respective professions and by identifying and removing incompetent and dangerous licensees from practice. But although health professions regulation served the health care system and its consumers well in the past, it is out of step with today's health care needs and expectations. As a result, the regulatory system is now being criticized for increasing costs, restricting managerial and professional flexibility, limiting access to care, and for being equivocally related to quality. Perhaps most seriously, regulatory bodies are perceived as largely unaccountable to the public they serve.

The lack of uniform regulatory language and laws among the states limits effective professional practice and mobility, confuses the public, and presents barriers to integrated delivery systems and the use of telemedicine and other new health technologies. These difficulties call for regulatory standardization across the individual states. Meanwhile, the public's changing perception of professionalism and its need for information about practitioners so that consumers can make informed choices about their care has challenged the structure and function of professional boards. The situation calls for improved accountability through increased public representation on professional regulatory boards and disclosure of practitioner information.

Current statutes grant broad, near-exclusive scopes of practice to a few health care professions and "carved-out" scopes for the remaining professions. These laws erect unreasonable access barriers to high-quality and affordable care. Accessible health care calls for flexible scopes of practice that recognize the demonstrated competence of various kinds of practitioners to provide the same health services.

Reports of incidents have raised concerns that the regulatory system may not protect the public effectively (Van Tuinen and Wolfe 1991). Continuing education requirements do not guarantee continuing competence. In addition, the complaint process is difficult to initiate for the consumer, and many complaints go without investigation. Finally, regulatory systems have largely failed to implement mechanisms to evaluate their effectiveness and correct their shortcomings. These problems call for effective continuing competence assessments and professional discipline processes, and a broad evaluation of regulation's effectiveness in protecting the public.

The Pew Health Professions Commission's Task Force

The Pew Health Professions Commission recognized that broader changes in the health care market would require reform in both workforce education and regulation.* The commission created the Taskforce on Health Care Workforce Regulation to explore the regulatory process and determine the effectiveness of the process in protecting the public's health. The goal was to propose new approaches to health care workforce regulation that would better serve the public's interest given the new health care environment. The task force believes that regulation would best serve the public's interest by

- Promoting effective health outcomes and protecting the public from harm.
- Holding regulatory bodies accountable to the public.
- Respecting consumers' rights to choose their own health care providers from a range of safe options.
- Encouraging a flexible, rational and cost-effective health care system that allows effective working relationships among health care providers.
- Facilitating professional and geographic mobility of competent providers.

The task force report was received by the commission in August of 1995

---

* The Pew Health Professions Commission was started in 1989 as a way of assisting the nation's health professionals to understand and respond to the challenges of health care change and reform. The commission is managed by the Center for the Health Professions at the University of California, San Francisco. The task force was started by the Pew Commission in 1994. Its members are Steve Boruchowitz, MPA, Health Systems Quality Assurance, Washington State Department of Health; Pam Brinegar, MA, Executive Director, Council on Licensure, Enforcement and Regulation; Bruce Douglas, JD, Director, Division of Registrations, Department of Regulatory Agencies, State of Colorado; Vic Harris, PhD, Executive Director, Colorado Health Professions Panel, Inc.; Paul Hofmann, DrPH, Senior Consultant, Strategic Health Care Practice, Alexander & Alexander Consulting Group, Inc., San Francisco; Judy Kany, MPA, Senior Consultant, Medical Care Development, Maine; Richard Morrison, PhD, Senior Research Associate, Williamson Institute for Health Studies, Virginia Commonwealth University; David Swankin, JD, President, Citizen Advocacy Center, Washington, DC.

and accepted for a year-long review and comment period by the professions, regulators, educators, state and Federal policy makers, and the public (Pew Health Professions Commission 1995). The task force envisioned four principles to guide any future changes in regulation. First, the members recognized the considerable variability of regulation, process, oversight, and evaluation among the professions and across the states. Future regulation must be standardized where appropriate and possible. Second, there was a legacy of little, if any, public input to the regulatory process. Future regulatory efforts need to be more accountable to the public. Third, the growing need for change in health professional practice requires a more flexible workforce regulation. This flexibility would support optimal access to a competent workforce, promote interdisciplinary cooperation, and support the cost-effective deployment of health care practitioners. Finally, the task force recognized the need for regulations that would protect the public's welfare in the most effective manner possible.

Based on these four principles, the task force made ten specific recommendations for an improved health professions regulatory system and also proposed policy options for states to consider implementing.

The Task Force's Ten Recommendations

1. STANDARDIZE REGULATORY TERMS: *Adopt a uniform health professions regulatory language for the public and the professions.*

States should use standardized, understandable language for health professions regulation and its functions to clearly describe them for consumers, provider organizations, businesses, and the professions.

Policy options for state consideration:
- Use the term "licensure" in state health professions regulatory acts.
- Use standard language in health professional licensing statutes that include references to
  - title protection
  - practice acts
  - regulatory terms such as "supervision" and "delegation"
  - enforcement and disciplinary processes and outcomes (e.g., uniform definitions for classes of alleged offenses and phases and outcomes of the adjudication process).
- Reserve the term "certification" for voluntary private sector programs that attest to the competency of individual health professionals.
- Identify and convene a body to codify regulatory terms and language.

States should consider models for standardizing and adopting terms such as those employed by the National Conference of State Legislatures, the National Governors' Association, or the Council on Licensure, Enforcement, and Regulation. This body should include representation from the regulated health professions, consumers, providers, and third-party payors.

2. STANDARDIZE ENTRY-TO-PRACTICE REQUIREMENTS: *Facilitate the physical and professional mobility of the health professions.*

States should standardize entry-to-practice requirements and limit them to competency assessments in order to facilitate the physical and professional mobility of the health professions.

Policy options for state consideration:
- Adopt entry-to-practice standards for each profession that are uniform throughout the fifty states.
- Adopt mutual recognition of licensure across the states by endorsement legislation, even without uniform entry-to-practice standards in place.
- Cooperate with the relevant private sector organizations and with other states to develop and use standard competency examinations for entry-to-practice. In developing these standards, states should not rely on accreditation or examination standards that do not directly and demonstrably measure the minimum knowledge and skill necessary for safe, contemporary practice.
- Recognize alternative pathways in education, previous experience, and combinations of these, to satisfy some entry-to-practice requirements for licensure.
- Eliminate entry-to-practice standards that are not based on the competence, skills, training, or knowledge of the professional.

3. REMOVE BARRIERS TO THE FULL USE OF COMPETENT HEALTH PROFESSIONALS: *Improve the public's access to a competent and effective health care workforce.*

States should base practice acts on demonstrated initial and continuing competence. This process must allow and expect different professions to share overlapping scopes of practice. States should explore pathways to allow all professionals to provide services to the fullest extent of their current training, experience, and skills.

Policy options for state consideration:
- Eliminate exclusive scopes of practice that unnecessarily restrict other professions from providing competent, effective, and accessible care. States should ensure that the regulation of health professionals allows different professions to provide the same services when competence, as measured by training, experience, and skills, has been demonstrated.
- Grant title protection without an accompanying scope of practice act to some professions. This would be appropriate for professions such as massage therapy that provide services that are not especially risky to consumers. Consumers will benefit from the assurance that the titled professional has met the state's minimum standards for initial and continuing competence.
- Allow individual practitioners to expand their scope of practice to an additional level of service found in other professional practice acts through a combination of training, experience, and successful demonstration of competency in that skill or service level.

4. REDESIGN BOARD STRUCTURE AND FUNCTION: *Respond to the changing expectations of the public and the health care delivery system.*

States should redesign health professional boards and their functions to reflect the interdisciplinary and public accountability demands of the changing health care delivery system.

Policy options for state consideration:
- Establish an interdisciplinary oversight board that has a majority of public members. The mission of this board should be to coordinate health professions regulation to meet an explicit state health policy agenda and provide oversight to ensure that the public's best interests are served. This board should have the authority to approve, amend, or reject decisions made by individual boards.
- Consolidate the structure and function of boards around related health professional or health service areas. These consolidated boards should be dedicated to consumer protection and quality assurance. Such consolidated boards, for example, might be medical/nursing care, vision health care, oral health care, rehabilitation, mental health care, or health technologies.
- Develop board membership profiles that include significant, meaningful, and effective public representation to improve board credibility and accountability. States should evaluate the board member appoint-

ment process to ensure that all appointments are fair and accountable to the public. All board members should be carefully recruited, well-trained, and supported.

- Staff and finance all boards and regulatory committees so that they can perform their missions effectively and efficiently. Support should include funding for appropriate technological needs.
- Compose boards with representatives of the state's urban, rural, ethnic, and cultural communities. Boards should also include representatives from the health care delivery system.

5. INFORM THE PUBLIC: *Provide practitioner information to improve board accountability and to assist the public in making informed decisions about their practitioners.*

Boards should educate consumers to assist them in obtaining the information necessary to make decisions about practitioners and to improve the board's public accountability.

Policy options for state consideration:
- Collect information about health professionals and make that information accessible and understandable to the public unless the law forbids disclosure or there is a compelling public policy reason that mandates confidentiality. The burden in disclosure decisions rests with those seeking to restrict access to information. The "compelling" criteria that prevent disclosure should be publicly available and specifically explained when an individual request is denied.
- Develop individual profiles for regulated health care professionals who deal directly with consumers. These profiles should include legally disclosable information about demographics, education, practice, employment, disciplinary actions, criminal convictions, and malpractice judgments.

6. COLLECT DATA ON THE HEALTH PROFESSIONS: *Support planning for an effective health care workforce.*

Boards should cooperate with other public and private organizations in collecting data on regulated health professions.

Policy options for state consideration:
- Use regulatory mechanisms to collect a workforce data set that would facilitate timely and informed workforce policy development. Regula-

tory agencies would not have the responsibility to analyze the data that they collect but, respecting disclosure and confidentiality laws, would share the information with other public and private agencies.
- Work in collaboration with other public and private agencies that use such data for health planning to identify a standard health personnel data set that is comparable, compatible, and accessible.

7. ASSURE PRACTITIONER COMPETENCE: *Assess the continuing competence of health care practitioners.*

States should require each professional board to develop, implement, and evaluate continuing competency requirements for health care professionals.

Policy options for state consideration:
- Require the regulated health professionals to periodically demonstrate competence through appropriate testing mechanisms.
- Competence testing could be triggered by a variety of markers, including the number of disciplinary actions, lack of specialty or private certification, length of time in solo practice, number of procedures performed, or other state-determined indicators.
- Testing could consist of random or targeted peer reviews for practitioners.
- Cooperate with the relevant private sector organizations and with other states to develop and use standardized continuing competency examinations.
- Support the expanded use of modern technological tools to enhance traditional competencies and their assessment.

8. REFORM THE PROFESSIONAL DISCIPLINARY PROCESS: *Protect and promote the public's health in an accountable, timely, and fair manner.*

States should maintain a fair, cost-effective, and uniform disciplinary process to remove incompetent practitioners from practice.

Policy options for state consideration:
- Detection
  - Establish an authoritative body, or assign such responsibility to an existing body, that would oversee the complaints, resolution, and discipline processes for all professions to ensure that boards are acting uniformly, equitably, and in the interest of public protection.

- Establish uniform complaint and discipline processes for all regulated health professions to ensure that investigations are handled in an objective, prioritized, and timely manner. The concerned parties should be informed of the progress of the complaint and investigation on a regular basis.
- Make public access to the complaint and discipline process simple and clear. Information about filing a complaint, the standards by which complaints are judged, investigation procedures, discipline, and appeals should be explained in a manner that is easily accessible to the public.

- Resolution
  - Employ resolution processes that are best suited to the parties and dispute, including alternative dispute resolution methods.
  - Discipline practitioners using the best available tools including rehabilitation, targeted education, settlement, and punitive actions.

- Disclosure
  - Ensure that the outcomes of complaints and resolution of investigations are available and understandable to the parties involved, and to the public where appropriate, unless the law forbids disclosure or there is a compelling public policy reason that mandates confidentiality. The burden in disclosure decisions rests with those seeking to restrict access to information. The "compelling" criteria that prevent disclosure should be publicly available and specifically explained when an individual request is denied.

9. EVALUATE REGULATORY EFFECTIVENESS: *Ensure that the health professions regulation protects and promotes the public's health.*

States should develop evaluation tools that assess the objectives, successes, and shortcomings of their regulatory systems in order to best protect and promote the public's health.

Policy option for state consideration:
- Regulatory bodies and processes should be subject to periodic external (e.g., sunset provisions) and internal (e.g., self-evaluation) evaluation. Criteria for evaluation might include:
  - Timeliness of adjudication process.

- Public perception of and satisfaction with regulatory processes and accountability.
- Effectiveness of boards at meeting their mission and objectives.

10. UNDERSTAND THE ORGANIZATIONAL CONTEXT OF HEALTH PROFESSIONS REGULATION: *Develop effective partnerships between state, Federal, and private regulatory systems to streamline health professions regulation.*

States should understand the linkages, overlapping responsibilities, and conflicts between their health professions regulatory system and other systems that affect the education, regulation, and practice of health care practitioners and work to develop partnerships to streamline regulatory structures and processes. States need to evaluate the links that should be forged or broken, the redundancies that could be streamlined or removed, the conflicts that can be resolved, and the gaps that demand attention.

Policy option for state consideration:
- Study the interplay between state health professions regulatory systems and the systems listed below:
  - Reimbursement
  - Accreditation
  - Professional associations
  - Legal system (civil and criminal)
  - Testing
  - Facility regulation
  - Federal government

The emerging market promises to realign much of what the people of the United States regard as a given about the health care system. It will drive changes in the way in which people receive care and in who delivers that care, where the care is available, what is included in the definition of care, what is the limit of individual responsibility, and what is the responsibility of private and public organizations to ensure access, efficacy, and safety. The particulars of these market-driven reforms are not available in precise detail, but the general direction changes will take are apparent.

Conclusion

The state-level processes of health professions regulation will need to reform to ensure their relevance in this new system. The recommendations of the Pew Health Professions Commission's Taskforce in Health Care Workforce Regulation should be the basis of a national dialogue addressing the reform of these processes.

Works Cited

Bledstein, B.J. 1976. *The Culture of Professionalism: The Middle Class and the Development of Higher Education in America.* New York: Norton.

Ludmerer, K.M. 1985. *Learning to Heal: The Development of American Medical Education.* New York: Basic Books.

Pew Health Professions Commission. 1995. *Reforming Health Care Workforce Regulation: Policy Considerations for the 21st Century.* San Francisco: UCSF Center for the Health Professions.

Rudolph, F. 1962. *The American College and University: A History.* New York: Vintage.

Van Tuinen, I. and S.M. Wolfe. 1991. *State Medical Licensing Board, Serious Disciplinary Actions in 1990.* Washington: Public Citizen Health Research Group.

Vesey, L.R. 1965. *The Emergence of the American University.* Chicago: University of Chicago Press.

Wiebe, R.H. 1967. *The Search for Order.* New York: Hill and Wang.

Developing Rational Health Professions Licensure

JUDY C. KANY

Rapid changes in the U.S. health system are causing changes in the way health professionals are trained and the way they should practice. In Maine and in most other states, however, practitioners are frequently restricted from providing needed services by an outdated regulatory system. A regulatory system, however, cannot be examined in isolation from larger issues regarding health care system cost, quality, and access. Although often unrecognized or unacknowledged, regulation affects a broad array of health care issues. For example, statutory "scope of practice" determines access and the ability to control health care costs. Scope of practice may prevent rural sites from developing new delivery models using extenders and aides, thus forcing health care systems to use overtrained and unduly expensive practitioners.

The Maine Licensure Development Project was established to propose changes in the state licensing system that would enable all health professionals to provide services at the level of their skill and ability, thereby allowing practitioners to be more responsive to Maine's changing health needs and help ensure quality during the transition to managed care. Over the past two years, the State of Maine has involved more than 2,000 citizens and health professionals in a series of meetings to identify problems with current regulatory laws and determine how they can best be addressed through changes in education, communication, and legislation. Planning for the project was undertaken in conjunction with the health professions, payors, faculty, legislators, consumers, and those in the executive branch of the state's government with responsibility for the health system and workforce. Project participants hope and expect a greater commitment to partnership and communication among the health professions as a result of this process.

The State Role in Regulating Health Care

The regulation of health system personnel is traditionally a state function. Licensing and defining a legal scope of practice authorized by licensure are the major roles of the states (McLaughlin 1994). Yet Governors, commissioners, and legislators have not traditionally provided leadership in developing more rational public policy in this area. Regulation is a key component of health care delivery, and states need to establish a process to ensure that regulation serves the common good, not special interests.

Morrison (1994) calls for significant change in state regulatory policies.

> The majority of the members of the health care workforce are licensed . . . by state governments. An unknown, but significant component of the cost of health care is caused by regulatory restrictions on the use of the workforce that are not necessary or important to the two legitimate goals of occupational regulation: consumer protection and quality assurance. Unnecessary regulatory barriers to cost-effective, accessible, quality health care must be identified and removed if the nation is to reach the important social goals of cost-containment, improved access, and the maintenance or improvement of quality of care. (p. 64)

Reforming Health Professions Regulation in Maine

Maine, like most other states, was working to improve its health care public policy when this project began June 1, 1993. Although many incremental reforms had been implemented—especially regarding health insurance—many issues still needed to be addressed, including the following:

- How to provide access to services in a rural state with personnel shortages and maldistribution.
- More efficient ways to deliver services to the rural population.
- The best mixes of personnel and delivery settings to deliver efficient and high-quality services.
- The outcomes of care and the relationship between cost of care and health status.

In Maine, we faced the following question: In a state greatly affected by a major recession, what public policy changes costing little in private or public funds could be implemented at the state level to help address some of these problems? The Joint Select Committee to Study the Feasibility of a Statewide Health Insurance Program, in its December 1992 final report to the legislature, called for an examination of health personnel allocation and health care delivery in Maine. But public policy surrounding the regulation of the health professions was an area of health policy yet to receive a thorough public discussion. A discussion about a more rational regulatory system for Maine, therefore, seemed ripe and appropriate.

Involving Mainers
The Maine Licensure Policy Development Project is patterned after a nine-year process used by the Province of Ontario. Ontario's process involved every possible interested party in discussions and meetings in an attempt to outline the important ingredients for a completely different regulatory system for the health professions.

Sponsorship of the project in Maine is by a not-for-profit research and development organization, Medical Care Development, which promotes discussion on health policy in an independent, nonconfrontational setting away from the partisan political limelight. Although the process has been anything but secretive, the press has not shown much interest. Consequently, there is little grandstanding or freezing of positions due to public statements.

A legislator from each party serves on the project's thirteen-member advisory committee, and so do the superintendent of insurance and the director of Maine's Division of Medicaid Policy and Programs. Choosing some of Maine's leading health policy experts for the project's advisory committee established immediate credibility for this potentially controversial undertaking.

An introductory conference in September 1993 brought about 250 people—health professionals and managers, faculty, legislators, insurers, state government employees, and citizens—to look at Maine's present system and Ontario's new regulatory model. Small group sessions were clear about the purpose of regulation: to protect the public and ensure quality and access. The sessions identified a wide array of issues—from education of health professionals to consumer choice and education, from access and reimbursement and cost issues to improving Maine's workforce database, and from focusing more on outcomes to focusing less on credentials.

Establishing a Task Force
A Task Force and Subcommittees on Reimbursement and Regulation of Practice emerged from the 1993 conference. Its goal was to develop and share an information base to allow a thoughtful examination of Maine's current health professions licensing laws and to encourage reasoned delib-

erations leading to an improved regulatory system. Education, accreditation, reimbursement, credentialing and privileging, liability, managed care, facility licensing and certification, quality improvement and assurance, supervision and delegation, and practice settings were among the topics addressed by the task force and its subcommittees.

The reimbursement subcommittee examined the effect of reimbursement on practice patterns and how it affects the availability and cost of care. Among topics the Subcommittee on Regulation of Practice covered were scope of practice and evolving requirements for interdisciplinary provider teams; members who were health professionals stressed that they were familiar with their own professions but needed to learn more about the skills, regulation, training, and responsibilities of other health professions.

A second statewide conference occurred in September 1994 with over 230 participants. Highlights included a description of the European professional regulation system and a presentation of computer tools for shared provider-patient decision making in medical practice. The results from a detailed, 100-question topics paper circulated to professionals and policy analysts throughout the state during the summer of 1994 were also reported. Those who responded agreed substantially on principles and most issues regarding the regulation of health professionals. Agreement emerged on the following views:

- In spite of changing practice settings, the focus of health professions regulation should be on licensure of individual practitioners, rather than institutional licensure.
- Overlapping skills between professions should be acknowledged, and consumers should be able to choose among professions for those overlapping services.
- We can expect the focus on health care delivery systems during the next few years to be on quality improvement, outcomes, and costs.
- Supervision and delegation of personnel, as well as competency, will continue to be troublesome areas for changing delivery systems.
- Health care and education need to be linked more effectively, and also be linked to health workforce planning and the regulatory system.
- States should have uniform regulatory standards; perhaps there should be national entry to practice standards or national competency exams.

Recommending Changes
In February 1995 the task force began tackling the difficult task of formu-

lating recommendations for policy change. We kept two basic premises in mind while forging recommendations for improving the regulatory system in Maine:

- *Licensing of health professionals should remain a principal means of protecting the public and providing accountability.* Licensure is a privilege granted by the state but not one to be withheld inappropriately. Any state license should be a legitimate credential ensuring that a minimum standard is met that all involved in the health system can count on when attempting to identify competent practitioners to perform particular health services.
- *Maine must create a simpler, streamlined, understandable, manageable, more efficient, and coordinated health professions regulatory system to serve the public and the participants in the health system.* The regulatory system needs to enable Maine's health professionals to use all of their skills. Communication needs to improve among the health professions and with the public, especially about the services that the various professions have the knowledge and competencies to provide on an individual basis or as members of a team.

Once we had drafted a set of recommendations, we asked some questions about the state's regulatory policy and our recommendations for improvement.

- Can we make more efficient use of the health workforce while adequately protecting the public from harm?
- Have we removed any unreasonable or anticompetitive requirements that produce no demonstrable benefit?
- What will be the overall effect of the proposal on access, quality, and the cost-effectiveness of the health system?
- Are these policy decisions made within the context of the total health system?

A final report with recommendations for regulatory changes was completed in June 1995. It recommended the following essential changes to the health professions regulatory system (Maine Health Professions Regulation Project and Task Force 1995):

1. **Streamline and clarify the health professions regulatory laws.** Promote understanding of the state's health professions regulatory system by participants and the public by making regulatory terms in the public sector distinct, transparent, and standardized. Lessen confusion by using transparent regulatory terms distinguishing government regulation from private-sector regulatory activities.

- Use the term "licensure" for public regulation of the health professions.
- Reserve the term "certification" for the private sector.

Problem: There is a great amount of confusion over some words associated with the regulation of health professionals. *Certification* is an especially confusing term, in part because it is used in both the private sector and the public sector and for facilities and many other purposes in addition to credentialing health professionals. There is a blurring in the public's mind—and in the minds of many in the health professions—where the line is drawn between (a) public-sector regulation, with its ability to impose legal sanctions and required accountability to the public, and (b) professional standards of private organizations that may be similar to public laws but whose sanctions are self-determined.

2. **Improve communication, coordination, and cooperation among the health professions and among the regulatory boards.** Establish a federation of Maine's health professions regulatory boards. Assign responsibility for regulatory "system" policy development to the commissioner of the department overseeing most of the regulation of Maine's health professionals and to the proposed federation of regulatory boards.

Problem: There needs to be better communication among the professions and regulatory boards. Communication is perhaps the area in greatest need of change. Few people fully understand the skills of another profession or individual practitioner unless they work together as team members in a system of care. The regulatory boards—even those administered by or affiliated with the same department—often do not communicate with each other. Interprofessional issues fall through the cracks. A vacuum is created by the absence of designated statutory responsibility for developing regulatory system policy. The individual boards recommend regulatory policy for their own professions, whereas regulatory issues affecting two or more professions or the entire health system are often unaddressed.

3. **Require demonstration of continuing competency to protect the public in order to improve health care services and help ensure quality during the change to managed care.** Support the continued and expanded use of modern technology, especially modern information technology, to enhance traditional methods of competency assessment.

Problem: Although it probably ensures minimal competency on entry into regulated practice, licensure as we know it provides no guarantee of continued competency, and there is no evidence that licensure is tied directly to positive outcomes (Morrison 1994). Although networks with peer review and practice standards are rapidly being established, there will continue to be a problem with practitioners who are not involved in professional networks.

4. **Acknowledge overlapping skills for the provision of health services and remove unnecessary monopolies for which there is no demonstrable benefit to the public.** Allow access to more overlapping services from health professionals when the necessary competence to protect the public has been demonstrated.

Problem: There are complaints that the current regulatory system creates too many monopolies and is unnecessarily exclusionary.* Consumers, managers, and payors need to know professional competencies and options for professional substitutability (table 1).

5. **Advocate the use of uniform terminology among the states and suggest uniform state practice standards** that could provide benchmarks for comparisons.

Problem: Health care managers, payors, other practitioners (sometimes others in the same profession), and consumers have immense difficulty understanding a health care professional's skills. Uniform standards and terminology across the states would lead to more consistency and understanding of professional practice.

Enacting and Implementing the Recommendations

Many of the recommendations will require changes in Maine law. There are three avenues for introducing legislation: the Governor, individual legislators, and the Maine Health Care Reform Commission. Governor Angus King stresses the need for new paradigms for state policy and is not wedded to old ways of doing things. Legislators from each political party served on

---

* The law states: Unless licensed by the board, an individual may not practice medicine or surgery or a branch of medicine or surgery or claim to be legally licensed to practice medicine or surgery within the State by diagnosing, relieving in any degree or curing, or professing or attempting to diagnose, relieve or cure a human disease, ailment, defect or complaint, whether physical or mental, or of physical or mental origin, by attendance or by advice, or by prescribing or furnishing a drug, medicine, appliance, manipulation, method or a therapeutic agent whatsoever or in any other manner unless otherwise provided by statutes of this State (32 MRSA 3270).

Table 1. Substitutes for Selected Health Professions

Profession	Substitute
Administrator, health care	General business administrator and clinician without health care administration entry education (P)
Administrator, long-term care	General business administrator and health care administrator without long-term care entry education (P)
Chiropractor	Physical therapist (P), physician (P)
Dental hygienist	Dentist (P), dental assistant (S)
Dentist	Dental assistant (S), dental hygienist (S), denturist (S), oral surgeon (S)
Denturist	Dentist (P)
Dietitian	Dietetic assistant (S), dietetic technician (S)
Medical record administrator	Noncredentialed personnel (P), medical record technician (S)
Medical technologist	Pathologist (P), medical lab technician (S)
Nurse anesthetist	Anesthesiologist (P)
Nurse-midwife	Lay midwife (P), obstetrician (P)
Nurse, registered	Physician assistant (P), physician (P), licensed practical nurse (S), nurse assistant and aide (S), physical therapist (S), recreational therapist (S), respiratory therapist (S), other therapist and technician (S)
Occupational therapist	Occupational therapy assistant (S), physical therapist (S), recreational therapist (S), registered nurse (S), other therapist (S)
Optometrist	Ophthalmologist (P), optician (S), optometric technician (S)
Pharmacist	Physician (P), pharmacy technician (S)
Physical therapist	Chiropractor (P), physician (P), occupational therapist (S), physical therapy assistant (S), other therapist (S), registered nurse (S)
Physician assistant	Nurse practitioner (P), physician (P), registered nurse (S)
Physician—DO	MDs (P), others listed as substitutes for MDs
Physicians—MD	DOs (P) chiropractor (S), dentist (S), nurse anesthetist (S), nurse-midwife (S), nurse practitioner (S), optometrist (S), physician assistant (S), podiatrist (S), psychologist (S), surgical assistant (S), various therapist and technologist (S)
Podiatrist	Physician (P), chiropractor (S)
Psychologist	Medical social worker (P), psychiatric nurse practitioner (P), psychiatrist (P), other counselor (P)
Radiologic technologist	Noncredentialed personnel (P), radiologist (P)
Recreational therapist	Occupational therapist (S), other therapist (S), therapeutic recreational assistant (S)
Respiratory therapist	Registered nurse (S), respiratory therapy technician (S)
Social worker, medical	Other counselors (P), social service assistant (S)
Speech-language pathologist & audiologist	Noncredentialed personnel (P)

P = substitute for the primary work domain of the profession; S = substitute for secondary tasks of the profession.
Source: Begun and Lippincott 1993.

the project advisory committee and on the task force. Two of the three members of the Maine Health Care Reform Commission served on the thirteen-member advisory committee. All these avenues, therefore, offer great potential. It is entirely possible that the reform commission will incorporate this project's recommendations in their entirety in its report due in January 1996.

We have already seen some substantial legislative activity. Effective January 1, 1996, Maine will have new legislation regulating independent practice for advanced practice nurses. Independent practice and prescriptive privileges will be granted to APNs who either have had two years of practice experience directly supervised by a physician or who currently work in an organization under the oversight of a physician.

Many recommendations can be implemented administratively through rules, policy, or informal means. Examples include the recommendations to establish a federation of health professions regulatory boards and to promote understanding of the regulatory system by initiating a newsletter for all stakeholders.

The private sector can also play a major role. It can promote understanding and coordination and assist in developing continued competency assessments. Advocacy for uniform standards and terminology can be a role played by both the public and private sectors.

Clearly, related issues need to be addressed in order to implement the recommendations. The task force will spend 1996 focusing on refinement and implementation of the recommendations. In addition, we hope to analyze further policy alternatives for regulating especially dangerous services and the competencies necessary to perform them safely, address the regulation of facilities, and develop recommendations for appropriate public policy regarding reimbursement issues.

In addition to Maine, Colorado, Nebraska, Virginia, and Washington all have ongoing projects to study and potentially reform their health professions regulatory systems.

Canadian Regulatory Reform

In the United States, states are just beginning to look at reforming their regulatory systems as part of health care reform. However, the most comprehensive reform has taken place in Canada.

Canadian provinces are undergoing many of the same changes in their health systems as we are in the states. Because of the need to address those changes, partially because of Ontario's precedent-setting work in the regulatory area, most of the provinces are seeking to reform their health professions regulatory systems. In addition to the reform that has been implemented in Ontario, discussion papers on the regulation of health professions are circulating in both Alberta and New Brunswick.

Ontario

Ontario's new health professions regulatory model went into effect January 1, 1994, and is quite different from the traditional, but varied, "practice acts" that have been enacted separately in each U.S. state and Canadian province. The new model is the outgrowth of a health professions legislation review announced by Ontario's minister of health in November 1982. The more than eleven ensuing years involved workshops, meetings, research, invitations for written submissions to the widest possible range of participants, at least six different ministers of health, enactment in 1991, and a period to prepare for implementation (Ontario Health Professions Legislation Review 1989).

Bohnen (1994) reports that the Regulated Health Professions Act of 1991 represents a decisive departure from the past pattern of professional regulation in Ontario: "The policy thrust underlying the Act—making more efficient use of all health professions without compromising public protection—is very different from the policy agenda underlying the statutes it has replaced."

Alberta

The Alberta Health Workforce Rebalancing Committee of the Province of Alberta (1994) has proposed a health workforce regulatory scheme based on four principles.

- The public must be protected from incompetent or unethical health professionals.
- The health professional regulatory system should provide flexibility in the scope and roles of professional practice so the health system operates with maximum effectiveness.
- The health professional regulatory system should be easily understood by the public. Information about professional regulatory structures should be credible and easily available to Albertans.
- The regulatory process for health professions must be fair and seen as fair in application. Principles of natural justice must be observed, and decision makers should be accountable for their decisions.

Central Features of the Ontario Law

Public Protection

- Restrictions on which practitioners may perform hazardous acts and procedures.
- Prohibition against unregulated practitioners providing treatment or advice when it is reasonably foreseeable that serious physical harm may result.
- Restrictions on the use of professional titles and designations.
- Processes to address complaints, discipline, and fitness to practice.
- Whistle-blowing obligations.
- Funding for victims of sexual abuse.

Mechanisms to Improve Quality of Care

- Mandatory quality assurance and patient relations program.
- Assessment of practitioners and their practices.
- External evaluation of the effectiveness of governing bodies.
- Broad regulatory authority given to governing bodies, including authority to set standards of practice.

Consumer Freedom of Choice and Flexibility and Evolution in Utilization

- Abolition of exclusive scopes of practice.
- Fewer restrictions on direct access to practitioners.
- Provision for delegation of hazardous acts and procedures.
- Exceptions to restrictions on who may perform hazardous acts and procedures.

Accountability and Openness

- Increased lay representation on councils of governing bodies.
- Requirements for open council meetings, discipline hearings, and complaint reviews.
- Requirements for the publication of discipline decisions and annual reports.

Policy Development

- Creation of the Health Professions Regulatory Advisory Council.
- Mandatory referral of various matters to the advisory council.
- Multiprofessional and public input into the advisory council.

Under the umbrella legislation prepared for Alberta, broad exclusive scopes of practice would be eliminated. Dangerous services that may place the public at significant risk could be provided only by regulated professionals specifically authorized to do so in legislation. The proposed list of dangerous services includes performing major medical or dental surgery, dispensing drugs to the public, and prescribing drugs.

Under the Alberta proposal, specific practitioner competencies required to provide dangerous services will be defined by professional legislation. Competencies include demonstrated knowledge, skills, and abilities. The professional regulatory associations will be responsible for determining which of their members have the appropriate competency.

New Brunswick

The aims of a discussion paper developed by the New Brunswick Department of Health and Community Services (n.d.) on health discipline regulation include improving public protection; enhancing accountability to the public; and increasing public understanding of, and confidence in, the regulation of health care providers. The discussion paper proposes two modifications; the most important is that all regulated health disciplines will be expected to meet standard requirements. The minimum requirements would apply to health disciplines that are now regulated by private acts as well as to emerging disciplines that would be regulated under a proposed health disciplines act.

Also included is a scope-of-practice proposal that would allow certain disciplines to provide services in the scope of practice of the self-regulating professions under certain conditions and with government approval.

Conclusion

Stakeholders must be involved in the development of health regulatory policy. It is amazing how much general agreement we can find if we together develop and then share an information base. It may sometimes be easier to change a whole system than part of it. When policy development looks at a whole system instead of small parts, there is less defensiveness about imperfections among the stakeholders. Criticism is not directed at one person— or at one profession. Instead, the focus is on looking for policy suggestions to make the overall system perform optimally in the public interest.

Regulating the health professions within an overall health care system is a complex task, considering the interrelationships with reimbursement, the tradition of professional association involvement in regulation by the individual states, accreditation of educational programs, and state and Medicare requirements for facilities. But if we take the time, make the effort, and involve all interested people in an attempt to educate ourselves, we are better equipped to make policy recommendations for reforming the regulation of the health care workforce.

Works Cited

Alberta Health Workforce Rebalancing Committee. 1994. *New Directions for Legislation Regulating the Health Professions in Alberta: A Discussion Paper.* Edmonton, Alberta: Alberta Labor.

Bohnen, L.S. 1994. *Regulated Health Professions Act.* Aurora, Ontario: Canada Law Book.

Maine Health Professions Regulation Project and Task Force. 1995. *Toward a More Rational State Licensure System for Maine's Health Professionals.* Augusta, ME: Medical Care Development.

McLaughlin, C.J. 1994. Health workforce issues and policy-making roles. In *Health Workforce Issues for the 21st Century*, P.F. Larson, M. Osterweis, and E.R. Rubin, eds. Washington: Association of Academic Health Centers.

Morrison, R.D. 1994. *The Causes and Consequences of Health Professional Regulation: Implications for the Allied Health Workforce.* Paper prepared for the National Commission on Allied Health, Health Resources and Services Administration. Washington: U.S. Department of Health and Human Services.

New Brunswick Department of Health and Community Services. N.d. *A Future Direction for Health Disciplines Regulation in New Brunswick: Discussion Paper.* Fredericton, New Brunswick: NBDHCS.

Ontario Health Professions Legislation Review. 1989. *Striking a New Balance: A Blueprint for the Regulation of Ontario's Health Professions.* Toronto: Ministry of Health.

THE VIRGINIA GENERALIST INITIATIVE

State Regulation of Physician Supply

R. MICHAEL MORSE

I n 1991, the House of Delegates of the Virginia General Assembly passed a resolution asking that the three medical schools in the state—Eastern Virginia Medical School, the University of Virginia, and the Medical College of Virginia—encourage medical students to become generalists and to practice in rural areas. Our collective response was a letter of commitment to a 50 percent generalist goal. However, there was no timeline for implementation, and within the schools this commitment was poorly communicated among faculty, students, and staff.

It was one of the better-kept secrets in Virginia that the state medical schools had made a commitment to generalist medicine. The schools were operating under the assumption that the 50 percent generalist goal would include medical students who matched in internal medicine, pediatrics, and family practice residencies. They were quite confident that they were already well on the way to meeting the goal and that achieving it would not be difficult.

The medical schools of Virginia have come a long way since then toward understanding and recognizing the implications of their commitment to generalism. In 1992, the Senate issued a joint resolution with the House asking the schools to create a plan for 50 percent generalist output. With the legislature starting to put our feet to the fire, the schools started thinking more seriously about their commitment. Fortunately, at about the same time The Robert Wood Johnson Foundation released a request for proposals for a generalist physician initiative. The schools were each independently planning to submit a proposal to the foundation. As we talked with each other, we also realized that we each were also independently planning to ask the state government for the matching funds.

This approach did not seem like a good plan because, first, it would pit each school against the others, and second, the issues were much broader than any one school could handle. It was going to take a collaborative effort to solve the problem.

The Medical Schools Come Together

This was the first time that the three schools had cooperated intensely in a large planning project of this sort. In the past, relationships among the schools were tense, at the least, with a lot of suspicion and concern about who was intending to do what. It was also unusual for the three schools to be getting together with the state government.

The three schools responded to the lawmakers' joint resolution with their own joint proposal for the Virginia generalist initiative, which they also sent to the foundation. It resulted in a commitment of state funds to match funds from the foundation for an eighteen-month planning phase. The state also guaranteed matching funds for the first year of the initiative once the six-year grant was awarded from the foundation. In the first year, out of a total budget of $3.8 million, the state appropriation was $2.24 million.

The Medical Schools Work With the Lawmakers

As this collaboration began, the state's Council on Higher Education came up with an idea for putting some teeth in the 50 percent goal since state dollars were involved. A unique formula was devised in which these schools would have to achieve 50 percent generalist output by the year 2000 in order to maintain their base level of state funding per student. This situation led to one of the first negotiations in which the schools were able to convince the state agencies involved that punitive incentives were not in the best interest of a future collaborative relationship. The result was a redesigned incentive plan. If the schools reach the 50 percent goal, there will be a 5 percent increment in money, but the schools' budgets will not be decreased as long as we achieve at least 40 percent generalist output. This plan gave us some maneuvering room as well as an incentive to move toward the 50 percent goal. It also changed a potentially negative interaction and negative relationship with the legislative and state agencies into a much more positive one.

Whenever you start asking for money, the people providing the money want you to document your need. We found that difficult. We looked at what we knew about workforce composition, which was not a lot, particularly at the local level within the state of Virginia. We used some big regional numbers, but we did not know the numbers relating to localities, and that is what legislators really want to know. They want to know about their constituents and what you are going to do to help them.

The outcome was our request to the state, through the Joint Commission on Health Care, to consider supporting a statewide census of practicing physicians. The census would not only determine where licensees are in practice, but also the primary focus of practice, and how many hours a week they spend in practice. This request was passed with some consternation. (It seemed like a fairly simple process but it certainly stirred up a hornet's nest among various professional groups.) Nurse practitioners and physician assistants will be included in the census. For the first time, we will be able to link the health care supply within the state to true workforce composition and people's health needs.

As a result of all these efforts, we were able to come up with a reasonable goal that can be recited by everybody in the initiative. That goal is to serve Virginia's health workforce needs. The issue of quality is important, and each partner has a slightly different perspective on it. From the view of the schools, there is a concern for ensuring quality. The quality issue does not stir up the same level of interest at the state legislature as does the discussion of numbers and location and areas of need, so we have here a tension and a dynamic that we have to deal with and respond to constantly.

Generalist goals are still tied to 50 percent, both in residency positions and eventual practice specialty. Working with another Robert Wood Johnson project, primarily through the Joint Commission on Health Care, the schools are dealing with the distribution of physicians across the state. Major strategies range from recruitment and admission to medical schools to the study of a consortium model for graduate medical education.

Tips for a Successful Collaboration

Consortiums have their risks. One of the key ingredients of the initiative's success was identifying the key players up front. At the institutional level were the deans of the medical schools. Each of the deans signed on as a coprincipal investigator in The Robert Wood Johnson grant, and each has been the lead advocate for the generalist initiative at the state level. We have also included the Virginia area health education centers in this process, believing that our outcome was uniquely tied to the success of the centers.

On the state legislative side, the Joint Commission on Health Care was clearly in the leadership position in health care issues in the General Assembly. The executive director of the commission was included as a member of the executive committee, and the director of the State Council on Higher Education and the state's Secretary of Education were added to represent the state executive branch.

These key players have been key advocates. Involving them early in the planning process as well as in implementation has been invaluable, and I am sure that we would not have achieved our funding levels without their support.

A major lesson we have learned at the medical schools is to look outside ourselves. We sometimes have a narrow view, particularly within faculty ranks not regularly exposed to workforce issues. It is important that we communicate to our faculties and staff that the center of all we do is deliver service to the communities of Virginia.

A critical component in our long-term success is going to be the longitudinal tracking system being developed by the three schools. The tracking system will demonstrate and support the outcomes of the generalist initiative. We believe that without this evidence, the probability of getting long-term funding and support from the state will be small. We are following not only our medical students and residents located within Virginia, but also all Virginia residents who are training outside the state; the hope is that we can bring them back to help the state meet its health care workforce needs.

The output goals for undergraduate medical education show some initial progress. Our graduate medical education goals are now tied entirely to shifts toward generalism within internal medicine and pediatrics.

Within the institutions, educational issues are critically important. To sell the initiative and implement it successfully, we had to deal with internal issues at each school. Each one is working to redefine and rebalance medical education to include many of the new skills, attitudes, and knowledge necessary not only for today's generalists but for the generalists of the future as managed care and the health care system evolve. These skills are much broader than the traditional skills we have been teaching.

Economic issues are of utmost importance for the health sciences centers in Virginia. They are being squeezed from a number of directions, and the usual sources of support are leveling off and in some cases significantly dwindling. An important message that we have tried to get through to state lawmakers is that the generalist programs we are developing and putting in place increase the cost of education because of the nature of the curriculum we are implementing. At the same time, the resources traditionally available from the ability to charge higher fees for patient care are going away. Within the state institutions, over 50 percent of the cost of undergraduate medical education is borne by revenue from clinical income. As that income is reduced, our ability to support medical education may be compromised. This important and global issue helps our legislators understand the internal economics of medical education.

Conclusion

Working in consortium is a lot like a dance. When agreeing to dance, it is a good use of time to determine what the music will be, and then work together. The act requires coordination, cooperation, and trust. Somebody's toes are probably going to get stepped on sooner or later. But as with any dance, it is important to take a break every once in a while, sit back and chat, and then go back and try again.

THE VIRGINIA GENERALIST INITIATIVE

The View From the Legislature

STEPHEN A. HORAN

The Virginia Joint Commission on Health Care is the state's major vehicle for health care reform. It is a legislative commission made up of fifteen members from both houses of the legislature. It is rather unique among state organizations for health care reform because it is based in the legislative branch; in most states undertaking major health care reform, the initiative has usually come from the Governor's office. In cases where the legislature has been involved, an executive branch agency has usually been designated to direct operations. In Virginia, legislators from across the state are driving the reform process.

Virginia is a state with a great deal of diversity. Because it is really three or four or five states in terms of geography and economy, it is difficult to develop statewide policies. Virginia tends to develop regional policies, a trend that is played out in the generalist initiative. We have three medical schools situated in different parts of the state; each has its own approach to the Virginia generalist initiative based on its geographic area, its level of integration with local communities, and other regional variations.

I would like to address some of the lessons learned from the legislative process. As legislative staff, I have been an information broker for the past year. I work with the medical schools to bring in a budget request, and I work with legislators and their staffs not only to get them to understand the budget request but also to help them gain a better understanding of the legislature's agenda for the medical schools. Ultimately, I try to get the two parties together to agree on a program.

Defining the Problem

One thing we learned is that the problem of physician supply must be clearly defined for state policy makers. The problem-definition process is a key factor in policy making in Virginia, particularly because we have a part-time legislature. It is difficult to sit down with a group of legislators for only a few minutes during the year and try to explain the details of health workforce reform. Legislative staff, therefore, play a strong role, and it is important to understand both the committee and staff structures in a state legislature.

In determining the goals for the generalist initiative, we focused on issues of imbalance in the generalist-specialist mix, primary care shortages, and the lack of preparation of medical graduates for managed care. We presented data to the legislators, emphasizing that an operable mix of generalists and specialists was 50:50. (Obviously this ratio is subject to much debate right now, but it is the goal toward which we are working.) Legislators questioned the source of this recommendation. We came back with the literature and expert opinion that support the ratio and advocate for this change in the overall mix.

We had to constantly remind people that the purpose of the generalist initiative went beyond simply solving access problems in medically underserved areas. It is also an issue that involves the overall physician mix in Virginia and across the country. Virginia is behind most states in terms of managed care, but it is penetrating the market quickly. The state employee program has moved towards managed care; the Medicaid program has adopted managed care and is now looking at capitation. The generalist initiative acquired new meaning for legislators when viewed in this context. Legislators started to wonder about and understand the need for primary care physicians.

Local Issues

It was important to bring the primary care shortage issue down to the local level. Data developed by the Department of Family Practice at the Medical College of Virginia estimated a shortage of about 353 primary care physicians in the nonmetropolitan areas of Virginia. The goal is one physician per 2,000 population.

A balance exists in the Richmond metropolitan area. However, Northern Virginia, an urbanized area, has a primary care physician shortage. After a lot of work putting together even the most rudimentary data about the current status of the state physician supply, we found that some of the national data bases, such as the data base of the American Medical Association, begin to fall apart when you start looking at local or regional issues.

We had to pull out telephone books in the Richmond metro area to see if some of the physicians in the AMA data base were still practicing; many were not. National data does not translate easily to an understanding of local issues.

Localizing issues cannot be emphasized enough. We put together a map of Virginia that showed the physician-to-population ratio at levels of one physician per 1,000, 2,000, and more than 3,000 residents. The map had numerous qualifications. If one subarea within a county has a shortage, it does not mean the whole county is short. All it means is that within that county there are areas where people lack access to primary health care physicians. These details are important to legislators if they are to understand the problems in their districts. It is time consuming and difficult to discuss such details with every legislator, so you end up picking the key legislators on the key committees and subcommittees and try to educate them as best you can.

It was helpful to talk qualitatively about the consequences of inadequate access to primary care. We used available research on these issues to illustrate the results of a primary care shortage: poor health status due to a high incidence of preventable health problems, higher health costs due to unnecessary hospitalizations and emergency room visits, a heavy indigent care burden resting on a few providers, long waits for appointments, and poor regional economic development prospects. The fact that businesses considering relocating in areas with a shortage of primary care have some serious questions about the health care infrastructure was of great concern to many legislators.

Practice Locations

To be supported and funded, the generalist initiative had to encompass undergraduate and graduate medical education reform, physician recruitment, and physician retention. Legislators and their staffs asked if these new physicians were going to practice in Virginia's areas of need. Some tension was created by legislative language that would have put quite a bit of responsibility on the medical schools for placing people in underserved areas and making certain they remained there.

We had to remind the legislators that the generalist initiative is a part of a broader strategy for Virginia involving other initiatives dealing with practice sites, recruitment, and retention of health care professionals. The Robert Wood Johnson Foundation has funded a practice site initiative, and the state acts as an umbrella to pull together several different initiatives for physician recruitment and retention. The Area Health Education Center program provides technical assistance and continuing medical education in outlying communities.

The Office of Rural Health in the U.S. Department of Health and Human Services has done a tremendous job to help community health centers in Virginia become Federally qualified health centers and receive cost-based Federal reimbursement; these centers are then able to be part of viable medical scholarship programs. Virginia has increased its commitment to medical scholarships significantly over the last several years and, in return, scholarship recipients agree to serve on a year-for-year basis in medically underserved areas.

Loan Repayments

We have established a state program for loan forgiveness but were unable to fund it. We hope to be able to do so in the future. Nevertheless, it was important to show the legislature that there are programs for enticing new medical graduates into underserved areas. However, the medical schools alone should not be held responsible for this task. Their role is to recruit prospective medical students and residents interested in serving in underserved areas and to get them trained in an appropriate community setting. But some individual incentives are also needed to get people to go to these areas and stay there to practice.

Lessons Learned

The generalist initiative must be presented with clear goals and reasonable expectations. Medical schools have limited ability to control where physicians ultimately practice, as well as the complexity of the economic and social disincentives in underserved areas. Even with the generalist initiative and other programs, it is going to be a major challenge to get more physicians to practice and remain there.

Policy makers must also consider market dynamics. As the market changes, and as we move toward health systems that employ salaried physicians, we must analyze how this change will help or hinder access to primary care in some underserved areas. Will we see some of the larger systems putting salaried physicians in the outlying areas for some period of time or in the inner cities that are short on primary care physicians? We don't know.

To win legislative support, the initiative needed the potential to solve local problems. The legislature wanted assurances that the medical schools would take some steps to ensure that these graduates would practice in Virginia. We ended up with a compromise: The medical schools would commit to graduating 50 percent of their graduates as generalists and doing what they can to make sure that half ultimately practice in Virginia. It means that about 25 percent of all Virginia medical graduates will practice in Virginia as generalists.

An important lesson that emerged from the process of negotiation is that academic health center funding must be justified with institutional performance data. Academic health centers are probably the most complicated units of state government. To most legislators, they are a black box in terms of their funding, the efficiency of their operation, and their need for more resources. (I have been working with the academic health centers for three years now and, to me, they are still a gray box.) Funding needs to be addressed with legislative staff on an ongoing basis.

Over time, the initiative must recognize broader state policy trends. This year all universities were asked to restructure to reduce the costs of education. This request was made at the same time that the generalist initiative approached the legislature with the data that, due to increased community-based training, restructuring medical education would increase the cost of education. It was difficult to reconcile those two different educational policies, and we had to spend a lot of time working with staff to explain medical education and justify the higher costs of community-based training.

As the state moves toward capitation in the Medicaid program, what will be the status of the academic health centers? We need to make sure that they continue to receive graduate medical education funding. In addition, information systems must be developed to demonstrate accountability. The Virginia generalist initiative is a long-term commitment on the part of the legislature. The legislature needs to see, year by year, some accountable data that show where our graduates are going and the progress that we are making.

THE VIRGINIA GENERALIST INITIATIVE

The Effect on Medical Education

C. DONALD COMBS

I will frame my analysis of the Virginia generalist initiative with two quotes. One is from Will and Ariel Durant who wrote a twelve-volume series, *History of Civilization,* and a short book summarizing what they called the lessons of history. Among their conclusions was the observation that "perhaps we could learn enough from history to bear reality patiently and to respect one another's delusions."

A second quote comes from Daniel Boone, a Virginia legislator who was also noted for his travels. Asked whether he had ever been lost, he said, "No, I have never been lost, but I was once bewildered for three days."

I can describe the effect of the Virginia generalist initiative on medical education in the state as somewhere between bearing reality patiently and being bewildered.

Origin of the Initiative

In 1991, it became clear that a consensus was building on the need for more generalist physicians in Virginia. It was also clear that there were no data to warrant this conclusion, only anecdotal evidence from distant rural areas with insufficient numbers of physicians overall. There also began to exist what I have called the policy orthodoxy that assumed we should move toward the 50 percent number for generalists.

At about the same time, the leaders of the three academic health centers made a commitment to the state legislature that we would work together to respond more directly to state health needs, rather than have the legislature mandate educational quotas for our institutions because they felt we were not responsive to the state's health workforce needs.

Challenges Faced by the Academic Health Centers

All three medical institutions in Virginia are committed to improving health care in the commonwealth. We have deans who are personally committed to doing that as well. Personal leadership is vital when undertaking a project as wide-ranging as the generalist initiative.

Having set a goal of generalized curricular reform in 1992, each school allowed the usual faculty process of curriculum design to proceed. The leadership simply stated that the curriculum had to move in certain directions and provided some ideas about how to make it move. We did not, however, mandate a series of specific changes from the top down. I believe this approach was an important means of moving faculties in the generalist direction.

Program Differences

Diversity of program emphasis among the three institutions is one of our challenges. Although all the schools are trying to do things that we think will produce both more generalist physicians and physicians who are better trained to practice in the late twentieth century and into the next century, we have some different theories about how to achieve that goal. One has to do with the use of community preceptors. My institution, Eastern Virginia Medical School, is a community-based medical school; we have made substantial use of community practitioners for the twenty years of our existence. We have never paid those preceptors for their services, we have never been asked to pay them, and we intend to not pay them for as long as we can.

Use of Community Faculty

The University of Virginia and the Medical College of Virginia have not made as much use of community faculty as Eastern Virginia Medical School. In discussions with faculty in their markets, these two schools found that community faculty expected to be paid for their services. They did not expect to profit from their teaching activities or make as much money as they did from patient care. But they expected some payment that took into account the reduction in their revenues that results from teaching. The University of Virginia and the Medical College of Virginia felt strongly about the payment issue and constructed budgets that included payments for community preceptors. It led to a fundamental difference in the budgets of the three institutions, and made it even more difficult to explain to legislators what

Eastern Virginia Medical School is doing with its money. At Eastern Virginia, we are putting our money into increasing full-time faculty, taking faculty effort out of patient care and devoting it to education.

Cost

Scarcity of resources is another challenge. When we designed this program, we envisioned a two-year project that would begin at $9 million in the first year and grow to over $12 million in the second year with the state paying about half of the costs in both years. It was the proposal that we submitted to The Robert Wood Johnson Foundation. After ten months of increasing awareness, we realized that no one was willing to pay $21 million over two years for us to do those things we thought we ought to do. We revised the proposal (figure 1).

We tried to be fairly clever and continue the pattern of cost-shifting that we have learned so well. School contributions shrank considerably in the later version. We tried to shift our expenses to the state, but the legislature adeptly shifted them right back to us.

Over the past year, what was envisioned as a full-blown program of slightly over $12 million a year has been reduced to one that is now about $5 million a year. This situation had raised some question for us as accountability measures are more clearly defined and the financial realities more clearly understood: What are we committed to do, and will we be able to do it?

It is a quandary; I understand from our student affairs dean that in the 1995 residency match, we will have over 59 percent of our students in primary care residencies. Data like that make it difficult to argue that we need more money to get to a 50 percent generalist output, since we are already there.

Such an outcome could be a single occurrence. And it does not explain anything about the variety of issues that need to be addressed about where training takes place and what this training comprises. (That said, the numbers will no doubt be noticed by legislators, especially when all three schools produce more generalists this year than last year.)

Determining Priorities

At each institution, competing legislative priorities are another challenge. All three institutions have made funding the initiative their highest legislative priority for the past two years. It has been easy for Eastern Virginia Medical School. We are a single-purpose institution, and funding the medi-

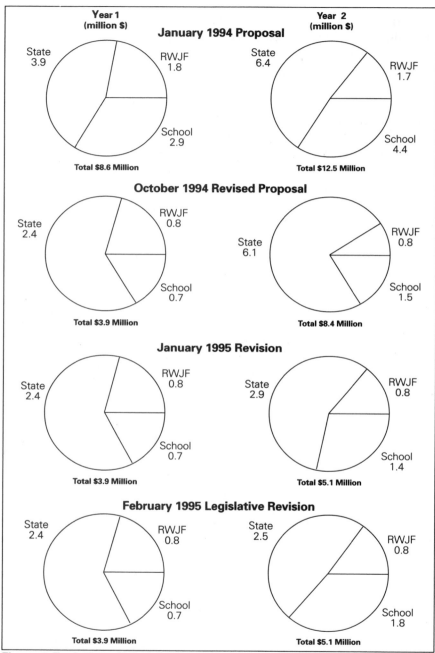

Figure 1. Evolution of Virginia Generalist Initiative Financing

cal school is our biggest concern. It is much more difficult for the University of Virginia and Virginia Commonwealth University to keep medical education funding as their highest institutional priority.

It is also difficult for the legislature, with a small and shrinking pot of discretionary money, to continue to carve out special dollars to fund this initiative. The governor has indicated that he is not interested in providing continuing levels of funding to higher education, let alone increased funding. In his opinion, there is still sufficient fat in the system to enable the institutions to fund all salary raises for the coming years, as well as to restructure themselves to support new programs.

There is a concern at each institution about competing priorities, mission, and accountability. We agreed a few years ago to look at what we were doing in undergraduate medical education that related to increasing the number of generalist physicians. We agreed to move toward the 50 percent generalist goal. At the same time, the need to place these physicians in practice in underserved areas in the state was increasingly linked to the generalist goal in the minds of the legislators. Retaining 25 percent of Virginia medical graduates in practice in the state is something we may not be able to achieve. We are not far off, but it is difficult to know how to improve. Issues related to the content and distribution of obstetrics and gynecology service keep arising, and we are looking at how to get more obstetrician-gynecologists to practice in underserved areas. Legislators want it to happen. In general, there is considerable tension between the set of hypotheses developed about a program in an academic institution and what the legislators are willing to support.

Fear of Micromanagement

State micromanagement of the academic health centers has not happened, but it is a potential concern. As a part of the generalist initiative, we have prepared detailed analyses of our budgets for the legislature; we have not yet received a detailed line-item budget from the legislature. But the initiative has forced legislative staff to look closely at what we are doing with every dollar appropriated to the institution. The state funds the generalist initiative with a certain amount of dollars, and then we are free to manage those funds. But there is always the risk that the state will say that we are getting money to do these specific things. They do not realize the fluidity and complexity of the situation in which we now find ourselves.

Conclusion

What are the future prospects for the generalist initiative? Is this approach wise? Will it work? I believe the best way to understand the generalist initiative is to say that it is a continuing conversation among the medical schools, state policy makers, and financiers about the relationship between social needs and educational programs. It is important that those involved understand that the conversation is important, likely to last awhile, and complicated. One goal is for at least half of graduating students to choose to become generalists. We may or may not achieve it. Retaining 25 percent of graduates in the state is also a goal. We may or may not achieve it. We will make good-faith efforts. We will gather good data. And we will continue to talk in good faith.

Roles of the Market

The marketplace for health care delivery has recently become a more active player in the health workforce field. The first paper in this section examines the effects that the changing marketplace is having on staffing policies in health delivery organizations and the resulting changes in demand for and supply of nursing professionals. The second and third papers describe the staffing policies of managed care organizations, which are stimulating much of the change in health care delivery. The fourth describes an area of workforce policy—academic accreditation— in which market players are beginning to challenge traditional decision-making authorities, especially the health professions themselves. And the fifth paper discusses the reforms in health professions education necessitated by the changing marketplace.

The Nursing Workforce in a Time of Change

Karl D. Yordy

Nursing is a particularly interesting example of a profession caught amidst the turbulent market forces creating radical change in the nation's health care system. This largest of the health professions had 1.8 million registered nurses employed in 1992 out of a total of 2.2 million RNs (U.S. Public Health Service 1994). Such a large group poses a substantial cost for the health care system and will, therefore, be a consideration in any effort to reduce costs and achieve greater productivity. My purpose in this paper is to examine the implications of one manifestation of these market-driven changes—the rapid move toward managed care and integrated health care systems—for the health professional workforce, using nursing as an example.

Growth of Managed Care

Managed care is a loose term that encompasses both tightly integrated systems, such as staff model health maintenance organizations, and more decentralized arrangements, such as preferred provider organizations. But in all forms of managed care arrangements, selected groups of providers are usually bound to a health plan by a contractual arrangement intended to provide economic advantages for the health plan and to maintain market share for the health care providers. The more structured forms of managed care have an enrolled population to be served by its group of providers and a commitment to some target for health plan expenditures, often in the form of a capitated payment. To meet their expenditure targets and compete successfully on price with other plans, managed care plans use various approaches to managing the rate of utilization of services, the site of service, or the coordination of services. These approaches may be internalized within

---

Note: The views presented in this paper are my own and do not represent the views of the Institute of Medicine Committee on the Future of Primary Care.

the professional group or run as a management function by the health plan.

In its most developed form, managed care is carried out by vertically integrated health systems in which there is central management and financing of a full array of health services. In such an arrangement, the organization has no ultimate vested interest in maintaining any organizational entities or facilities, such as hospitals, but is motivated by the desire to offer effective services that both satisfy enrollees (as well as the organizations paying for the care) and are produced efficiently. However, many arrangements that are less integrated are also offering various forms of managed care.

Because the particulars of managed care arrangements are constantly evolving and are typically viewed by the health plans as proprietary information, measuring the growth of these plans is difficult. But there is no doubt that the growth is substantial. An estimate by Howard Bailit (1995) of Aetna indicates that total enrollment in managed care is about 125 million, with all but about 11 million in private plans (table 1). However, the rate of growth of public plans has been more rapid than that of private plans: In 1994, there was a 13 percent increase in Medicare managed care enrollment and a dramatic 100 percent increase in Medicaid managed care enrollment; private plans grew by only 10.4 percent. For private plans, en-

Table 1. Enrollment in Managed Care, by Payor, 1994

Payor	Total Enrollment (in millions)	Managed Care Enrollment (in millions)	% Change Managed Care, 1993–94
Private	180.0	115.0	10.4
Medicare	36.0	2.8	13.0
Medicaid	32.0	8.0	100.0

Source: Bailit 1995.

Table 2. Enrollment in Private Managed Care Plans, by Product, 1994

Product	Members (in millions)	% Change 1993–94
HMO	49	10.0
Point-of-service plan	10	13.0
Preferred provider organization*	56	9.0

Source: Bailit 1995.

* Estimate based on discussions with Gordon Wheeler of the American Preferred Provider Organization.

Table 3. Enrollment in Managed Care by HMO Type, 1992–93

HMO Type	Enrollment (in millions) 1993	% Increase 1992–93
Staff	5.1	-8.9
Group	10.8	6.9
IPA	21.3	12.1
Network	7.9	19.6

Source: Bailit 1995.

Table 4. Penetration of Managed Care in the 95 Largest Cities, 1993

% Managed Care	Number of Markets
0-10	4
11-20	18
21-30	35
31-40	19
41-50	16
51-60	3

Source: Bailit 1995.

rollment in HMOs and point-of-service plans totaled 59 million in 1994 (table 2). Fifty-six million more enrolled in looser arrangements such as preferred provider organizations. Enrollment in HMOs and point-of-service plans is growing more rapidly (table 2). Looser HMO types, independent practice associations, and networks are growing more rapidly than group models; staff-model HMOs actually lost enrollment in 1992–93 (table 3).

Bailit also estimates managed care penetration in the ninety-five largest cities (table 4). In nineteen of these markets, penetration exceeds 40 percent. In another fifty-four markets, penetration exceeds 20 percent. It seems likely that these penetration rates will grow substantially in coming years, especially since the pressures for cost containment are unlikely to abate and the passage of national health care reform mandating a choice of fee-for-service plans seems doubtful.

Major Issues

Nursing expanded rapidly during the period when hospitals, the employment setting for the largest number of nurses, were funded primarily on a basis of reimbursement for costs. In 1970, 722,000 RNs were employed. By 1980, the number of employed RNs had grown to 1.3 million (IOM 1983). Since nursing is the largest cost center in most hospitals, there should be little surprise that nursing is a target for cost-cutting in the hospital sector (Henneberger 1994).

Educational Pathways

Three principal educational pathways for becoming a registered nurse are a matter of considerable controversy within the profession. In 1992, 30.1 percent of employed RNs had a diploma (hospital based), 31.0 percent had an associate degree, 31.0 percent had a baccalaureate degree, and 7.9 percent had a master's degree or doctorate. The proportion from diploma schools has declined since 1980 (figure 1), while the other categories have increased.

In broad terms, diploma and associate degree programs would seem to be more in tune with the usual functioning of a labor market, and these educational environments would seem to be more oriented to the traditions of vocational training. In contrast, the baccalaureate programs would seem to be more in the tradition of professional education. The graduate degree programs, especially those for nurse specialists, are close to the professional model, including the intent to prepare some of the graduates for independent practice. Some nursing organizations and leaders have advocated that basic entry-level training should be at the baccalaureate level on classic professional grounds (IOM 1983).

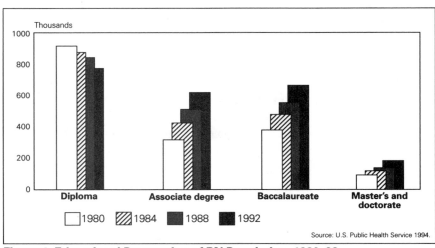

Figure 1. Educational Preparation of RN Population, 1980–92

Table 5. Hospital Work Units Where Nurses Spend Most of Their Time, 1992

Unit	% of Time
Outpatient department	5.5
Home health unit	0.4
Hospice unit	0.2
Intensive care	18.1
General/specialty	40.1
Operating Room/post-op	11.4
Labor/delivery	5.7
Emergency room	6.8
Other	11.8

Source: U.S. Public Health Service 1994.

Assuming that higher levels of training lead to higher compensation, the tendency of a cost-competitive health care system would be to employ the people with the lowest level of training who can do the job. Nursing uses the same cost argument when arguing that nurses should substitute for physicians in providing of primary care (Aiken and Sage 1992). These pressures to find the lowest-cost personnel capable of performing a particular function may mean that nurses with less training will lose jobs while those with advanced training find new opportunities. Aggregate projections of nursing supply and demand may have little meaning if different components of the nursing workforce are having different experiences in the marketplace.

Employment Settings

In 1992, 1.2 million nurses, about two-thirds of all employed nurses, were employed in hospitals. These data include nurses employed by hospitals in other than acute inpatient care. Only about 6 percent of nurse time in 1992 was spent in outpatient, home health, and hospice services (table 5). Nurses spent 6.8 percent of their time in the emergency room. Acute inpatient functions took about 75 percent of nurse time. The remaining 11.8 percent of nurse time was spent in such functions as transition beds. Furthermore, while other employment settings for nurses have grown since 1980, there has been little change in the proportion of nurses employed by hospitals, although, as figure 2 shows, the absolute number has grown more than the absolute increases in other settings (figure 2).

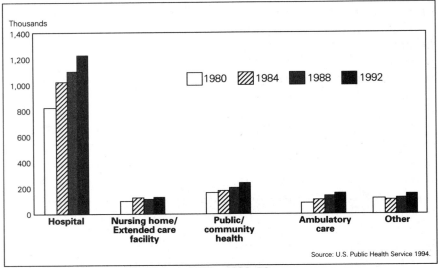

Figure 2. Employment Settings of RNs, 1980–92

These data should make clear that much of the current employment of nurses is vulnerable to staff reductions in acute inpatient services and the emergency room, both of which are specific targets for reduction by managed care plans. Total inpatient days in U.S. hospitals fell from about 384 million in 1982 to about 295 million in 1992, a decrease of 23.2 percent (AHA 1993). The number of hospital beds fell in the same period from 1.36 million to 1.178 million. Despite this drop in beds, occupancy rates in acute general hospitals fell from 77.4 percent in 1982 to 68.5 percent in 1992. These trends have important implications for the employment of nurses. The data suggest that the full burden of these changes, and other changes brought about by the spread of managed care, has not yet been felt by the profession.

A compensatory factor is that the intensity of hospital services has increased as less sick patients are either seen in other settings or discharged earlier. This intensity usually translates into a higher ratio of nurses per patient, which has certainly been the trend, as more nurses are treating fewer patients in the inpatient setting. It should be noted, however, that one of the results of the great increase in research on outcomes and effectiveness being supported by the Agency for Health Care Policy and Research and other groups may be to question further the rate of use of procedures requiring hospitalization. Advances in surgical and other invasive techniques and wider use of new noninvasive approaches may continue to justify moving procedures out of the hospital setting. Managed care plans have a strong incentive for development and use of such advances.

The small proportion of nurses employed in settings other than hospitals means that large proportional increases in these employment opportunities would have to take place in order to absorb even a modest reduction in hospital nursing employment. One can also question whether the educational preparation, experience, and skills of many hospital nurses can be applied in nonhospital settings without substantial retraining. The sources of financing for such training on a large scale are also unclear.

Salaries

Nursing salaries increased by about one-third in real terms between 1980 and 1992 (figure 3), a period when growth in real incomes for many Americans stagnated or declined. The average annual salary for a hospital staff nurse in 1992 was $35,212. Nurses with specialized training earn substantially more. The salaries of nurse anesthetists averaged more than $76,000 in 1992, and those of nurse practitioners and nurse midwives averaged about $44,000.

When the total increase in numbers of nurses is coupled with the increase in their incomes, the total increase in expenditures for nursing salaries since 1980 is substantial. The increase in salaries makes nursing an even more attractive target for cost reductions, especially in a hospital sector that

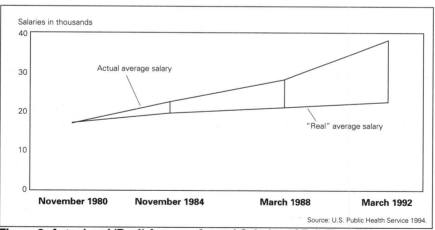

Source: U.S. Public Health Service 1994.

Figure 3. Actual and 'Real' Average Annual Salaries of Full-Time RNs, November 1980–March 1992

is downsizing under pressures from managed care. Cost reductions can be achieved through layoffs, salary reductions, productivity increases, substitution of lower-cost personnel, or a combination of these measures. Anecdotal evidence suggests that all of these approaches are in fact being used.

Outside the hospital sector, nurses have argued that they can substitute for more expensive physician services, especially in primary care where nurse practitioners have been carrying out many functions that once were the exclusive domain of physicians. However, the higher that salaries rise for NPs, the less attractive is this substitution from a purely economic standpoint. And substitution is a two-way street. A managed care plan may choose to train its own nursing personnel for the functions it wants performed and may not buy into a general increase in entry-level training.

As in fields outside health care, nursing may face choices and trade-offs with regard to salary demands. Within the hospital setting, nurses can justify higher salaries on the basis of higher productivity, but they are already complaining about overwork in situations where fewer do more. This choice may be similar to that made by the General Motors workers at the Buick plant in Flint, Michigan. They went on strike in 1994 to achieve a reduction in mandatory overtime, even though that overtime was resulting in annual incomes exceeding $60,000 for many workers.

In downsizing situations, nurses may be faced with a choice between lower salaries or less jobs; similar situations have led to salary give-backs in the airline and other industries.

In fields such as ambulatory care and home health care, where employment opportunities for nurses are growing, nurses will need to justify higher salaries on the basis of higher productivity.

Implications for Workforce Planning and Policy

As noted, the rapid spread of managed care is almost certain to bring about a substantial downsizing of the hospital capacity in the United States. In mature competitive markets such as Minneapolis-St. Paul, as much as a third of hospital capacity has already been eliminated. This downsizing implies that the nursing workforce in hospitals will also be subject to reductions, given that hospitals are still the employers of about two-thirds of all registered nurses and that nursing is the largest cost center in a hospital. While estimating exact numbers is difficult, a realistic assumption would be that this decline is likely to be substantial, even with the increase in the intensity of care in hospitals. If one used an approach similar to that used by

Weiner (1994) in projecting future demand for physicians and extrapolated the experience of the Twin Cities to the rest of the nation, the reductions of nursing employment in the hospital setting would be very large.

Even if opportunities for employment of advanced practice nurses in primary care settings and in the provision of obstetrical care increase by a factor of three or four rather quickly, the increase is unlikely to be large enough to provide employment for more than a small portion of the nurses losing positions in the hospital sector. Furthermore, the argument of the nursing profession that NPs and nurse-midwives be substituted for physicians presumes advanced training. Therefore, conversion of the hospital nurse workforce would require a major retraining effort. Given the great variety of arrangements that managed care plans may make for the use of nursing personnel in the primary care setting and the rapid changes that are likely to be made in those arrangements as they are tested in the marketplace, managed care plans may choose to develop their own approaches to advanced training rather than accept the profession's model. Substitution is a very fluid and flexible concept that will vary as circumstances change, such as the price of the substitute and the impact on productivity and outcomes. Managed care plans, especially the more integrated ones, have a broader framework and management structure for making trade-offs in the use of professional health care personnel than the typical health care institution or practice setting of the past. The plans have strong economic incentives to use expensive personnel efficiently in accomplishing their competitive objectives. The more advanced and integrated managed care plans are likely to be impatient with any professional model that interferes with their ability to innovate and respond quickly to market conditions.

The relationship of costs to desired outcomes is likely to be subjected to intense scrutiny in the competitive managed care environment. This means that nursing, along with the other health professions, will need to emphasize the development of objective measures of practice cost-effectiveness that are convincing to managed care plans, rather than depend on professionally mandated standards of practice, which have often been the exclusive purview of the learned professions. Future salaries for nurses will be established in this context, and as competitive markets in health care function more completely, salaries will send signals about the demand for nursing professionals.

This is not to imply that health care will ever be a perfect market, or that nursing and the other health professions will ever completely lose their role in establishing professional standards and educational pathways. But the days of almost exclusive professional control of such matters are passing. In the future, the professions are likely to share the shaping of professional functions with managed care plans increasingly accountable for efficient achievement of many health care objectives. This scenario will likely occur in spite of the fact that some of the health professions are launching campaigns to provide new legal barriers to market changes (e.g., any-willing-provider laws).

Managed care plans are also likely to be partners in determining the desired educational pathways for nursing. The plans are also likely to be an ally of the nursing profession in removing legal and regulatory barriers to the scope of practice for nurses to allow room for practice innovations that enable the plans to compete effectively.

In the absence of comprehensive health care reform, managed care plans will almost certainly not deal with the growing number of uninsured Americans. Although the continued existence of a large number of uninsured people may be unfortunate from the perspective of the broader public interest, the situation may create additional opportunities for nurses to function as providers of last resort funded directly by public sources. Nursing has a long and honorable history of fulfilling this function, still carried out by public health nurses in many settings. Managed care plans may play a role, as shown by some of the approaches being developed under Medicaid waivers (e.g., TennCare).

Long-term care seems to be another growth opportunity for nursing, given the growth of the elderly population and the traditional interest of integrated health systems in long-term care. However, the number of RNs involved up to now has not been great and has not grown rapidly. As long as long-term care remains an orphan of public and private health care financing schemes, extreme pressures to keep down costs will motivate long-term care organizations to continue to substitute less costly care providers for RNs.

Need for Timely, Substantive Data

The changes being wrought by the growth of managed care are rapid. Because decision making is highly decentralized, many innovations in the use of nurses will be hard to track. These circumstances call for better and more timely data on health care arrangements, including the use of nurses and other health professionals. The pace of change requires that, to be useful, new data must be available on at least an annual basis and have sufficient detail to describe developments in many types of practice settings and locations. National averages may obscure important local or regional developments. Data on the use of resources, such as health care personnel, should be linked to data on the use of services by individuals across health care settings and to measures of the outcomes and costs of care.

The Institute of Medicine (IOM-NRC 1992) recommended some approaches in this direction several years ago, and the health care reform discussions during 1994 included some useful ideas about data requirements under reform plans. Even if comprehensive reform does not take place, improvements and expansion of health data collection should proceed as an essential function of the Federal government. Without such improvements in data collection, health workforce planning and policy will be flying blind.

In a rapidly moving and highly decentralized health care environment—driven by market forces that may be forceful, even brutal, and capable of many surprises as innovations are made and tested in the market—simple estimates of demand are impossible and misleading, and professionally determined need will be subject to validation in the market. The function of workforce planning in such circumstances should be the provision of valid, timely information that reflects uncertainty by presenting "what if" analyses. Such an approach requires improved data as well as an understanding that many different decisionmakers will act on the insights and analyses derived. The approach encompasses professional organizations, individual professionals, current and prospective students, educators, regulators, managed care plans, and funding organizations, such as employers and governments, that provide direct or indirect payment for education programs as well as for health care. The data and analyses can serve both "liberal" and "conservative" policy agendas and help this democratic society make more informed choices about the future directions of health care and the health professions. In my view, assisting these decisions through the provision of better data is more appropriate, given the rapid and often chaotic changes, than the establishment of highly specific estimates or targets for numbers of nurses as a basis for workforce policies.

Conclusion

Although this paper has focused on nursing, the profession has much in common with the other health professions with regard to workforce policy, even if the particulars are different. In a competitive health care system where managed care plans and integrated delivery systems are seeking to be more productive, the roles and functions of the various health professions in those care arrangements will be continually reassessed. The future interactions among the health professions in carrying out health care innovations call for an integrated approach to data-gathering, analysis, and workforce policy formation. No longer can each health profession utilize only its own professional norms to project its future in isolation from market forces and from related developments within other professions. Balancing professional standards with the pressures for change and innovation will present a formidable challenge for workforce planning for all the health professions.

Works Cited

Aiken, L.H. and W.M. Sage. 1992. Staffing national health care reform: A role for advanced practice nurses. *Akron Law Review* (fall).

AHA (American Hospital Association). 1993. *Annual Survey of Hospitals. 1992.* Washington: AHA.

Bailit, H.L. 1995. Market strategies and the growth of managed care. In *Academic Health Centers in the Managed Care Environment*, D. Korn, C.J. McLaughlin, and M. Osterweis, eds. Washington: Association of Academic Health Centers.

Henneberger, M. 1994. For nurses, new uncertainties: Managed care means fewer openings, specialized needs. *New York Times* (August 21).

IOM (Institute of Medicine). *1983. Nursing and Nursing Education: Public Policies and Private Actions.* Washington: National Academy Press.

IOM-NRC (Institute of Medicine and National Research Council). 1992. *Toward a National Health Care Survey.* Washington: National Academy Press.

U.S. Public Health Service. 1994. *The Registered Nurse Population, 1992.* Washington: Government Printing Office.

Weiner, J.P. 1994. Forecasting the effects of health reform on US physician workforce requirement: Evidence from HMO staffing patterns. *JAMA* 272.

Deploying Primary Care Personnel in Managed Care Plans

More Art Than Science

BERNARD J. MANSHEIM

Extensive, excellent analysis performed recently on U.S. physician workforce requirements for the future (Weiner 1994) suggests the need for 120 to 140 total full-time employed physicians per 100,000 population, with a ratio of 60:40 or 50:50 specialists to generalists (Dial et al. 1995). These data are derived from staffing patterns from various models of health maintenance organizations, mostly staff and group models.

Such predictions appear to be relevant as more and more Americans enroll in HMOs, prepaid group practices, and other types of plans. The premise on which the workforce prediction is based, namely, that over 50 percent of Americans will be enrolled in managed care plans by the year 2000, appears to be on target (Weiner 1994). Staffing patterns in HMOs provide a measurable estimate of physician workforce needs since HMOs contract with or employ a set number of physicians to care for a defined population. Their data offer a glimpse of the physician need and could be considered an est'mate that approaches the minimum requirement in our patchwork health care system. Nevertheless, the recent national health-reform debacle, coupled with powerful market forces and a highly disjointed, uniquely American health care system, all conspire to render predictions about physician workforce needs a "guesstimate" at best.

Survey Methods

To provide a "real world" view of how HMOs and prepaid group practices decide on primary care physician staffing, I conducted an unscientific, yet reasonably representative, study. Senior managers of HMOs and prepaid group practices, representing the care of several million Americans in managed care environments, responded to my questions.

Scope of Inquiry

The information I gathered encompasses health care provided for Medicare, Medicaid, and "commercial" members (i.e., patients) in rural, suburban, and urban environments. The responses are augmented by my personal experience in both academic medicine and private practice, as a manager in both group- and independent-practice associations-model health maintenance organizations, and as CEO of two prepaid, primary care group practices with health centers in three different states.

I make no claim to statistical validity. Results reported are a distillation of experience from assorted real-world experts.

Types of Respondents

It is not surprising that the way a managed care organization determines its primary care staffing needs depends on the delivery system itself. It is important, therefore, to define the types of organizations that I surveyed.

A managed care organization is "an integrated delivery system that manages health care services, rather than simply financing or delivering them" (Weiner 1994). For this paper, this definition is synonymous with an HMO. Preferred provider organizations and indemnity insurance plans are purposely excluded; the former tend to be a reduced fee-for-service variant of the latter. Neither purports in any significant way to "manage" care, and the physician panel, therefore, is relatively unlimited.

Three basic types of HMOs are represented, though individual organizations are more often a combination of the three. The independent practice association (IPA) model, in most cases more appropriately referred to as a direct-contract model, accounts for over 60 percent of all HMO membership. In this model, solo practitioners or small primary group practitioners contract with an HMO to provide services for its members (Group Health Association of America 1994). In some cases, a large number of individual physicians band together as an association to form a legal vehicle through which the single entity can contract on behalf of the entire physician group. This IPA model is currently dominated by direct contracts, although associations are making a resurgence.

The group model HMO derives its name from the practice of contracting exclusively with a group practice or number of groups. In this model, the physicians are employed not by the HMO but by the medical group, which, in turn, contracts for services with the HMO. This model is sometimes referred to as a network.

The third and oldest type of HMO is the staff model. In this organization, the physicians who supply care are actually employed by the HMO.

Results

How an HMO or prepaid group practice decides on the appropriate number and types of primary care physicians is usually a complex decision. Statistical analysis plays only a partial role.

Factors Plans Take Into Account

The following considerations are typical:

- *Geography.* In a physician-scarce area, the selection process is necessarily less rigorous. Virtually every willing physician may be chosen as strict credentialing is abandoned. Similarly, in such a situation of scarcity, specialists who are willing may be allowed to practice primary care. (Naturally, the selection process is more rigorous where there is a glut of physicians.)
- *Customer desires.* Despite reasonably accurate knowledge of the ideal physician-patient ratio, customers (employers) who select health care plans for their employees often have a profound influence on the number and type of primary care physicians. It is not unusual for large employers to demand a thick provider directory, simply to accede to the employee perception of greater choice. In other words, the decision is made based on what the employees want, not on what they need.
- *Regulatory requirements.* The Health Care Financing Administration (HCFA), which regulates HMOs that serve the Medicare population, has issued rules that define physician staffing requirements for Medicare-eligible HMOs. HCFA has mandated that an HMO must have sufficient primary care physicians for its members to be able to access a physician by car within twenty minutes, or travel less than seven miles, unless geographically impossible. By virtue of its authoritative nature, this HCFA requirement defines the minimum staffing need for an HMO. Some states have similar mandates.
- *Staffing ratios.* Numerous studies acknowledge a primary care physician-member ratio between 1:1700 and 1:2200. This purported opti-

mal primary care ratio refers to adult non-Medicare patients. A purely pediatric HMO practice can have a ratio that ranges between 1:1300 and 1:2500. A Medicare population physician-member ratio is approximately 1:1500. Obviously, staffing ratios are complex in themselves. Most family practice physicians care for children and adults of all ages. Likewise, in an IPA model, a typical primary care physician may participate in one or more HMOs and have a vast assortment of other payor relationships (e.g., PPO, indemnity, insurance). Such ratios are meaningless unless an assigned membership for a given physician is known. After all, a fee-for-service member does not become a known member until he becomes a patient).

Some IPA-model HMOs have developed specific strategies that aim to control the number of members assigned to a primary care physician. One example is the notion that no more than 10 percent to 30 percent of a physician's entire patient panel should consist of members of a given HMO. Consequently, an HMO may strive to include primary care physicians who carry no fewer than 100 and no more than 200 of its members. The purposes of such strategies are three-fold: first, to maximize the partnering relationship between the HMO and the physician; second, to insulate the physician against the possible loss of large numbers of patients; and third, to be able to exert economic influence on the physician to cooperate with utilization and quality improvement programs, clinical practice guidelines, formulary use, and other efforts to "manage" care.

- *Physician accessibility.* Aside from regulatory guidelines on geographic accessibility of physicians, more pragmatic measures are often applied. For example, the length of time it takes for a patient to get an appointment for an elective (or urgent) visit is a realistic measure of potential need for additional physicians.
- *HMO membership potential.* Predictions of membership are often a wild card in a primary care physician staffing plan. Swings of several thousand or more members can occur unpredictably, especially at the peak enrollment months of January and October.
- *Use of nonphysician providers.* Physician assistants and nurse practitioners are often incorporated into staff- and group-model HMOs. Generally, they are considered able to carry a workload equal to one-half that of a physician. In practice, it is often much greater.
- *Competitive need.* Among the quasiscientific approaches used to determine primary care needs, managed care organizations often

compare their own panels to those of their competitors. In some cases, it is considered strategically appropriate to develop a physician panel that the competition closely mimics. Other times, physician panels are developed in an effort to achieve differentiation. In such cases, ratios and actual need become secondary considerations.

Practices Among Plans Surveyed

Among the HMOs solicited, all used more than one of the methods just described to determine staffing need for primary care physicians. Which methods are used depends significantly on the type of delivery system. For example, use of physician-patient ratios is far more common for, and applicable to, staff- and group-model HMOs. It is important not to underestimate factors such as the managed care company strategy (e.g., a large primary care panel versus limited group practice panel) as well as employer dictates regarding the size of the primary care physician panel, which can play a major role in the workforce plan.

As noted earlier, an IPA-model HMO may want a broad physician panel to assuage patient concern about being provided a sufficient choice of doctors. Alternatively, a group-model HMO may purposely limit the physician panel in order to promote the unique nature of the group practice setting. Another strategy that has been embraced is the open-access panel: every possible primary care physician who meets credentialing standards in a community is sought and cost control focuses on contractual arrangements with hospitals and specialists.

The Tenuous Nature of Workforce Predictions

The complex, if unpredictable, way managed care organizations go about the business of developing a primary care workforce will have a profound influence on workforce predictions for the future. Two other issues make workforce projection even more difficult. First, what kind of a health care system will we have in ten years? Such issues as universal coverage, re-formed Medicare and Medicaid programs, and the potential growth (or shrinkage) of managed care will all come into play.

Second, what kind of delivery system will we have? If nonphysician providers (e.g., nurse practitioners and physician assistants) and nonallopathic care givers (e.g., chiropractors and herbalists) play an increasing role, the need for primary care physicians could be altered drastically. In addition, should concepts such as "demand management" and "virtual health" be implemented, workforce needs could change considerably. Thus, like the practice of medicine itself, any predictions about primary care workforce requirements for the future may involve a lot more art than science.

Works Cited

Dial, T.H., S.E. Palsbo, C. Bergsten, J.R. Gabel, and J. Weiner. 1995. Clinical staffing in staff and group model HMOs. *Health Aff.* (summer).

Group Health Association of America, Research and Analysis Department. 1994. *HMO Industry Profile, 1993 Edition.* Washington: GHAA.

Weiner, J.P. 1994. Forecasting the effects of health reform on U.S. physician workforce requirement. *JAMA* 272.

A Staff-Model HMO Perspective on Health Care Staffing

KATHLEEN COONEY

Staffing decisions are among the most critical decisions that any health plan makes. This paper describes the process by which Health-Partners, a large parent corporation for health plans and pro-viders serving a total of 650,000 members in Minnesota, determines provider staffing in its nineteen staff-model medical centers. Also described are some of the staff attributes particularly needed by health plans in general.

The HealthPartners corporation was created in 1993 through mergers of two health plans and a major teaching hospital: Group Health, a health maintenance organization with a staff-model health plan in existence since 1957 that has evolved to include contractual arrangements with other clinics; MedCenters, a health plan formed in the early 1970s as a group-model plan centering on the Park Nicollet Clinic; and the St. Paul Ramsey Medical Center.

Today, HealthPartners operates nineteen Group Health Medical Centers. They are staff-model centers that include full-range family practice centers, internal medicine and pediatrics centers, and regionalized subspecialty centers. These centers serve 240,000 HealthPartners members of health maintenance organizations and preferred provider organization members in the Twin Cities. They are exclusive providers, i.e., the staff serve only HealthPartners members and do not see other patients. Staff includes 350 salaried physicians, including 250 primary care physicians. A wide variety of medical specialties and subspecialties are currently on board, including:

Allergy	Obstetrics and Gynecology
Cardiology	Oncology and Hematology
Chemical health	Ophthalmology
Dermatology	Pediatrics

Endocrinology	Psychiatry
Family practice	Pulmonary
Gastroenterology	Rheumatology
Infectious disease	Surgery
Internal medicine	Urology
Neurology	

Issues Affecting Staffing

Staffing decisions are determined by a combination of internal management decisions and external market-driven pressures. Internal decisions are generally made on the following factors:

- *Projected membership growth.* Growth is estimated by the marketing department and the clinic's staff to meet the demands of the projected membership.
- *Estimates of physician turnover.* Annual turnover at the centers runs a low 6 percent. This low rate is attributed to the positive practice environment and the intensely competitive Twin Cities market.
- *"Make/buy" decisions.* The health plan considers "make or buy" decisions by specialty. It can either recruit a particular type of specialist or subspecialist or contract for those services in the community.

Key external, market-driven pressures also affect physician staffing patterns. Two are of particular importance.

- *Cost concerns.* Employers continue to exert strong pressures on the health plan to control its costs. Annual premium increases, which were more than 15 percent a few years ago, are down to the low single digits in many accounts.
- *Comparison shopping.* Employers are seeking service and value for the dollar, and they compare health plans to ensure that they get the best value. They want better access for fewer dollars, and the health plan has to respond.

To respond in this manner, the health plan must focus on maximizing its value in three areas.

- *Reduce hospital utilization.* Group Health currently provides about 235 inpatient days for every 1,000 adult, nonsenior enrollees. The goal is to reduce that utilization level to about 180 to 200 days in response to employer demands.
- *Limit specialty referrals.* Because of the intense competition among providers for patients, especially in the subspecialty areas, the health

plan has been able to keep contracted referral fees down.

- *Increase ambulatory care efficiency.* The ambulatory care centers also face a difficult budget squeeze, operating within total budget increases of 1 to 2 percent, while absorbing some contracted salary increases of up to 5 percent.

Staffing Patterns

The use of midlevel practitioners—nurse practitioners, physician assistants, and nurse-midwives—varies dramatically among the adult medicine, pediatric, and obstetrics/gynecological practices (table 1). In 1994, the adult primary care practice has made far less use of nurse practitioners and physician assistants than the pediatric and obstetrics/gynecological practices have. The health plan is now seeking to expand significantly the use of nurse practitioners and physician assistants for adult primary care, aiming for one NP or PA for every three to four MDs. However, the plan faces some constraints on supply because there are no physician assistant training programs in the Twin Cities.

The pediatrics department has been somewhat more aggressive than adult medicine in its use of pediatric nurse practitioners. In general, the pediatricians practice in the medical centers, while the pediatric nurse practitioners spend about one-half of their time providing care for newborns in hospitals.

The obstetrics/gynecological department has made extensive use of midlevel providers–with a total of thirty nurse practitioners and nurse-midwives compared to twenty-six obstetrics/gynecological physicians. Patients

Table 1. Professional Makeup, Group Health Medical Centers, 1994

Department	Physician providers	Number	Midlevel providers	Number
Adult Medicine	Internist	78	Nurse practitioner	8
(primary care)	Family practitioner	75	Physician assistant	2
Total:		*153*		*10*
Pediatrics	Pediatrician	58	Nurse practitioner	6
Total:		*58*		*6*
Obstetrics/Gynecology	Obstetrician/ Gynecologist	26	Nurse practitioner	11
			Nurse midwife	19
Total:		*26*		*30*

Table 2. Target Ratios, HealthPartners, 1994

Age of Member	Patients per Physician
0–15	1,200
16–64	2,000
65+	650
Full range (family practice)	1,600

are very satisfied with the care provided by the obstetrics/gynecological nurse practitioners and nurse-midwives, and this service is one of the most popular programs the health plan offers.

In the past, staffing was typically based on the volume of medical center visits, but enrollment-based staffing ratios are now used as well. These target ratios provide a rough indicator of staffing needs, although I believe that the ratios are always problematic and must be viewed in context. For example, a medical center that is under its target ratio is not necessarily understaffed, nor is a center over its ratio necessarily overstaffed. One important issue is the availability of midlevel staffing, which obviously affects physician ratios.

In general, HealthPartners has benchmarked its staffing ratios (table 2) against the ratios of other competitive plans. The typical ratio among other plans is about one physician for 2,000 patients, although some plans have a ratio as high as 1:2,400. HealthPartners' current target ratios must be updated regularly, and HealthPartners is doing so.

Trends in Staffing

Recent staffing patterns focus on three trends: The first, as noted, is an increased use of midlevel practitioners in providing care and service for patients and enrollees. The second is a set of significant changes in the roles of nurses, as follows:

- *Education.* Nurses are being used increasingly to help educate patients about both prevention and care. For example, during a typical forty-minute visit to the women's clinic or the diabetes clinic, a nurse provides about twenty minutes of risk assessment and health education, followed by a twenty-minute visit with a physician. This routine is beneficial for the patient and also makes practice more rewarding professionally for both the nurse and the physician.
- *Health maintenance.* Twenty percent of ambulatory care is estimated

to be routine health maintenance, and nurses can play an increasing role in providing this care.

- *Chronic care monitoring.* A special focus of nursing care is the monitoring of chronic care patients, such as those with chronic heart failure.
- *Specialty and condition-specific tasks.* Nurses also assume specific roles related to certain medical conditions or specialties. For example, following prescribed protocols, nurses are responsible for Coumadin monitoring.

The third important trend is the redefinition of the primary care physician. HealthPartners is moving to a split between primary care physicians who have an inpatient hospital practice and those with a purely ambulatory care role.

The hospital primary care physician program includes Group Health physicians who are "on site" at the hospital, admitting most Group Health patients twenty-four hours a day, seven days a week. The goal is to improve case management. A team of five physicians is assigned to the patients of that hospital (about thirty-five inpatients) for a period of seven days—providing an opportunity for active care, monitoring, and discharge planning.

The ambulatory care physicians serve as managers of the care teams, leading the patient care teams, delivering care, and directing the care of others. The team includes physicians, nurses, nurse practitioners, physician assistants, and health psychologists.

Unmet Needs in Staffing

The highest priority request that a health plan like HealthPartners can make of the health professions education community is more primary care providers—physicians (general internal medicine and family practice), physician assistants, and nurse practitioners. In addition, particular experience and skills that are in demand by health plans are often seen as lacking in physicians coming out of residency programs. For example, health plans could benefit from new staff who arrive with

- *More ambulatory care experience during training.* HealthPartners is discussing ways to work with the University of Minnesota to better prepare general internal medicine residents for the ambulatory care setting.
- *Understanding of and experience with managed care.* Such understanding encompasses how managed care plans work, what types of proto-

cols are used, and how resource allocation decisions are made.

- *Appreciation for the role of health psychology and the need to integrate mental health with primary care.*
- *Understanding of the care-team concept.* The physician functions as a leader of a team of professionals, delegating to midlevel providers and serving as a resource for them. The physician must learn the skills required to work in such a collaborative arrangement.
- *Interest and capability in management.* Physicians will be called on to function as managers in health plans.

One HMO's Involvement in Resident Education

To help improve the education of physician residents so that they can be more effective when entering practice in an organized, integrated setting, HealthPartners has established a managed care clinic elective. This one-month course is offered with the St. Paul Ramsey Medical Center's family practice residency program. It attempts to improve both knowledge and skills in the following areas:

- Resource allocation in an integrated delivery system, including concepts of cost-effectiveness and cost-efficiency.
- Appropriate triage of patients, a function often performed by nurses in integrated systems.
- Medical decision making.
- Use of medical practice guidelines, which HealthPartners has been developing as part of a joint initiative through an Institute for Clinical Systems, operated with the Mayo Clinic and the Park Nicollet Medical Center.
- Health plan governance and management.
- The value of outcome studies.
- Use of automated medical records.
- The ethics of health care distribution.
- Management of patient expectations through shared decision-making.
- Group practice organization and management.
- Quality improvement theory, such as continuous quality improvement.

The elective also attempts to improve skills in certain defined areas, including efficient use of resources, appropriate management of referrals, interaction with consultants to whom patients are referred, and clinical expertise in office surgery, dermatology, orthopedics, and sigmoidoscopy.

Conclusion

Staffing decisions in staff-model HMO health plans are influenced by both internal management decisions and external competitive factors. For plans in markets like the Twin Cities, these demands often lead to comparing staffing ratios and benchmarking of the competition. In such an environment, staff-model HMOs need to hire health professionals who are experienced and comfortable working in an efficient, outcome-driven environment. To ensure an adequate supply of these professionals, health plans have a responsibility to encourage change in the health professions education process as well as participate in the process.

The Corporatization of Health Care

Effect on Accreditation and Academic Integrity

C. EDWIN WEBB

U.S. health care delivery is rapidly evolving from a system of individual and group practitioners, functioning primarily as entrepreneurs, to one dominated by corporate conglomerates. The status of practitioners, regardless of discipline, is shifting from being an owner to being an employee. As pressure to control costs and manage care increases, practitioners, institutions, and the supporting infrastructure for educating health professionals are inevitably coming under scrutiny by these employers. As "customers" for the graduates of health professions education programs, what role should these organizations play in the educational process? And specifically, what effect will they have in determining educational content, outcomes, and standards?

Among the health professions experiencing this phenomenon, pharmacy perhaps has the longest experience. The rise of the chain drug store corporations since the 1960s has significantly influenced where and how pharmacists practice in the community setting. In recent years, emboldened by their dominance in the marketplace, these entities and the national organization representing their interests have become active in a variety of issues historically the purview of the profession and its educational system. A key target of these activities has been the accreditation standards revision process for professional degree programs in pharmacy, together with the movement of schools of pharmacy toward the professional doctorate as the entry-level educational preparation for pharmacists. As a result, the American Council on Pharmaceutical Education as well as individual schools and colleges of pharmacy have faced substantial additional barriers in their efforts to implement change widely embraced by the profession and the academy.

Do similar threats exist for other health professions disciplines? If so, what are they and how are they to be addressed? How might the health professions work together, both by themselves and with corporate entities, to meet new workforce requirements while ensuring educational quality and academic integrity?

The Role of Accreditation in Higher Education

Accreditation, the voluntary self-assessment of institutions that provide education or services to students, clients, or others, represents one of the truly distinguishing features of the American higher education and professional communities. It is entirely consistent with contemporary theories of continuous quality improvement and provides a basis on which quality above minimum standards can be assessed, both by peers and, increasingly, by the public at large.

As it has evolved in higher education over the past century, accreditation has focused on such issues as clarity of academic mission, institutional financial integrity, adequacy of human and physical resources, institutional quality, and student achievement. Although not without flaws, the accreditation process has gained significant acceptance within higher education over the past several decades. Its purpose and value have generally been accepted within the academic and professional communities.

Accreditation is much less clearly understood by and definable to the world outside these spheres. Consequently, its purposes and goals may be sources of confusion, misapplication, or, in some cases, targets for social or political agendas. As an example, the public may perceive that an assurance of "quality" for an institution provides a "warranty" for the graduates of its programs, ensuring both their performance ability and their employability. Yet neither is a purpose of the accreditation process. In addition to ensuring and improving the quality of professional education programs, specialized accreditation effectively links with and enhances the process of state licensure of health professionals. The so-called three-legged stool of education, accreditation, and regulation is generally regarded as an effective model for higher education.

These characteristics contribute to the current state in which accreditation of higher education programs finds itself as America moves into what Peter Drucker has described as an age in which " . . . knowledge, not labor or raw material or capital, is the key resource." As society's most valuable future asset, knowledge and its dissemination through higher education systems will be eagerly sought and jealously held. Assessment of educational program quality will be an increasingly important process in this environment.

Systemic Problems in Accreditation

Accreditation in higher education faces many challenges as expressed in a recent document produced by the National Policy Board on Higher Education Institutional Accreditation. The principal challenge is the need to restore public confidence in accreditation as the means by which institutions of higher education regulate themselves. Over the past few years, several key problems arising within the accreditation system have contributed to the image of accreditation as a failing process. Among these problems are:

- Lack of a shared sense of what accreditation is and what it is supposed to ensure.
- Questions about the rigor and consistency of accreditation in a regional structure.
- Government dissatisfaction with its own ability to monitor student assistance programs, with corresponding efforts to shift that burden and responsibility to accrediting bodies. Accrediting agencies find themselves being asked increasingly to serve as regulators or police for programs and criteria established by the Federal government.
- Significant and growing concern among college and university administrators about the proliferation and demands of specialized and disciplinary accreditation programs.
- Internal disputes within the higher education community that have resulted in the demise or ineffectiveness of coordinating bodies such as the Council on Postsecondary Accreditation.

None of these problems is particularly surprising. However, the failure of higher education to address them effectively leaves the system of voluntary accreditation vulnerable to such outside threats as increased governmental oversight, competing or conflicting standards, and outside political and social pressures.

Specialized Accreditation: Unique Problems and Threats

Specialized accreditation plays a unique role within the health professions education community. The proliferation of specialized accrediting bodies has paralleled the emergence of numerous professional and academic disciplines. Consequently, as noted above, institutions that provide several specialized educational programs face additional burdens and challenges. For example, a relatively small but comprehensive university with 4,000 to 5,000 students may deal with as many as fifteen to twenty different accrediting bodies in addition to its regional accreditor. In any academic year, the institution may undergo several programmatic or institutional reviews. Each review consumes significant resources in terms of preparation, self-study, evaluation, and follow-up. Significant financial costs, both direct and indirect, also accompany the accreditation process.

Despite these problems, specialized accrediting bodies, especially those in health professions education, have generally been successful in demonstrating that their efforts have contributed to improvements in the overall quality of the accreditation process. But because specialized accrediting bodies often deal with relatively small numbers of programs, they may be vulnerable to powerful interests or other unique situations within the discipline. In some cases, economic support for the accreditation process is tied, sometimes too closely, to the discipline and its professional organizations. In a period of changing economics, technology, and government regulation, specialized accrediting bodies in health professions education are likely to face increasingly challenging times. The revolutionary changes in health care financing, delivery, and organization that are creating massive change and anxiety within the existing community of providers serves only to further heighten these concerns.

Pharmacy as a Case Study for the Health Professions

The case of pharmaceutical education provides one example of the types of issues that may increasingly face educators and accreditors in other health professions.

Drawing on the vision of pharmacy's professional and educational leadership of the past twenty-five years, pharmaceutical education's accrediting body, the American Council on Pharmaceutical Education (ACPE), in 1989 established an open, structured process for revising accreditation standards for a four-year professional doctoral education program. Accrediting bodies must now conduct such regular review of accreditation standards to maintain their recognition by the Department of Education. Movement to a single program at the professional doctorate level (from the current two-tiered program of both baccalaureate and entry-level Pharm.D. programs), debated within the profession for four decades, is supported through formal policy statements of the vast majority of national professional organizations in pharmacy.

The single most active, powerful opponent to this mandate for change in pharmaceutical education has been the chain drug store industry. Chain drug stores employ large numbers of pharmacy graduates each year in order to conduct the retail distribution of prescription drugs in accordance with existing practice laws. Although such corporations have been financially successful in this mode of operation, much of pharmacy's leadership envisions dramatically different models for the delivery of pharmaceutical care in an emerging health care system. Pleased with its financial success and satisfied with the status quo, the chain drug industry has exerted tremendous pressure on pharmaceutical education to stop, if not turn back, the clock of professional evolution.

A primary target of pressure by the chain drug industry has been the ACPE and its process for revision of pharmaceutical education standards. Using both print and video communications with state education departments, governing boards of higher education institutions, state legislatures, the U.S. Department of Education, and congressional committees, together with threatened legal actions, the chain drug industry has engaged in a deliberate pattern of intimidation, misinformation, and interference in both the ACPE standards revision process and the academic decisions and integrity of institutions and professional schools. Disregarding the effect that its actions might have on students' eligibility for financial aid, as well as the wishes of the faculty and the professional community at large, the chain drug industry has publicly announced its intention to pursue decertification of the ACPE by the Department of Education, if necessary, to accomplish its objective.

The threat to the accreditation process for professional programs in pharmacy is real. However, a more problematic effect of these tactics may be the loss of academic integrity and overall responsibility for curriculum development, evolution, and improvement within individual schools and colleges. This oversight that has historically been the purview of faculties working cooperatively with the professional community. In a recent case involving a state-supported school of pharmacy, legislation developed and supported by the state's chain drug industry was introduced that would have prohibited the school from implementing its plans for curriculum reform and implementation of a single professional degree program. The changes had been planned for several years, with meticulous attention to input by the state's practitioners, the school's alumni, and professional pharmacy associations within the state. The legislation failed to be passed out of its appropriate committee by a single vote, and then only after the school's administrative leadership and faculty had devoted time and resources that could have been more effectively applied to the change process itself. Several other schools of pharmacy have encountered or are currently experiencing similar problems and tactics.

Sadly, such tactics have fallen on at least partially receptive ears in some institutions. Because of the current state of affairs within accreditation generally and the financial pressures facing university administrators and governing boards or agencies, some are initially receptive to arguments for the status quo. Fortunately, many others, recognizing the profoundly negative consequences of allowing narrow and special-interest thinking to subvert the reasoned and orderly change process underway in the majority of the nation's colleges and schools of pharmacy, have successfully defended and advanced the change process. Such success has often required substantially greater effort, political activity, and financial resources than would normally have been anticipated or required.

The Situation in Other Health Professions

Is the example presented by pharmacy unique within the health professions? A review of recent literature in medical, nursing, and dental education yields little definitive discussion concerning corporate influences on the education and training of these health professionals or the accreditation of their academic programs.

Medicine

The president of the Association of American Medical Colleges has called on academic medicine to develop enhanced partnerships with managed care and other health-system groups to address both curricular and clinical training needs. Such efforts can also help to ensure that graduates of medical education programs will understand the emerging health care delivery system and be more valuable to entities seeking to provide medical care services. Personal communications with other members of the association's staff suggests no evidence of direct attempts at present by corporate health care entities to influence academic programs or the medical education accreditation system inappropriately. One does hear, however, the occasional rumblings of entities considering "starting our own medical school." Such pronouncements probably should not be dismissed lightly.

Nursing

In some ways, nursing presents a profile similar to that of pharmacy in the emerging corporate health care environment. Members of the nursing profession have for many years been predominantly "employed" rather than engaged in "private practice." Employer and other groups frequently debate the types of nurses and skill sets required for various nursing functions within a particular practice setting. In fact, nursing's past includes a significant role for employers (for example, hospitals) in the financing and provision of certain types of nursing education. This model has, of course, diminished considerably in recent years.

The emergence of primary care nurse practitioners and clinical nurse specialists makes analysis of the potential effect of corporate health care influence on nursing education even more complicated. There is some evidence that health care systems and managed care entities are positively disposed to utilizing such nursing professionals in the delivery of many primary care services. The nursing profession, of course, strongly supports efforts to enhance and increase education and training programs in these areas. The opportunity for partnerships appears strong. Such partnerships, however, may present challenges to nursing education as well.

Dentistry

The dental profession has undergone substantial upheaval and change in recent years as a result of changing technologies, new, preventive strategies, and gradual inclusion of dental services within health care plans. It appears, at least on initial observation and investigation, that health care systems are relatively pleased with dentistry's educational infrastructure and "product." There is essentially no discussion in the recent dental education literature concerning corporate influences on dental education and training. The efforts in recent years of dental hygienists to develop models of independent practice appear to have stalled at this point, although one might speculate that such models might have some attractiveness to corporate health care entities seeking to provide preventive health services at reduced costs.

The Need for Positive Action—and Vigilance

The health professions education enterprise should aggressively rethink its historical elitism and become more collaborative with and responsive to the health care marketplace. The active involvement of all legitimate stakeholders in advancing the effectiveness and value of health professions education should be encouraged. Such stakeholders, including those who employ graduates of specialized and professional programs, can ideally provide perspective, vision, and support for the educational process.

Such involvement should, of course, respect the legitimate prerogatives and professional and academic integrity that are part of the nation's higher education system. It must be tempered with a recognition of the potential for corporate or economic interests within the health care system to adversely affect the academic and accreditation processes for economic purposes. Such a threat to any discipline or institution is a threat to all.

A New Health Professions Curriculum for a New Delivery System

RICHARD J. DAVIDSON

We are in an era of the most rapid change in the history of the modern health care system. This change, driven by powerful market and political forces, is having a profound effect on the hospitals and emerging health care systems that make up the membership of the American Hospital Association. The title of this paper raises an unspoken question: "In the current rapidly changing health care market, can we make delivery system and curriculum changes fast enough?" I have serious doubts that all of us can. And I will briefly outline these changes from my vantage point as the president of the American Hospital Association. I will then give you my thoughts on the role academic health centers can play in helping the health care system react to—and constructively adapt to—these changes.

Today we have hospital excess capacity, and we have health professions education excess capacity. Current market shifts toward care delivered in community settings and greater attention to primary and preventive services are going to increase the excess capacity. Only those hospitals, health systems, and academic health centers who can adapt to the new health delivery structure are going to survive because the market and political forces driving these changes are powerful. Standing still is not an option.

Those health care entities who do survive will focus their strategic thinking beyond their institutional walls and look at the market for their products. For academic health centers, it means building a curriculum that produces a graduate who meets the needs of the customer, whether the customer is a hospital, HMO, or public health agency.

I used to be repulsed by the health care field's adoption of the business-school terms "the market" and "the product." But we do produce a product, and there are customers for our product. Your product—one of the most important in American society—is the graduates of your programs, whether they are physicians, nurses, pharmacists, or any of the other health professionals you train. And the customer can be a whole variety of health care settings.

So you're producing a product—graduates—for a set of customers, and your product needs to be prepared to service the communities in which they're going to work. How do you determine the needs of these communities? You do it by doing market research, the way GE and Ford and Microsoft do. We even do it at the American Hospital Association. If we don't do market research, we're likely to produce an obsolete product. Academic health centers may have a fine faculty, but if the faculty is not focused on producing the right kind of graduate for today's health care market, the value of that faculty is diminished.

Let's look at today's health care environment to get a better sense of where we've been and where we need to go.

Americans have become increasingly skeptical of their institutions, and health care is no exception. Polling data tell us that Americans feel disconnected from the health care delivery system. They no longer feel that physicians and hospitals care about them personally. Instead, patients feel lost in a fragmented system. They see our health care system—really a nonsystem—as a jumble of rocks in a stream. They have to jump from one rock to the other, not sure if they're seeing the right provider at the right time or whether they're seeing too many or too few providers. They have a lot of anxiety about whether anyone is actually *caring* for them or *overseeing* their care.

Traditional health professions education has fed into this delivery system fragmentation. Our health professions schools have by and large reinforced a traditional "guild" mentality, in which each discipline has stood alone. Graduates have gone out into the world prepared to operate only within an increasingly specialized division of labor that lacks coordination with other divisions, and it is this system that forces patients to jump from rock to rock.

Principles to Guide the Health Care Delivery System

Over the past four years, the American Hospital Association has focused its energies on addressing the public discontent and the system fragmentation. We have crafted a vision of the health care future in which a broad range of local health care providers—hospitals, physicians, nursing homes, and home health and community health agencies—come together to form locally based networks. Our goal is to have local networks provide a single entry point for the health care consumer, with a care coordinator to help sort out the confusing array of specialists. As they evolve, networks will accept a capitated payment to provide care to the enrolled population. This up-front, per-person fee does an extremely important thing: It shifts more of our health care resources to the front end of the care spectrum, where dollars go further as we head off debilitating illness and injury.

The following are some of the organizing principles behind local health care networks:

- Draw together a broad range of health care providers so that patients receive the most appropriate services in the most cost-effective settings.
- Manage all health care requirements of a person throughout life.
- Improve the health status of the community while continuing to manage acute, chronic, and episodic illness.
- Develop measures of health care performance that ensure quality.

In progressive health care systems, such as Sentara, based in Norfolk, Virginia, you will find new professional job categories, such as community outreach specialist and patient care coordinator. And you will find familiar professionals deployed in new ways. Home health nurses will visit Medicare managed care patients, for example, to look for household hazards that may cause falls and to check medicine chests for dangerously incompatible medications.

Visionary leaders in health professions education will understand this new, integrated, community-based approach to providing care. They will make institutional commitments to building and sustaining community-based delivery systems, paying special attention to disadvantaged inner city and rural areas. These delivery systems will ensure timely access to a comprehensive array of services and supports, with community-based primary care sites at their core.

Leaders in health professions education sense that health professions curricula need to change in order to better prepare graduates to take their place in the evolving health care system. Institutions and faculty, however, often feel most comfortable following the traditional academic model of insular decision making within the institution. Institutions need to go into their communities and talk to community leaders and find out what they're looking for in products from the health professions education system.

Here's what you're likely to hear, according to innovative hospital and health system leaders I've talked to. They need people who are

- Technically competent, with a broad range of skills.
- Effective communicators, both in the hospital and in the community.
- Biased toward team work and away from a health professions "guild" mentality.
- Comfortable with organizational and community accountability.
- Dedicated to improving health.
- Trained in schools that make a culturally diverse workforce a priority, and who are, therefore, comfortable working in culturally diverse settings.
- Dedicated to continued self-improvement because continuing education is going to be essential to success.
- Flexible and able to function with the ambiguities inherent in an ever-changing health care world.

A Model of Tomorrow's Health System

Let me take you on a quick tour of a hospital of the future that has gone through self-examination and then reshaped its services and workforce.

Patient-Centered Care

The basic idea behind patient-centered care is twofold: to move previously centralized services closer to the patient, and to train staff broadly so that services that previously had to wait for specialists—some respiratory therapy tasks and IV insertion, for example—can be done by nurses on the patient's unit. Also, instead of pharmacy being centralized in the basement, there may be a number of satellite pharmacies. This change can cut the time needed to fill routine medications and increase pharmacists' professional interactions by putting them in closer touch with both physicians and patients.

Many nonprofessional jobs may have both primary and secondary responsibilities. For example, housekeeping staff may also transport patients, stock supplies, and help patients walk after surgery. Medical secretaries may process admissions and even help pass food trays. Is this all theory? No. Take a look at Western Pennsylvania Hospital in Pittsburgh, and you'll see it in action.

The changes help the hospital adjust better to a growing managed care market. Service, patient satisfaction, and quality will eventually be the criteria on which managed care plans choose providers, although "price, price,

price" may initially play the largest role.

At the American Hospital Association we prefer to put the concept of managed care in the larger context of community-based "coordinated care." Whatever its form, the basic thrust toward reorganizing care with a greater emphasis on cost-effectiveness and outcomes measurement is not going to go away. We *have* to do a better job of using our health care resources; the nation can no longer afford to deliver such a large portion of its health care through traditional fee-for-service medicine as is currently the case for Medicare.

A *Washington Post* editorial on September 12, 1995, noted that "Medicare and Medicaid will become the accounts that ate the [Federal] budget if nothing is done to curb their continuing growth." Moving Medicare beneficiaries into managed care, already well under way in Medicaid, is one of the steps to be taken. Of course, employer-sponsored health plans are also steadily moving in this direction.

It is our job as health care providers and health professions educators to help ensure that these changes are done right.

Interdisciplinary Care Teams

Another concept that shows promise is the interdisciplinary care team. At the University of Utah, a grant from The Robert Wood Johnson Foundation and The Pew Charitable Trusts allowed University Hospital to plan and implement several prototypes of its vision of patient care, organized across care settings and over time. The mechanism that makes this approach possible is a staff team of caregivers drawn from a range of hospital departments.

After a year of planning and some fine-tuning to more clearly define roles, University Hospital developed the STAR model (Service Team with Appropriate Resources). At its center is a new nursing role: the patient care coordinator. Core members of the team vary according to patient focus. For example, the spinal cord injury STAR may consist of a rehabilitation physician and nurse; a resident; physical, recreational, and occupational therapists; an orthopedic surgeon and neurosurgeon; and the patient care coordinator. Additional consultative members are brought in as needed.

Although gathering comparative data on the STAR's performance is difficult because most data are reported according to the hospital's old departmentalized structure, early, subjective judgments by the STAR members themselves are encouraging. Three-quarters believe that quality of care has improved. They cite in particular improved patient education, smoother transitions within the hospital, extension of the care continuum to include readmission and postdischarge care, and improved overall patient outcomes. A third of the STAR members believe that costs have been reduced. They point to smoother and faster patient transfers, shorter lengths of stay, fewer unnecessary admissions, and the elimination of unnecessary procedures.

Urban Community Partnerships

A growing number of hospitals and health systems are forming community partnerships to increase access to care. A few years ago, the American Hospital Association established a special award to recognize outstanding hospital-community collaborative efforts. The range of entrants' accomplishments provides truly inspiring examples of what can happen when people work together to solve problems. For example, Presbyterian Hospital of Dallas, part of the Presbyterian Healthcare System, had seen its neighborhood change from a prosperous community to one of the poorest and most crime-ridden in the city. The hospital, meanwhile, had flourished. The hospital decided to use some of its many resources to help turn the neighborhood around.

The hospital began with a community assessment, interviewing residents, landlords, and business owners and reviewing census data to identify the most significant problems. Three problems surfaced as the most pressing: an unstable population base and a high crime rate, a lack of social services and recreational activities, and a high rate of infant mortality.

As the largest landowner in the neighborhood, the hospital successfully petitioned the city to designate the area an improvement district, with the primary goal of reducing crime. A self-imposed hospital "improvement tax" provided the $26,000 needed to hire a full-time manager to get the effort off the ground.

The hospital took the lead in forming a coalition of local churches, schools, police, neighborhood businesses, residents, apartment owners, community groups, and its own employees. The goal of the coalition is to pool neighborhood resources to improve quality of life. Tangible results include an after-school program that provides safe and constructive activities for schoolchildren and a city-sponsored summer recreational program. The hospital has also "adopted" a local middle school. Hospital employees volunteer as tutors in an effort to keep children in school. The hospital also arranged funding for a community nurse, who works with the after-school program and will also bring health screening and health education to people where they live.

Rural Collaborative Efforts

With dramatically fewer resources, rural areas, too, have also worked to improve health and quality of life in their communities. Bladen Community Care Network, a project of Bladen Community Hospital in Elizabethtown, a southeast North Carolina community, is proof that rural health care delivery can be improved even in the face of some tough odds—odds like ranking 91st out of North Carolina's 100 counties in income and having 44 percent of the population without a high school diploma.

Seven years ago, medical and health care were on the verge of becoming extinct in Elizabethtown. An old and decaying hospital was about to close, physicians were leaving, and there was no partnership between public and private agencies to take up the slack. But with community support, the hospital turned the corner. The county overwhelmingly approved its first bond issue in forty years. The hospital used the money to straighten out its finances, develop new programs, and make quality improvements.

Bladen Healthwatch, a neighborhood health outreach approach, was developed with two key components: a volunteer "neighbor helping neighbor" health outreach program in isolated rural communities; and a consumer resource center that helps promote access to a range of health, wellness, and social services, and also offers a consumer library.

The hospital's board of trustees agreed to fund a full-time staff person to run the center for a year and to look for additional funding. Now, funding is a shared responsibility between the county health department and the division on aging, with other local agencies expected to join. New programs developed by Healthwatch include those targeting diabetes, immunizations, and teen pregnancy. Healthwatch volunteers identify people in need of services from a network of rural health centers staffed by nurse practitioners and physician assistants who are supervised by primary care physicians. The county hospital's urgent care center serves as a weekend emergency backup to the rural health centers.

Care Outside Hospital Walls

Cambridge Hospital, affiliated with Harvard Medical School, is an example of another important trend: the transformation of hospitals from high-volume, acute care centers to community-oriented primary care institutions. The community surrounding Cambridge Hospital has an unusually high proportion of poor families and a shortage of primary care physicians. Despite the presence of prestigious institutions of higher learning and world-class health care facilities, residents experience a host of health problems associated with poverty and unemployment.

Cambridge Hospital has developed a range of service programs to deal with these problems staffed by primary care doctors and nurse practitioners, social workers, and community health specialists. To help ensure an adequate number of primary care physicians for its work, the hospital sponsors a primary care residency program.

One of the strongest characteristics of the hospital's programs is providing care to a culturally diverse community through a multicultural and bilingual staff. The multidisciplinary AIDS program and the linguistic mental health teams especially benefit from this approach.

Workforce Diversity

The hospital of the future should deliver culturally sensitive health care services in diverse communities. Doing it well requires a culturally diverse staff at every level.

To help prepare leaders for a culturally diverse workforce, the American Hospital Association joined forces with the American College of Healthcare Executives and the National Association of Health Services Executives to create the Institute for Diversity in Health Management. In just two years, the institute has founded a number of programs to help minority high school, college, and graduate students move toward educational and work experience in health services management. For example, the institute's Summer Enrichment Program provides an internship at a hospital or other health care institution with rotation duties under the supervision of a health care administrator, as well as other career-enhancing training. One hundred fifty students have taken part in this program in its two years of operation, with more than one hundred health care institutions providing enrichment opportunities.

Innovations in Health Professions Education

Academic health centers can be leaders in helping their students adapt to a changing health care delivery system, or they can be rear-guard resisters—a role that some segments of unionized nursing have primarily adopted. Workforce change *is* threatening to health professionals and to the institutions that train them. A dig-in-your-heels reaction may be understandable, but it doesn't contribute to solving the significant problems of access and financing that are undeniably part of this country's health care system despite our many dazzling accomplishments.

I urge educational institutions to look to innovators in the health care workplace—innovators delivering care outside hospital walls, designing multidisciplinary care teams, and cross-training flexible staffs to improve patient satisfaction and hold down costs. I urge you to look to innovators in education who are adapting their programs to make it easier for students to enter a new community-based, decentralized health care environment—an environment that is likely to become the standard for care.

Two innovators are providing opportunities for students from different disciplines to study together. The University of Texas Health Science Center at Houston is pioneering a "core curriculum" course, as part of an overall realignment toward prevention and health promotion among its six health professions schools. Students in the course design the best treatment plan for complex health problems contained in individual mock case histories. Each class has four teams made up of one person from each health professions school. More facts about the case are revealed each week; students give each other homework assignments as they work toward designing their treatment plan. After considerable initial skepticism, a group of faculty members is now enthusiastic about the potential of the approach and is investing significant time to carefully evaluate whether the course turns out to be worthwhile for students.

The Johns Hopkins University School of Medicine is another pioneer in improving preparation of health professionals, having just revamped its entire medical school curriculum toward that end. The new curriculum has seven objectives.

- Integration of basic science and clinical experiences.
- Expanded use of case-based, small-group learning sessions.
- Early experience with community-based practicing physicians.
- Development of a four-year, longitudinal course on the physician and society, including study of legal issues, finances, political issues, and the history of medicine, as well as ethics and fine arts as they relate to medicine.
- Computerization of learning and teaching.
- Expanded experiences in ambulatory settings in required clinical courses.
- Greater faculty rewards for teaching.

The Trend Toward Outcome-Oriented Care

Despite efforts to match health professions education with the evolving health care marketplace, I understand that some of today's health care trends, namely, those toward generalization, erasure of professional boundaries, and delivery of the best care cost-effectively, go against the academic grain. The hallmark of increased education has been increased expertise and autonomy, along with a belief that increased salary should follow. But the evolving marketplace is looking at outcomes, not levels of training. If we are short of physical therapists, and the work of physical therapist assistants shows similar results, the marketplace is going to say, "Let's have more physical therapist assistants."

In the face of public health studies showing that 50 percent of deaths in people under seventy-five years old are due to personal behaviors that can be modified, we need to stop and think about our current allocation of health resources. Shouldn't more resources go to getting people to stop smoking and to consume less fats and toward greater environmental cleanup?

The health care market is increasingly moving toward measuring outcomes. Studies have shown that large differences exist from one state to another in the use of angiograms and subsequent angioplasties and bypass operations, with no evidence that the more aggressively treated patients live longer or better. These studies will influence us as we examine how this nation uses its increasingly squeezed health care resources.

New Thinking About Licensure and Certification

I'd like to suggest some lines of thinking about licensure and accreditation. The first focus of managed care plans is going to be price. But price will not remain the focus if employees are not happy with the quality and service provided under employer-sponsored health plans. In the not-too-distant future, health care providers will be compared not simply on the basis of price, but also on the basis of value. Although we're not there yet, new information systems will increasingly allow consumers and purchasers of care to make these comparisons. The focus will be on results: Did the patient get better? Was the treatment handled in the most effective and cost-efficient way?

The result could be a shift in perception about what entity is most appropriate for certifying or licensing who is qualified to deliver care. The health care delivery network may ultimately become responsible for these tasks. Society may come to think about health care delivery as it does about automobile or aircraft manufacturing. Government has a prescribed role, but the public trusts companies like Ford and Boeing to ensure that their design engineers are qualified. As the emphasis in health care delivery moves to community-based networks held accountable for measurable results, that kind of "institutional licensure" may make sense.

Shifting Roles and Settings

Another trend with implications for curriculum development is the shifting roles and settings of health professional practice. Registered nurses who previously practiced in hospitals are moving to home health, community-based nursing, and company worksites. In addition, whole new job categories will develop as the health care delivery system reinvents itself over the coming years.

The need for mobility and flexibility may argue for initial basic education in a core set of knowledge and skills. Then, as careers develop and the needs of the system change, health professionals may want to advance, fine-tune, or retune their skills. To facilitate such midcareer development, courses should be offered at convenient sites. This approach is being successfully used in Sioux City, Iowa, where two local private colleges have brought their Bachelor of Science in Nursing completion programs to Marian Health Center. According to Marian Vice President of Patient Services Verna Welte, RN, nurses are much more likely to earn their degrees if they can stay at the hospital to attend class after leaving a 4:00 P.M. shift rather than drive across town to a college campus.

Hospitals, too, need to do a better job of encouraging lifelong learning for employees and staff. The University of Chicago Hospitals have established an internal "academy" to foster continued personal and professional growth and to educate employees in the mission and evolving role of the hospital. Courses prepare employees for new roles and responsibilities in patient-centered care, wellness programs, and computer-based programs. The hospitals are also working with local community colleges to develop additional courses to further employee learning.

Conclusion

For many of us, events are moving so rapidly that we have a sense of disorientation, of not being certain where things are going and how they ought to go. And we're going to continue to be faced with change that we can't forecast. What we can do is work with change. We can learn to adapt, and we can apply our values to change. In fact, we need to become bold leaders of change. I don't think anybody wants to become a dinosaur jockey, sitting atop something about to become extinct. We want to be riding a sleek horse that can take us to the future.

That is why academic health centers and hospitals and health systems need a close working relationship. The system is changing so rapidly, and the health care workforce along with it, that only by sharing our strengths and our insights can we stay relevant and avoid the fate of the dinosaurs.

Roles of the Health Professions

One way that the health professions influence the character of the health workforce is by creating and institutionalizing new roles for themselves. The papers in this section show how different professions have emerged over time to meet clinical needs, and the professional and political conflicts that come into play when professions with similar clinical roles see each other as competitors.

The Evolution of New Health Professions

A History of Physician Assistants

JAMES F. CAWLEY

In the turbulent 1960s, a decade of change in many areas of American society, a fundamental rethinking of the division of medical professional practice came about. The introduction of nurse practitioners and physician assistants and the reemergence of certified nurse midwives* represented a major alteration in American medical practice, with these providers assuming an enlarging scope of practice that included performing medical diagnostic and therapeutic tasks heretofore reserved only for physicians.

In this paper, I examine the social, medical, and public policy forces that converged in the U.S. health system and brought about the introduction of these new health professionals. Using the PA experience in the United States as a general model, I also draw on selected comparable experiences from other countries to explore the following questions:

- What is the evolutionary process by which new health professions are created?
- How are decisions made regarding scope of practice, legal status, professional credentialing, educational program support, and methods of payment?
- What elements predict successful incorporation over time of new health professionals into a nation's health system?
- What lessons for health workforce policy making and medical education can be drawn from the PA experience?
- What does the future hold for PAs?

---

* A number of terms have been proposed or collectively used to refer to the new professions of physician assistants, nurse practitioners, and certified nurse-midwives, including physician extenders, nonphysician providers, midlevel providers, and associate practitioners. None is wholly satisfactory.

The Appropriate Climate

Although physicians typically are regarded as the "captain of the ship" in the health systems of most countries, and their status may be thought of as the "gold standard" of health care professionals, numerous other health professionals assume roles in clinical practice that sometimes overlap considerably with those of physicians.

Particularly after times of societal and cultural turmoil such as war and revolution, when doctors are in short supply, new professionals are introduced, often initially as generalist physician substitutes. Some are later incorporated into health systems where their utilization and status become institutionalized and their roles evolve to include a broad range of clinical practice activities.

Generally, nonphysician providers have fewer years of formal training than physicians; a regulated, dependent status; and, in some cases, a largely technical practice scope. In nearly all instances, a major rationale for the introduction of such providers is to supplement and extend the delivery of medical care services. The clinical roles of some nonphysicians blend medical care tasks with skills imported from other health care paradigms and disciplines; their practice is not merely substitutive of physician functions; it also expands to encompass services that may be termed physician-complementary, (i.e., health and medical services not performed by physicians).

International Examples

Physicians have trained and employed many types of assistants throughout the history of medicine. In many countries during the past two centuries (table 1), a number of nonphysician health providers have played important roles in meeting a nation's medical services needs (Roemer 1993). Their introduction into the health care system has been shown to be an effective health workforce stopgap measure in several health systems (Pene 1973; Seidel 1972; Cawley and Golden 1982).

The successful introduction of new health professionals in other countries, however, has varied, depending on individual circumstances within a country's health system. In some cases, nonphysician providers have been well accepted and are fully integrated in health systems; in others, they have not achieved permanence.

Although it appears at first glance that there are a number of similar social and historical precedents in the development of health care providers

Table 1. Types of Nonphysician Health Practitioners in Various Countries, 1802–present

Health Provider	Country	Period
Officier de santé	France	1802–1892
Feldsher	Russia, Eastern Europe	1790–present
Nurse midwife	U.S., Europe, others	1900s–present
Barefoot doctor	China	1960s–present
Physician assistant	U.S.	1965–present
Nurse practitioner*	U.S., Canada[†]	1966–present

* Includes nurse midwives whose roles began in the United States and Great Britain around the turn of the century and reemerged formally in the 1960s as part of the nurse practitioner movement.

[†] After rapid growth during the 1970s, Canada in the early 1980s adopted workforce policies that effectively eliminated NP practice. By 1992, there were fewer than 250 NPs in practice in Canada.

like the Russian feldsher, the Chinese barefoot doctor, and the U.S. physician assistant—e.g., a postrevolutionary/military-connected foundation, workforce response to a primary care physician shortage, and dependent practice orientation—the creative forces contributing to the emergence were unique to the specific time and sociomedical climate of that nation. Some, like the officier de santé of nineteenth century France, emerged largely because of the low number of physicians in the postrevolutionary years, and ultimately died out because they failed to meet their expected social mandate to assume generalist practice roles and practice in rural and underserved areas. Officiers had two years less training than a French medical doctor, could prescribe and perform minor surgery, and were semiautonomous in practice stance (Heller 1978).

The feldsher is a military-derived health practitioner developed and utilized in Eastern Europe and Russia in the armies of Peter the Great. Feldshers were used in the medical care system of the former USSR throughout the twentieth century. To this day, they practice mostly in remote villages and rural regions and perform a wide range of generalist and specialty functions. They have two years less formal training than physicians, and a long-term but somewhat tenuous status, as physician numbers continue to increase in most of the countries formerly making up the USSR (Roemer 1993; Seidel 1968).

Creation of the Physician Assistant

In describing the creation and natural history of new types of health care professionals, I propose that there may be at least five, somewhat overlapping, stages in the evolution of new health professionals.

Stage 1. The Era of Ideology (1961–65)

When PAs were introduced into medical practice in the United States in the 1960s, the principal hope of their creators was to improve primary health care delivery in the wake of generalist physician shortages brought about by the demise of the general practitioner. The physician assistant was envisioned as a new type of medical generalist, one whose role could build upon prior medical experiences, who could be trained in a reasonably short period of time, and who could be rapidly deployed to a practice location in a medically needy area.

The concept of new types of health personnel to extend physician services in the United States was first suggested by Charles L. Hudson (1961), then President of the National Board of Medical Examiners, in a speech to the House of Delegates of the American Medical Association in 1961 and in a subsequent article in the *Journal of the Medical Association*. Hudson articulated the rationale for new health personnel based on changing medical labor-hospital staffing personnel demands and advancing technology. Later, Eugene Stead and Harvey Estes noted the short supply of primary care physicians and the increasing specialization of physicians. It led them to propose a new category of personnel to augment physician capacity to deliver needed generalist/primary care services (Stead 1966).

Eugene Stead, chairman of the Department of Medicine at Duke University in the 1960s, recognized changing medical service and personnel needs in and around Duke University Medical Center. A highly respected figure in academic medicine, Stead became interested in developing training programs for new health care personnel. He envisioned a new type of midlevel generalist medical clinician (between the level of a doctor and a nurse) who could be trained in a relatively short time to assist physicians in a broad range of practice settings. Stead believed that such providers should work closely with physicians, and established the PA role in a configuration that would not directly threaten physicians. He first approached nursing leaders at Duke and developed an advanced medical education program for nurses designed to expand their roles in generalist care delivery. This program could have initiated the nurse practitioner movement, but was opposed by the National League of Nursing and never became operational due to a lack of national accreditation (Ballweg 1994).

In 1965, Stead founded the PA profession in the United States when the new Duke PA program enrolled four ex-Navy medical corpsmen in a two-year, intensive medical generalist curriculum. Education was divided into a basic and preclinical science year and a year of clinical rotations.

Shortly after Stead introduced the physician assistant model at Duke, other versions of the PA concept emerged, such as the Child Health Associate Program developed by Henry Silver in 1966 at the University of Colorado and the Medex program founded by Richard Smith at the University of Washington in 1969 (Gifford 1984).

Sociocultural Factors

During the 1960s, the demise of the American general practitioner, perceptions of an overall shortage of physicians, glaring shortcomings in access to health care for many citizens, and war-related medical personnel issues combined with that decade's counter-cultural ferment and citizen activism to forge the development of new types of health personnel.

The determination to create new professionals meant many things to many groups, and many configurations of health workers were proposed. The consensus was that introducing the PA and similar providers created new health practitioners whose role focused on providing primary care/generalist services in physician practices, thereby expanding medical care access to needy populations and regions.

Support of Organized Medicine

The PA concept would not have germinated had it not been for the overt support and active involvement of major physician groups in the United States. The AMA, in particular, contributed substantially to the development of PA educational program accreditation standards, professional credentialing mechanisms, and the formation of PA professional organizations. Support in shaping and supporting the infrastructure of the profession also came from the American College of Surgeons, the American Academy of Family Physicians, and the American Academy of Pediatrics, among other groups.

These formative stages saw an impressive degree of collaboration among organized physician groups, PA educators and professional leaders, public policy agencies, and national medical regulatory bodies in building the critical components of the PA profession's structure. Physician groups worked with government agencies, the National Board of Medical Examiners, the

Federation of State Medical Licensing Boards, and members of the general public. PA practice certification mechanisms were patterned to a large degree on their counterparts in the medical profession (Gifford 1984).

Stage 2. The Era of Implementation (1966–73)

The Federal government also provided strong support for the development of PAs. Domestic policy in the early 1970s sought to improve citizen access to health services by increasing health care personnel. Most Federal policy makers believed there was an overall shortage of physicians and a falling proportion in general practice. The new Federal workforce approach comprised two major elements: (1) increasing physician supply by expanding support for medical education, and (2) promoting the introduction of new practitioners whose roles would focus on primary care.

At the Federal level, important leadership in the early nurturing of the PA concept was provided through grant support for PA educational programs. Legislative initiatives included the Allied Health Professions Personnel Act of 1966 and the Health Manpower Act of 1968. PA programs quickly sprang up in medical centers, hospitals, and colleges; programs were also supported by state legislatures and private foundations.

The Comprehensive Health Manpower Act of 1973 was an important milestone; it marked the inclusion of PA program-funding support programs under Title VII of the Public Health Service Act. Since then, Federal PA grant awards have totaled $140 million supporting PA educational programs; in FY 1994, programs received a total of $6.56 million (Cawley 1992).

STATE REGULATION

The introduction of the PA into the American health system brought with it the need to consider legal and regulatory approaches enabling emerging health practitioners to enter clinical practice. Important decisions centered on determination of the professional scope of practice of these new professionals, the appropriate level of state board recognition (licensure, registration, certification), and stipulations for supervision and prescribing activities (Curran 1970). To support the entry of PAs into clinical practice, the AMA House of Delegates in 1970 passed a resolution urging state medical licensing boards to amend health occupation statutes and regulations to permit PAs to qualify as medical practitioners.

The legal basis of PA practice is codified in state medical practice statutes granting authority to licensed physicians to delegate a range of medical diagnostic and therapeutic tasks to individuals who meet educational standards and practice requirements to qualify as a PA. Beginning in 1969, states began to amend medical practice statutes allowing PAs to enter clinical practice legally. Among the first states to amend medical acts allowing PAs to practice were California, Colorado, New York, and North Carolina. Authority for medical task delegation is based on the legal doctrine of *respondeat superior*, which holds that it is the physician who is ultimately liable for PA practice activities; it also requires that doctors who employ PAs define and supervise PA clinical actions appropriately.

PRACTICE QUALIFICATION

Qualification for entry to practice as a PA in nearly all states requires that applicants graduate from an education program accredited by the Committee on Accreditation of Allied Health Educational Programs (CAAHEP), pass the Physician Assistant National Certifying Examination (PANCE), or do both. The PANCE is a national standardized examination in primary care medicine, administered annually by the National Commission on Certification of Physician Assistants (NCCPA). It comprises both written and practical components, and its content and standards are developed in cooperation with the National Board of Medical Examiners. At present, NCCPA certification is a required qualification for PA practice in forty-seven states; over 92 percent of all PAs in active practice hold current certification. To maintain certification, PAs must obtain continuing medical education hours annually and recertify by formal examination every six years.

EDUCATION STANDARDS

Formal standards for PA educational programs were initially established by CAAHEP's predecessor in the AMA in 1971 with the publication of *Essentials of an Approved Educational Program for the Assistant to the Primary Care Physician* (CAAHEP 1990). Compliance with the *Essentials* is the basis for awarding accreditation to PA educational programs. It defines the core components of PA educational programs (level of institutional sponsorship support, curriculum content, clinical training affiliations, basic and clinical science course offerings, faculty qualifications, and admission and selection guidelines) that must be fully met prior to award of accreditation. It has also allowed PA educational programs some latitude to create curricular configurations based on a structure awarding several types of academic degrees. Reflecting the many changes affecting educational preparation in a rapidly developing field, the *Essentials* were revised and updated in 1978, 1985, and 1990.

Stage 3. The Era of Evaluation (1974–80)

A great deal of health services research during the 1970s examined the effect of PAs on medical practice. Early results showed that PAs were safe and competent practitioners in primary care, there was a high degree of patient acceptance of the PA role, and most PAs were in primary care practices in medically needy areas (OTA 1986).

Initial PA practice distribution tended to reflect the Federal and medical sector intent that PAs assume primary care roles in areas of need. Early recruits to the PA profession were often individuals with extensive levels of prior health care experience (e.g., military medical corpsmen, registered nurses) that contributed to their ability to function effectively with minimal levels of physician supervision. Upon graduation, most tended to select work with primary care physicians typically located in a rural or medically underserved community (Willis 1990).

Many of the clinical performance aspects of PA evaluation were performed in ambulatory practice and health maintenance organization settings. In such settings, PA clinical performance was impressive. Their productivity (number of patient visits) approached levels of primary care physicians. Record (1981) carefully documented PA productivity rates in a large staff model HMO. She determined that the physician-PA substitutability ratio, a measure of overall clinical efficiency, was 76 percent. The study assumed a practice environment where PAs were utilized to their maximum capacity to perform medical services (consistent with educational competency and the legal scope of supervision) and worked the same number of hours per week as physicians.

Although PA cost-effectiveness was not studied in all clinical practice settings, Record et al. (1980) clearly showed that within their spheres of practice competency, PAs could lower health care costs while providing physician-equivalent quality of care.

By the end of their first decade in practice, experience and empirical research indicated that American medicine's adoption of the PA had been generally positive. PAs were responsive to the public and medical mandate to work in generalist/primary care roles in medically underserved areas. As their numbers grew to 10,000 in 1980, PAs were gaining recognition as being competent, effective, and clinically versatile health providers (Schafft and Cawley 1987).

Stage 4. The Era of Incorporation (1981–90)

The PA role broadened during the 1980s when utilization extended beyond primary care into inpatient hospital settings and specialty areas. The trend toward such specialization was due, in part, to their clinical versatility and in part to medical workforce demand (Jones and Cawley 1994). PA utilization increased, despite the rising number of physicians in the workforce as predicted by the Graduate Medical Education National Advisory Committee (GMENAC 1981). As more PAs entered specialty or inpatient practices, the numbers of PAs in primary care began to fall. In 1981, the proportion of PAs working in the primary care specialties (defined as family practice, general internal medicine, and general pediatrics) was 62 percent; by 1994, it had fallen to 45 percent. Over the same period, the proportion working in surgery and the surgical subspecialties rose from 19 percent to 28 percent; PAs in emergency departments rose from 1.3 percent to 8.5 percent (Jones and Cawley 1994).

This period also marked milestones indicating increasing recognition of PAs in the workforce: approval of PA services for reimbursement for services in certain settings under Medicare Part B of the 1986 Omnibus Budget Reconciliation Act, commissioned officer status in the U.S. uniformed services, passage or updating of medical practice acts in many states, and authorization of health professional licensing boards to regulate PA practice in many states.

Stage 5. The Era of Maturation (1991–present)

Having achieved a remarkable degree of acceptance and incorporation in U.S. medicine, the PA profession has grown from infancy in the 70s, through adolescence during the 80s, into a mature health profession in the 90s. Together with primary care physicians and NPs, PAs are today considered essential members of America's primary care workforce (Osterweis and Garfinkel 1993). Their integration into American medicine is confirmed by the growing demand for their services in the health marketplace and by recent strides in achieving full legal, professional, and health payor acceptance of their roles (Cawley 1994).

There are 26,000 PAs in full-time active practice in the United States, representing more than 94 percent of PA graduates. PAs are recognized by the medical licensing boards in forty-nine states and the District of Columbia; only Mississippi does not sanction PA practice. PAs may prescribe medications in thirty-seven states, the District of Columbia, and Guam. Over 92 percent passed the PANCE, 72 percent hold at least a bachelor's degree, and 13 percent have a master's degree or higher. About 5 percent of PA graduates have gone on to medical school; 30 percent are military veterans.

The typical PA is a male, age 40, in practice as a PA for nine years. Practicing with a physician group in a primary care specialty located in a small community, he works an average of forty-two hours per week, has been in his current position for four years, sees about twenty-two ambulatory patients per day, and earns a salary of $56,300 per year (AAPA 1993). Women make up 44 percent of the profession, a marked increase from the less than 10 percent in the 1970s. Nearly three-fourths of PA students are women.

PAs are employed on the clinical staffs in community hospitals, academic health centers, emergency departments, and ambulatory care clinics. PAs also fill critical clinical service gaps as primary care providers in such other places as correctional health systems, substance abuse clinics, student health services, occupational health clinics, and geriatric settings.

Lessons From the PA Experience

The first quarter-century experience with PAs in the U.S. health system holds several lessons for health workforce decision makers and policy stakeholders. The lessons may apply in medical education, systems of professional regulation and public accountability, deployment of providers in primary care, professional relations, and strategies in long-term workforce policy issues.

Lesson 1. Medical and Primary Care Education

For health professions educators, experience with PA education programs demonstrates that it is possible to develop an effective, practically focused, medical generalist curriculum that builds on prior student skills. PA programs have designed a medically rigorous, socially relevant, and multidisciplinary approach. Their cumulative experiences, including those in academic health centers as well as those sponsored by free-standing teaching hospitals, colleges, and universities, have been deemed to be largely successful educational endeavors. The nation's sixty-one accredited PA programs prepare clinically competent and versatile generalist providers capable of handling a majority of the patient problems encountered in primary care. Medical school deans and faculty considering curriculum revision to increase primary care experiences for medical students have been encouraged to consider the medical educational approaches developed and utilized in PA programs (Estes 1988).

Innovation has flourished in PA programs because of both their multidisciplinary design and their greater latitude to make curricular adjustments than the typical medical school. PA programs over the years have kept pace with advancing biomedical and population health trends; they have been pioneers in incorporating topic areas recognized to be of increasing importance in medical curricula: behavioral sciences, communication sciences, the humanities, epidemiology/biostatistics, public health, preventive medicine/health promotion/disease prevention, geriatrics, community-based practice/community-oriented primary care, clinical decision sciences, medical literature research/interpretation studies, and health services research and policy.

PA programs have also been innovators in developing effective strategies in deploying graduates to primary care medicine in medically needy areas.

Lesson 2. Social Responsibility

American medicine has been criticized as being overly specialized and unresponsive to the health needs of many citizens. Workforce policy reform discussions have focused attention on the question of the effectiveness and accountability of America's health workforce to meet societal health needs. Some people have concluded that the present system of health professions education and the composition of the workforce seem ill-fitted to meet the nation's future needs. Policy makers are frustrated because, despite a substantial expansion of physician numbers over the past twenty years and the long-standing Federal Medicare subsidy for graduate medical education, America has failed to produce a balanced physician workforce and fallen short of meeting the need for generalist medical care services and universal access to care. The Council on Graduate Medical Education (COGME) among other groups, estimates that America will have an oversupply of physicians by the year 2000, with too few in primary care and too many in specialties (GMENAC 1981; PPRC 1994; Weiner 1991; COGME 1994).

In 1981, Harvey Estes emphasized that the key reason for the widespread acceptance, utilization, and overall success of the PA concept in U.S. medicine thus far had been fulfillment of the expectation for PAs to serve in primary care roles extending health care access to medically needy populations. He noted that it would be critical for PAs to retain their generalist/primary care practice focus or else risk a loss of medical establishment and public support.

PAs and PA educational programs have demonstrated social responsiveness: PAs are more likely than physicians to be in primary care specialty practice (46 percent versus 32 percent); PAs (34 percent) are more likely than either allopathic (12 percent) or osteopathic physicians (15 percent) to be working in rural communities (populations under 50,000); 18 percent of PAs are practicing in communities with fewer than 10,000 people (Cawley 1994).

Lesson 3. The Critical Issue of Autonomy

Autonomy is regarded by leading medical sociologists as the defining attribute of a professional within the health occupations (Hafferty and McKinlay 1993). Physicians have long been regarded to be among the true professions: doctors possess their own language and have a distinct body of knowledge, collect direct fees for their services, function autonomously, and are largely self-regulated.

The decision to establish the role of the PA as a dependent professional was a product of the collective wisdom of the profession's founders. They recognized that acceptance and utilization of these new providers was directly related to the perception of physicians as to the threat PAs may present in terms of income and turf. Dependent practice for PAs continues be a major factor in the acceptance and integration of PAs in the medical system. PAs have recently reaffirmed their acceptance of a dependent practice role seeking closer formal ties with the AMA (Ballweg 1994).

In contrast, some NP advocates steadfastly maintain that NPs can perform primary care or other services independent of physicians, a posture clearly threatening to physicians and strongly opposed by medical groups. Even medical groups known to be generally supportive of nonphysician utilization have questioned NP preparation for independent practice. For example, after a recent series of strong exchanges between nurse practitioner leaders and physician organizations, the American College of Physicians reaffirmed its support for the roles played by both PAs and NPs in the health system and encouraged a collaborative mode of practice between physicians and these providers, but found it "cannot support independent practice of NPs or direct fee-for-service payments to them" in either primary care or inpatient care settings (ACP 1994).

Lesson 4. Team Practice

There can be little question that part of the success of the experience with PAs is due in part to their close educational and professional practice relationship with physicians. There are many similarities in the medical training approaches of physician assistants, nurse practitioners, and primary care physicians. PAs (and NPs) are now well integrated into many medical practices; all PAs and most NPs work with physicians, nurses, and others on the health care team.

Conventionally defined "barriers to practice" (i.e., restrictive state regulations and payment ineligibility) clearly affect levels of PA clinical productivity in a broad sense. However, evidence also suggests that differences in the delegatory styles of physicians are important determinants of PA practice effectiveness. Physicians now share a great deal of their medical diagnostic and therapeutic responsibilities with PAs—more than they did twenty, or even ten, years ago.

What's Ahead for PAs?

Physician willingness to share medical functions is a result of forces affecting the way division of medical labor has evolved in the U.S. health system. What is the future for PAs in America's health system? Broadly speaking, future demand and utilization of PAs (as well as NPs), is likely to be shaped by a combination of medical, economic, and political factors affecting their relationships and interactions with physicians.

Challenging Barriers to Practice

State medical practice acts defining the boundaries of PA practice activities tend to vary considerably by state, particularly with regard to scope of practice, supervisory requirements, and prescribing authority. This variation leads to barriers to PA-practice effectiveness in a number of states (Sekcenski et al. 1994).

As originally envisioned, the role of the PA encompassed working with physicians in the full range of clinical practice areas: office, clinic, hospital, nursing home, surgical suite, and the patient's home. Laws in many states were written to allow physicians to delegate a broad range of medical tasks to their PAs. This latitude allows PAs to exercise a degree of clinical judgment and decision-making autonomy within the parameters of state scope-of-practice regulations.

By necessity, geographic practice isolation in rural and frontier settings may result in varying degrees of off-site physician supervision and require the PA to exercise more autonomy in clinical judgment. Regulatory reluctance to support such MD-PA relationships in satellite and remote clinical settings restricts the PA from providing services that might otherwise be unavailable in medically underserved areas.

Maintaining Relations With Other Professions

As forces continue to shift in the medical marketplace. It will be a challenge to both the PA and NP professions to remain on friendly terms. There will be an increasing amount of competition between PAs and NPs for positions in settings like HMOs and other managed health care systems. Policy consensus and health research evidence suggest that, in such settings, NP and PA roles in primary care appear to be virtually interchangeable (PPRC 1994).

But in other clinical practice settings there appears to be an increasingly divergent pattern of utilization between NPs and PAs. PA training and practice is increasingly tending toward PA utilization in surgery, surgical subspecialties, medical subspecialties, and emergency medicine. NP practice now leans toward ambulatory care, chronic disease management, pediatrics, women's health, and school-based health services. One recent study shows that among 255 Council of Teaching Hospital (COTH) members surveyed, 116 use PAs, 77 use NPs, and 62 use both types of professionals. PAs are employed more usually on general medicine services (11 versus 8), surgical services (50 versus 7), and emergency departments (14 versus 2), while far more NPs worked in pediatric services (28 versus 1) (Riportella-Muller, Libby, and Kindig 1995).

Comparisons by a number of authors also show variance by clinical specialty distribution, practice setting, legal and regulatory parameters, educational orientation, credentialing mechanisms, and geographic distribution (Clawson and Osterweis 1993).

Seeking Ongoing Federal Support

The oversupply of physicians correctly forecast by GMENAC in 1981 casts a chill on the prospects for long-term success of the PA movement. With too many physicians, what would be the continuing need for PAs? In 1983, pessimism regarding the future market for PA services led GMENAC to revise its initial projections of utilization downward. Yet there is ample evidence to indicate that the actual utilization of PAs has expanded considerably during the past 15 years. A critical question will be whether what has been termed Federal "entitlement" funding going to PA educational programs will continue, and, if so, if it will be continued under Title VII reauthorization or contained within an alternative funding structure for nonphysician professions educational support.

Enhancing the Primary Care Workforce

Some people believe that it is unrealistic to expect that physicians in any appreciable numbers will reverse trends of professional specialization under current or anticipated incentives (Andes and Cooper 1994). Doctors may continue to avoid primary care practice, and it is unlikely that a significant number of well-established specialist physicians will convert to generalist roles. Even if the long decline in interest among young physicians in primary care careers and generalist practice is reversing, it will take decades before adjustments in training outcomes affect service delivery (Kindig 1993).

If physicians remain increasingly specialized, PAs are likely to assume a higher profile in delivering primary care services, particularly in HMOs, managed care systems, and other organized systems such as the Veterans Administration, state and Federal correctional systems, and the military. If physicians are no longer in the primary care business, PAs, and perhaps NPs, working with physician "managers," may be the provider types best equipped to meet the need for primary care personnel. Proponents of this view have recommended increasing PA educational program output to augment capacity in the primary care workforce (Miekle 1992).

Reacting to GME Reform

Conventional workforce policy direction aims to bolster the supply of primary care physicians principally by restructuring the size and financing of physician GME, but this approach will take many years to affect the primary care workforce significantly. The effect of a reduction in the number of GME residency positions has led some policy analysts to project an increased demand for PAs in teaching hospitals. Although the costs and medical aspects of PA substitution for residents in GME programs is an area in need of more study, a 1993 COTH hospital survey indicates that a majority of GME residency programs already employed, or planned to employ, PAs, NPs, or both to replace physician residents (Kindig 1993).

Meanwhile, there is the perception that there are too few PAs available for primary care and that the increased utilization of PAs in downsizing GME programs could further strain the short supply of PAs. In addition, positions available for PAs in inpatient/specialty roles currently tend to be more plentiful in the medical marketplace and pay higher salaries than in primary care; such a trend could adversely affect the availability of both NPs and PAs to meet projected requirements in primary care. In spite of the fact that the costs and medical aspects of PA substitution for residents in GME programs is an area in need of more study, workforce policy groups project that there could be an increasing demand for PAs in hospitals and by specialty physicians. A reduction in physician resident numbers in GME programs could increase requirements for PA services to meet anticipated personnel requirements in teaching hospitals and academic health centers. How many PAs would be needed in downsizing GME programs, considering workforce requirements in other sectors, such as primary care? Workforce policy reform may also include revisions of mechanisms of funding support for PA training and modified financing mechanisms to reimburse hospitals for PA inpatient services.

Responding to Market Forces

Many analysts agree with Moore (1994) that market forces will be the major determinants of the growth and long-term survival of the PA profession. As our health care system changes from one encompassing a disease-oriented and economically open-ended structure to one with a more preventive, patient-centered, and cost-conscious direction, PAs could assume a higher profile. Their professional roles could also be influenced significantly by changing trends in the division of medical labor and public perceptions of physician responsiveness to societal health care problems. One health economist predicts that "an enlightened and cost-conscious society may compel medicine to relinquish some of its monopolies," denting the "physician monopoly on medical services delivery" (Levine 1993).

Conclusion

The emergence of PAs in the 1960s, along with other new categories of health care practitioners, was a signal event in the division of medical labor in America's health system. In the future, it is likely that medical practices, hospitals, managed health care systems, and other health facilities will seek ways to become more economically efficient and to utilize professional expertise and capabilities better. Workforce requirements for PAs, as well as for NPs and generalist physicians, are projected to increase to meet future demand for primary care. PAs are comfortable with their roles as dependent practitioners and have not wavered in that stance. The fundamental elements of PA practice—use of a referral system and frequent consultation with periodic review by a physician—appear to be synonymous with a well-designed health system (Starfield 1992).

In addition, the level of acceptance and integration of PAs in American medicine appears to be directly related to their willingness to practice in settings, locations, and clinical areas deemed by physicians to be less preferable. Thus, it is probable that the utilization of PAs in the U.S. health system will continue as long as they extend medical services in physician practices without challenging ultimate physician authority.

Works Cited

AAPA (American Academy of Physician Assistants). 1993. *Annual Census Data on Physician Assistants, 1993.* Alexandria, VA: AAPA.

ACP (American College of Physicians). 1994. Physician assistants and nurse practitioners. *Ann. Intern. Med.* 121.

Andes, G. and H. Cooper. 1994. Why specialists won't switch to primary care. *Wall Street Journal* (June 7).

Ballweg, R. 1994. History of the profession. In *Physician Assistant: A Guide to Clinical Practice*, R. Ballweg, S. Stolberg, and E. Sullivan, eds. Philadelphia: W.B. Saunders.

CAAHEP (Committee on Accreditation of Allied Health Educational Programs). 1990. *Essentials of an Accredited Physician Assistant Educational Program.* Chicago: AMA.

Cawley, J.F. 1992. Federal health policy and PAs. *J. Am. Acad. Phy. Asst.* 5.

Cawley, J.F. 1994. *Physician Assistants in the Health Workforce: Report of the Ad Hoc Advisory Group on Physician Assistants and the Workforce.* Final Report. Rockville, MD: Council on Graduate Medical Education, U.S. Department of Health and Human Services.

——— and A.S. Golden. 1982. Nonphysicians in the United States: Manpower policy in primary care. *J. Public Health Policy* 4.

Clawson, D.K. and M. Osterweis, eds. 1993. *The Roles of Physician Assistants and Nurse Practitioners in Primary Care.* Washington: Association of Academic Health Centers.

COGME (Council on Graduate Medical Education). 1994. *Fourth Report to Congress and the Department of Health and Human Services: Recommendations to Improve Access to Health Care Through Physician Workforce Reform.* Rockville, MD: Health Resources and Services Administration, U.S. Department of Health and Human Services.

Curran, W.J. 1970. New paramedical personnel—to license or not to license? *N. Engl. J. Med.* 282.

Estes, E.H. 1988. The PA experiment after 25 years: What have we learned? *Federation Bulletin* 88.

Gifford, J. 1984. The development of the physician assistant profession. In *Alternatives in Health Care Delivery*, R. Carter and H.B. Perry, eds. St. Louis: Warren Green and Company.

GMENAC (Graduate Medical Education National Advisory Committee). 1981. *Nonphysician Heath Care Provider Technical Panel*. Vol. 6. Washington: U.S. Department of Health and Human Services.

Hafferty, F.W. and J.B. McKinlay, eds. 1993. *The Changing Medical Profession: An International Perspective*. New York: Oxford University Press.

Heller, R. 1978. Officiers de santé: The second-class doctors of nineteenth century France. *Med. Hist.* 22.

Hudson, C.L. 1961. Expansion of medical professional services with nonprofessional personnel. *JAMA* 176.

Jones, P.E. and J.F. Cawley. 1994. Physician assistants and health system reform. *JAMA* 271.

Kindig, D.A. 1993. What Does the Literature Tell Us About The Potential and Feasible Substitution of Nonphysician Providers for Physicians?: A Policy Perspective. Unpublished paper.

Levine, S. 1993. Some problematic aspects of medicine's changing status. In *The Changing Medical Profession: An International Perspective*, F.W. Hafferty and J.B. McKinlay, eds. New York: Oxford University Press.

Miekle, T. 1992. An expanded role for the physician assistant. *Bellwether* 3(3).

Moore, G.T. 1994. Will the power of the marketplace produce the work force we need? *Inquiry* 31.

Osterweis, M. and S. Garfinkel. 1993. *The Roles of Physician Assistants and Nurse Practitioners in Primary Care: An Overview of the Issues*. Washington: Association of Academic Health Centers.

OTA (Office of Technology Assessment), U.S. Congress. 1986. *Nurse Practitioners, Physician Assistants, Certified Nurse-Midwives: A Policy Analysis*. Health Care Technology Case Study No. 37. Washington: National Technical Information Service.

Pene, P. 1973. Health auxiliaries in francophone Africa. *Lancet* 811.

PPRC (Physician Payment Review Commission). 1994. *Annual Report to Congress*. Washington: PPRC.

Record, J.C. 1981. *Staffing Primary Care in 1990: Physician Replacement and Cost Saving*. New York: Springer.

————, M.E. McCally, S.O. Schweitzer, R.M. Blomquist, and B.D. Berger. 1980. New health professionals after a decade and a half: Delegation, productivity, and costs in primary care. *J. Health Polit. Policy Law* 5.

Riportella-Muller, R., D. Libby, and D.A. Kindig. 1995. Substitution of physician assistants and nurse practitioners for physician residents. *Health Aff.* 14 (summer)

Roemer, M.I. 1993. *National Health Systems of the World.* Vol. 2. New York: Oxford University Press.

Schafft, G.E. and J.F. Cawley. 1987. *The Physician Assistant in a Changing Health Care Environment.* Rockville, MD: Aspen.

Seidel, V.W. 1968. Feldshers and feldsherism: The role and training of the feldsher in the U.S.S.R. *N. Engl. J. Med.* 278.

———. 1972. The barefoot doctors of the People's Republic of China. *New Engl. J. Med.* 286.

Sekcenski, E.S., S. Sansom, C. Bazell, M.E. Salmon, and F. Mullan. 1994. State practice environments and the supply of physician assistants, nurse practitioners, and certified nurse-midwives. *N. Engl. J. Med.* 331.

Starfield, B. 1992. *Primary Care: Concept, Evaluation, and Policy.* New York: Oxford University Press.

Stead, E.A. 1966. Conserving costly talents—providing physicians' new assistants. *JAMA* 198.

Weiner, J. 1991. *The Effects of Future Health Care System Trends on the Demand for Physician Services: An Assessment of Selected Specialties.* Prepared for the COGME. Rockville, MD: Health Resources and Services Administration, U.S. Department of Health and Human Services.

Willis, J.B. 1990. Is the PA supply in rural America dwindling? *J. Am. Acad. Phy. Asst.* 3.

The Interplay Between the Supply of Physicians and Advanced Practice Nurses

GERALDINE D. BEDNASH

Although legislative efforts for health care reform failed in the 103rd Congress, the need for primary care providers cited in those proposals has not declined. In his recent article on managed care and the implications of this shift for academic health centers, Iglehart (1995) details the aggressive recruitment and retention efforts of academic health centers as they strive to acquire a greater number of primary care physicians for practice in their managed care organizations.

The growth in managed care and continuing concerns about the cost of health care services has intensified the debate regarding the appropriate supply and mix of physicians. This debate has overlapped with discussions regarding the collective supply of health professionals, most notably nurse practitioners, other advanced practice nurses, and other nonphysician providers who can safely and effectively provide a broad range of primary care services. Efforts to increase the supply of primary care physicians, therefore, have also raised questions about how an increased supply of primary care physicians would affect the employment and production of NPs and physician assistants.

NPs and Physicians: Complementarity or Substitutability?

Questions regarding the interplay of the physician and nurse practitioner workforces come from two different perspectives. First, if attempts to reform the physician education production stream to increase the number of primary care physician providers are successful, will there be a need for fewer or more nurse practitioners? Second, what roles will NPs fill in a system with an abundance of primary care physicians? These questions clearly arise from a view that NP care is heavily biased toward functions that substitute for physicians. They imply that if physicians are available to deliver the needed primary care services, NPs will no longer have an added value for the delivery system.

This view of NP practice is clearly a function of its history. In the early 1980s, much of the rhetoric focused on the complementary functions that NPs could add to the total care process (Edmunds 1979, 1981, 1984). NPs were characterized as having skills and knowledge similar to that of primary care physicians. However, NPs were not viewed simply as substitutes; rather, they added the advanced nursing functions that created a complementary role. Many reports about NP practice focused on the value added to care delivery when NPs were a part of the care team. NPs provided something unique: They provided patients the time, education, explanations, lifestyle information, and other services that physicians were either not inclined or not educated to provide.

By the late 1980s and early 1990s, the cost of care became the overriding concern of policy makers. As a result, NPs were told that complementary roles were a luxury that the system could not afford. NPs were directed to prove their substitutability. Could NPs, or for that matter other advanced practice nurses, safely and effectively provide care traditionally provided by physicians? This concern was the major impetus for a report by the Office of Technology Assessment (OTA 1986) frequently cited as proof that NPs can do 60 to 80 percent of primary care.

Much of the debate regarding the use of NPs is focused on substitutability. Clearly, the health care system's experience with NPs has created confidence in NPs as an effective and efficient group of providers. The report by the Office of Technology Assessment concluded that NPs are safe and effective providers who can greatly decrease the cost of delivering primary care services. In addition, the growth of managed care organizations, which have a strong focus on controlling the costs of services, has increased interest in having NPs serve in substitutive roles. An econometric model of the costs of underusing APNs in care delivery developed by Nichols (1992) and the report by the Office of Technology Assessment have provided greater weight to the argument for expanding utilization of NPs as an effective means of keeping health care costs in check.

The concern for good outcomes of care has also increased interest in using NPs for roles in primary care delivery. This view does not imply that physician care keeps patients unhealthy. Rather, it recognizes that managed care organizations are becoming aware that medical care can be greatly augmented when good nursing care is part of the total team effort.

In fact, it is not an either-or question: NPs and other APNs can both complement and substitute for primary care physicians. It is therefore unlikely that a large increase in the number of primary care physicians will, in turn, decrease the interest in APNs either. APNs of all types will continue to play a vital role in the delivery of care in a managed care world teeming with primary care physicians.

The Supply of APNs

Any discussion about the role of NPs and other APNs must consider the demographic characteristics of the entire APN population and how many APNs the education programs are preparing. According to the U.S. Department of Health and Human Services (1992), 139,065 APNs had received formal post-basic nursing education as either NPs, clinical nurse specialists (CNS), certified registered nurse anesthetists (CRNA), or certified nurse midwives (CNM) in 1992. Of this number, 48,237 had been educated as NPs. Although it appears to be a large number, only 29,965 held national or state certification to practice as NPs, and only 23,659 worked in a position with the title of NP. And fewer than 22,000 certified nurses were providing patient care as nurse practitioners in 1992 (Washington Consulting Group 1994).

These figures suggest that a large percentage of NPs are not in the workforce. There is some evidence that barriers to practice deter NPs from either practicing or locating in certain geographic regions (Sekscenski et al. 1994; New York Rural Health Research Center 1995).

Where APNs Work

Despite the intensity of discussions related to independent practice by NPs and other APNs, the reality is that almost all of these clinicians work in organized care delivery settings, not in independent practice. According to a survey of certified NPs and CNSs conducted by the Washington Consulting Group (1994) in conjunction with the American Association of Colleges of Nursing, almost 90 percent of NPs were employed in ambulatory care settings in 1992. The remaining 10 percent, most of whom were adult and neonatal NPs, worked in hospital inpatient settings.

According to the same survey, 23 percent of NPs in 1992 received most of their income through fee-for-service arrangements billed under their name to a practice in which they were employed. Only 3 percent received all their income from fee-for-service arrangements. In 1992, the mean salary for NPs was $45,088. NPs employed in hospitals had salaries averaging $48,502, whereas the average salary for those employed in ambulatory care settings was $45,102.

Education

Nurse practitioner education began outside the mainstream of degree-granting nursing education programs. For many years during the early development of NP programs, NPs were educated in certificate-granting programs. Nurses entering these programs came from a variety of educational backgrounds, and eligibility for recognition through a national certification process did not require a master's degree. In 1992, only 45 percent of NPs held a master's degree as their highest level of nursing education (Washington Consulting Group 1994). NP education gradually made a transition to formal, degree-granting nursing education programs. Today, nearly all NPs graduate from nursing programs granting a master's degree. Moreover, the requirement that candidates for national certification hold a master's degree has been adopted by all but one NP organization.

Recognition of NPs as important primary care providers and increased demand for these clinicians have led to an increase in both the number of NP programs and the number of graduates. In 1993, the American Association of Colleges of Nursing received a contract to develop a network of faculty at master's-level NP programs to facilitate recruitment of NPs into the National Health Service Corps. At that time, the association identified seventy-eight graduate-level institutions that housed approximately 150 NP programs covering the full range of primary care specialties (i.e., family, gerontology, adult, and pediatric) and a small number of NP programs for acute care practice (American Association of Colleges of Nursing 1993). In 1994, AACN conducted a more comprehensive assessment of the number and types of NP programs in four-year colleges and universities (Berlin and Bednash 1995). In addition, enrollments and graduations in the various master's-level APN programs were assessed. Master's-level enrollments in 1994 totaled almost 30,000 students in 449 programs in 252 institutions. More than 11,000 students were enrolled at 190 institutions, with a total of 462 NP programs.

The types of programs offered in these institutions reflect the usual characteristics of the NP population, with family NP programs the most common primary care specialty. A new and increasingly popular curriculum offering is the acute care NP program. This program prepares NPs for practice in the hospital setting and is an evolutionary offshoot of the neonatal NP programs that have existed for some time. In addition, a small but growing number of programs have been developed for CNSs desiring NP education and training. An additional 250 students are enrolled in these post-master's certificate programs (Berlin and Bednash 1995).

NPs and Other APNs in a Managed Care World

The growth in the types and numbers of NP programs and the increase in enrollment in master's-level nursing programs is evidence that the market, at least for now, is creating tremendous demand for these clinicians. In addition, growth is occurring even without full utilization of these clinicians.

Utilization

A report in *HMO Practice* (Frampton and Wall 1994) details efforts by the Harvard Community Health Plan to assess how NPs as well as APNs were utilized. The article notes that although NPs and other APNs could have managed 60 percent of patient visits, they were handling only about 25 percent of all visits. For instance, NPs were managing 9.1 percent of patients presenting with bronchitis or pneumonia, whereas the authors believed that these clinicians could have effectively managed 72 percent of patients with these problems. After evaluating a wide range of common primary care needs, the authors concluded that the health plan was seriously underutilizing an important primary care provider. They recommended greater use of these clinicians to decrease costs, the same conclusion reached by the 1986 report by the Office of Technology Assessment.

However, the 1986 report was criticized for relying on old research and not using physician practice as the standard of comparison. A more recent meta-analysis of NP research (Brown and Grimes 1992), conducted to overcome some of the criticisms of the earlier report, supports the conclusion that NPs produce care that is not simply a substitute for physician care. The findings of this latest meta-analysis have particular importance for a managed care world. Like the study by the Office of Technology Assessment, it reveals that NP knowledge of clinical care and desired outcomes is equivalent to that of physicians. But NPs scored better than physicians on health promotion activities, functional status of patients, and patient satisfaction and compliance with care.

If managed care organizations have a financial interest in keeping patients healthy and out of the care system, then NPs are the providers who can give that unique focus to care.

Moreover, a population of highly skilled NPs for the acute care environment will also benefit an integrated network. A growing body of research provides evidence that NPs who substitute for house staff or residents provide high-quality—and in some instances, better—care than residents. One study assessing the effect of substituting NPs for house staff in trauma care provided evidence that using NPs is associated with a decrease in length of stay and a concomitant decrease in cost of care (Spisso et al. 1990). In addition, the study reported improved documentation of patient care, decreased patient waiting time in clinics, decreased patient complaints, and a saving of 352 minutes per day for house staff when NPs were on duty.

A second study of the effectiveness of NPs in a level III neonatal intensive care unit revealed that although infants cared for by NPs had significantly lower birth weights and gestational age, they averaged 2.4 fewer days in the hospital and $3,491 less in total hospital charges than did infants cared for by house staff (Schulz, Liptak, and Fioravanti 1994).

These studies give a strong indication of the unique capabilities of NPs, which could offset some of the effects of physician education reform, such as a loss of residents and house staff. Moreover, these findings indicate that in some instances care may be enhanced by this substitution. These NPs were providing both substitution and complementarity.

Some Invisible Providers

Much discussion has occurred recently about one APN—the clinical nurse specialist—and whether this clinician group should disappear entirely, merge into the NP role, or remain as a specific clinician group (Cronenwett 1995). The CNSs make significant contributions to an integrated process of care delivery. They help the patient traverse and negotiate the complexities of health care services. They are the APNs who provide not only specialized clinical skills but are savvy about the resources patients need, the kinds of social referrals necessary to facilitate good discharge or transfer, the out-of-hospital care system that needs to be established, and the assessment that must be made of the patient's capacity for the transition.

CNSs, however, are often the invisible provider group. Much of their work occurs behind the scenes and is not often evaluated in terms of the costs and benefits of CNS intervention. One case study of the contributions made by CNSs serving as case managers has been documented at Sioux Valley Hospital in Sioux Falls, South Dakota (Gardner 1992). This 400-bed hospital is the largest and only teaching hospital in South Dakota, and provides the full range of sophisticated care for that state. It has been recognized by the Health Care Financing Administration as one of the fifteen hospitals in the United States with the lowest three-year mortality rates for coronary artery bypass, and was cited in a study of the top 100 hospitals in the United States by Lexecon Health Services as one of nine "superperformers" for bypass procedures. A follow-up report of the top 100 hospitals again included Sioux Valley as one of the outstanding hospitals in the United States with model care outcomes for coronary artery bypass graft patients (*Modern Healthcare* 1994). Only twenty-five of the hospitals cited in the first group achieved a second citation in the Lexecon study. The study concluded that if all U.S. hospitals performed at the benchmark levels set by these superperformers, the cost of hospital care in the United States would decline by $21 billion, average length of stay would drop by more than one day, mortality rates would drop by 17 percent and complication rates by 14 percent. Hospital charges would decrease by $43 billion.

The Lexecon study cited the nursing system as a significant factor in the hospital's exemplary outcomes. Sioux Valley Hospital employs a differentiated practice nursing system in which nurses are assigned roles based upon their education, skills, and experience. Nursing staff are employed as associate, primary, and advanced practice nurses with differentiated salaries. Sioux Valley employs fourteen APNs, a fairly substantial number for a system of that size. The CNS clinicians established the Center for Case Management after an assessment of a small patient population that had played a significant role in the hospital's Medicare losses. The clinicians used referrals, home care, home visits, and a number of other nursing interventions to avoid high-cost hospitalizations and emergency room visits.

The CNS panel follows patients who meet the following criteria:
- Chronic illness with a high probability for sudden physiological imbalance.
- Cognitive/developmental imbalance.
- Emotional/coping deficit.
- Inadequate caregiver/community support.
- Fixed financial resources.
- History of frequent hospitalizations or ER utilization.

In one six-month period, a significant reduction took place in pre- and post-intervention costs, admissions, length of stay, and Medicare losses. Good referral to home-based care alternatives also saved costs to the Medicaid system.

Conclusion

The clinicians discussed above were engaging in the pure nursing activities that will make APNs a significant force in any managed care environment, whether or not the medical educational system produces significantly greater numbers of primary care physicians. Simply producing more physicians will not provide the most cost-efficient and effective care process.

As advanced practical nursing programs increase in number and type, it is vital that they maintain a strong focus on the nursing aspects of the APN's role. Moreover, academic health centers seeking to establish managed care organizations will benefit from strong ties to the nursing education enterprise. These programs can offer the resources for a balanced health care delivery system.

Discussions will undoubtedly continue regarding the interplay between physician and APN supply. However, the focus should not be on a simple substitution model. NPs and other advanced practice nurses will not be, and should not be, purely substitutive. Their roles are complementary. As the care delivery system continues its dramatic movement to a structure organized around principles of cost and appropriateness, the need for these clinicians will grow, helping put the highest quality, lowest cost provider next to the patient.

Works Cited

American Association of Colleges of Nursing. 1993. *National Health Service Corps Advisory Network Data Base.* Washington: AACN.

Berlin, L.E. and G.D. Bednash. 1995. *1994–1995 Enrollment and Graduations in Baccalaureate and Graduate Programs in Nursing.* Washington: American Association of Colleges of Nursing.

Brown, S.A. and D.E. Grimes. 1992. *A Meta-Analysis of Process of Care, Clinical Outcomes, and Cost Effectiveness of Nurses in Primary Care Roles: Nurse Practitioners and Nurse-Midwives.* Washington: American Nurses Association.

Cronenwett, L.R. 1995. Molding the future for advanced practice nurses: Education, regulation, and practice. In *Role Differentiation of the Nurse Practitioner and Clinical*

Nurse Specialist: Reaching Toward Consensus. Washington: American Association of Colleges of Nursing.

Edmunds, M. 1979. Junior doctoring. *Nurse Pract.* 4(5).

———. 1981. Nurse practitioner–physician competition. *Nurse Pract.* 6(2).

———. 1984. Do nurse practitioners still practice nursing? *Nurse Pract.* 9(5).

Frampton, J. and S. Wall. 1994. Exploring the use of NPs and PAs in Primary Care. *HMO Practice.* 8(4).

Gardner, E. 1992. Study amends lore about CAG volume, cost. *Modern Healthcare* (November 30).

Iglehart, J. 1995. Health policy report: Rapid changes for academic medical centers, part 2. *N. Engl. J. Med.* 332(6).

Modern Healthcare. 1994. 1994 report: Top 100 offer guidance. (January 17).

New York Rural Health Research Center. 1995. Nurse practitioners: Potential to help is diminished by array of state limits. *New York Rural Health Courier* 2(1).

Nichols, L. 1992. Estimating costs of underusing advanced practice nurses. *Nursing Economics* 10(5).

OTA (Office of Technology Assessment), U.S. Congress. 1986. *Nurse Practitioners, Physician Assistants, and Certified Nurse-Midwives: A Policy Analysis.* Health Technology Care Study 37. Washington: Government Printing Office.

Schulz, J., G.S. Liptak, and J. Fioravanti. 1994. Nurse practitioners' effectiveness in NICU. *Nursing Management* 25(10).

Sekscenski, E., S. Sansom, C. Bazell, M. Salmon, and F. Mullan. 1994. State practice environments and the supply of physician assistants, nurse practitioners, and certified nurse-midwives. *N.Engl. J. Med* 331(19).

Spisso, J., C. O'Callaghan, M. McKenan, and J.H. Holcrof. 1990. Improved quality of care and reduction of house staff workload using trauma nurse practitioners. *J. Trauma* 30(6).

U.S. Department of Health and Human Services. 1992. *The Registered Nurse Population: Findings From the National Sample Survey of Registered Nurses.* Washington: Government Printing Office.

Washington Consulting Group. 1994. *Survey of Certified Nurse Practitioners and Clinical Nurse Specialists: December 1992.* Prepared for the Division of Nursing, Bureau of the Health Professions, Health Resources and Services Administration, Rockville, MD.

Health Professions Substitution

A Case Study of Anesthesia

JERRY CROMWELL

S ubstitution in health professions is an extremely important issue, particularly in today's practice environment. For a long time, we in the health economics profession specifically, and in the nation generally, have been looking for the Holy Grail—the elusive optimal provider mix. By optimal, I mean the most cost-effective mix of provider inputs, not simply the lowest cost. As an economist, I see a number of market failures that lead to a less than optimal provider mix. These market failures can be attributed to three general causes.

The first cause is insurance. When patients are not paying the full cost of their care, they are not as price-sensitive to cost, and hence to the input mix, as they might otherwise be.

Second, is the tremendous amount of ignorance on the part of both patients and providers of the kinds of services the patients actually need and the most cost-effective provider input mix needed to provide these services. Much of the health services research in the Federal government today is devoted to research in this area.

Third, is the interesting relationship that has developed between doctors and the hospitals where they practice. Hospitals historically have been doctors' workshops where they can use all the services of the hospital basically for free. This situation has resulted in less cost-effective management of hospital resources than otherwise might be possible.

Identifying Possibilities for Physician Substitution

Research on physician substitution has been going on since the advent of Medicare and Medicaid. In some areas, extensive substitution is already going on. We know that nurses provide a significant amount of substitution for physicians in both the office and the hospital. They are midwives, assistants at surgery, and physician extenders. An extensive number of allied health professions also contribute to substitution.

The Federal government has played a role in determining the workforce mix, primarily in support of physician and allied health education. They have also conducted a number of studies of workforce trends and productivity, research that was more prevalent in the 1970s than thereafter. But the area in which the government has affected the workforce mix most profoundly has been in its service reimbursement policies.

The private sector's role in workforce management has been relatively minor until recently. Except for the large health maintenance organizations like Kaiser Permanente, there hasn't been too much consideration in the private sector of what constitutes an optimal provider input mix. Currently, the private sector, through managed care, is starting to worry about that mix.

Anesthesia Substitution

Anesthesia is an excellent laboratory for studying substitution. Anesthesia is a traditional nursing function that has been replaced, in fair part, by physicians over the past 20 to 25 years. There are significant cost implications to the wrong provider input mix in anesthesia, simply because of the tremendous differences in cost between nurse and physician providers (Rosenbach and Cromwell 1988). Anesthesia, therefore, provides an excellent example of what can go wrong with the workforce mix when you pay for inputs (i.e., types of providers) rather than outputs (i.e., the services delivered). Federal and third-party reimbursement have paid for anesthesia inputs rather than outputs. This major flaw in the reimbursement system explains the inefficient mix we've developed in anesthesia (Cromwell and Rosenbach 1988).

There are three basic models of anesthesia practice.
1. In the solo anesthesiologist model, the physician, practicing alone, handles all the cases in the hospital. In some instances around the country, solo nurse anesthetists practice alone and handle all of the cases.
2. In the second model, a hospital has a mix of the two providers, yet each may be practicing solo on any one case depending on the case and the time of the day.
3. In the anesthesia team arrangement, a physician anesthesiologist (MDA) supervises a certified registered nurse anesthetist (CRNA).

Extent of MDA-CRNA Substitution

Significant regional differences in the mix of the two anesthesia providers leads me to believe that there are significant opportunities for provider mix improvement. In California, there are two anesthesiologists for every CRNA. In South Dakota, there are seven and a half CRNAs for every anesthesiologist (Rosenbach et al. 1988).

What do these two types of providers do in their delivery of anesthesia? The following data are based upon the federally funded Anesthesia Practice Survey, a 1986 survey of roughly 500 each of anesthesiologists and CRNAs randomly selected around the country (Rosenbach et al. 1988). To my knowledge, there is no more recent comprehensive random survey of anesthesia practice patterns.

CRNAs provide a substantial amount of anesthesia activities. They evaluate patient-risk factors in at least half (51 percent) of their cases; in more than half of their the cases (61 percent), they discuss the anesthesia plan with the patient or the family. In roughly half of their cases (45 percent), they evaluate the patient in recovery. They administer regional anesthesia roughly a third (29 percent) of the time. They insert arterial lines about a third (36 percent) of the time, but they are much less involved in inserting other invasive monitoring devices such as central venus pressure lines and Swan-Ganz catheters. These data tell us that the CRNAs are actively involved in just about all of the major anesthesia activities.

When cases are stratified by anesthesia complexity and model of practice (e.g., solo CRNA, solo MDA), three conclusions are noteworthy (Rosenbach et al. 1988; Rosenbach and Cromwell 1988). First, solo CRNAs are far more involved in vaginal deliveries than are anesthesiologists. Second, anesthesiologists are only slightly more likely to perform the more complex anesthesia procedures in the nation. And third, a significant percentage of solo anesthesiologists are doing simple anesthesia procedures (e.g., dilation and curettage, vaginal delivery, and hernia repair).

A favorite economic method of study is activity analysis. In the Anesthesia Practice Survey, respondents provided a daily log of roughly 4,000 operations. Figure 1 categorizes these operations in terms of percent of MDA time devoted to each case on the vertical axis; CRNA time is depicted on the horizontal axis. At the top of the vertical axis are about 1,200 cases in which the anesthesiologist was practicing alone. On the horizontal axis are about 700 cases in which the nurse anesthetist was practicing alone. The 45° line is the full-time equivalent (FTE) line, which is a one to one substitution of anesthesiologist time for CRNA time.

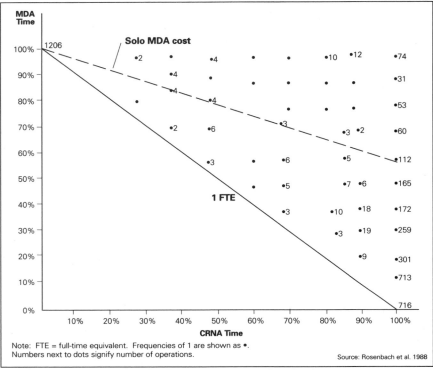

Figure 1. Percent CRNA-MDA Time (4,000 operations), 1986

All of the observations are either on these two corner points, the two solo points, or above the point where more than one FTE is on a case. All dots represent numbers of cases with more than one FTE practitioner on a case. The dashed cost line represents the solo MDA cost line. Given the relative cost difference of the two providers, the dashed line represents all of the combinations of the two providers that would be equivalent to the cost of an anesthesiologist practicing alone. Thus, all cases above the dashed line effectively cost more than an anesthesiologist practicing alone. A large proportion of cases are in the gap between the 45° FTE line and the solo MDA cost line at varying percentages of MDA-CRNA activity. The procedures that fall in the range above the MDA cost line are those in which managed care organizations, and every other payor, will seek cost-savings by changing the provider mix to get much below the MDA-cost line, and in some cases, particularly in simpler ones, to much below the MDA cost-line. It illustrates opportunities for potential professional arbitrage.

CRNA practice raises MDA productivity; it is the kind of situation that managed care organizations look at closely. The solo anesthesiologist sees an average of 3.7 patients per shift (Cromwell and Rosenbach 1990). Working in a team with a CRNA, the MDA sees 6.5 patients per shift, a 75 percent increase in the number of patients per shift (Cromwell and Rosenbach 1990). Even adjusting for the complexity of certain surgeries, there is a 63 percent greater increase in anesthesiologist productivity when the MDA works in a supervisory capacity. The anesthesiologist in a team works with a CRNA for the equivalent of more than 8 hours of CRNA time during the anesthesiologist's shift. Only about 60 percent of the procedures that the anesthesiologist does are concurrent. The other 40 percent of the time, the anesthesiologist is working on his or her own cases and is not directly supervising a CRNA. Thus there are still opportunities for additional productivity even in the team scenario.

Relative Cost of Each Provider

There have been tremendous increases in the nominal incomes of both MDAs and CRNAs. The average reported income for anesthesiologists increased roughly 80 percent during the ten-year period 1983 to 1993 (AMA 1994). The actual increase in income for CRNAs was 100 percent in this period (AANA 1988; AANA 1994).

Comparing hourly incomes, the more relevant marginal measure for economic analysis, we see some compression in the relative cost difference in ten years. In 1983, anesthesiologists cost 2.2 times what a CRNA cost ($51.84 per MDA hour, $23.80 per CRNA hour). The MDA cost difference has compressed somewhat to approximately 1.8 times that of a CRNA ($87.44 to $49.20). The compression is due to the relatively large increase in CRNA salaries over the ten years. Nevertheless, managed care organizations and government payors may take advantage of the resulting arbitrage gap.

Forecasting Shortfalls in CRNAs

In 1980, there were approximately 17,500 CRNAs and 13,000 MDAs in practice in the United States. There was some increase from 1980 to 1985 in the number of full-time equivalent CRNAs practicing. From 1985 to 1992, the supply was effectively flat at approximately 20,000 (Cromwell et al. 1991). Over that same period, there was a rapid growth in the number of anesthesiologists practicing in the United States. By the early 1990s, the number of full-time active CRNAs and MDAs was basically the same (ASA

1995; AANA 1995). Given the demonstrated opportunities for MDA-CRNA substitution, equal supplies of the two providers imply an increasingly non-cost-effective provider mix.

The main reason for the flattening in nurse anesthetist supply is the significant decline in the number of training programs. From 1981 to 1985, thirty-eight programs closed (AANA 1989). From 1986 to 1990, another twenty programs closed. During that same decade, from 1986 to 1990, the average number of graduates per year declined from almost 1,000 per year down to 633. A low point of about 575 graduates was reached in 1987. The situation has turned around in the 1990s. The number of CRNA programs has begun to rise again slowly, and the size of those programs have begun to grow again. In the period from 1990 to 1994, programs were averaging 866 graduates, and for 1996, the AANA is projecting well over 1,100 CRNA graduates (AANA 1995).

In a study for the Division of Nursing in the U.S. Health Resources and Services Administration, I analyzed the forecasted shortfall in CRNAs by the year 2000 under various low and high scenarios of CRNA supply and need (Cromwell et al. 1991).

Under any forecast, there is a significant CRNA shortfall, ranging from 6,852 to 9,816 FTEs. If one wants to move towards what is perceived to be a more economically efficient provider mix, then the shortfall of CRNAs doubles to about 18,000 to 21,000 FTEs by the year 2000. This forecasted decline in supply has concerned public policy makers as well as the private sector. Although it appears that educational institutions are responding to the shortfall, growth in CRNA supply is far below what is required to support widespread adoption of the team concept.

Factors Driving Future Demand

Some of the factors driving future demand for anesthesia providers include

- Health Care Financing Administration (HCFA) payment reductions for anesthesiologists have been going on for six to eight years in various forms. These reductions are forcing more supervision on the part of anesthesiologists so they can meet any target incomes they may have.
- There is a strong movement toward competitive bidding or bundled payment for inpatient services. In the HCFA heart bypass demonstration, the government pays a single rate for bypass surgery to seven hospitals in the country. This single rate covers both the hospital component as well as the surgeon, the anesthesiologist, and all the consult-

ing physicians in the hospital. The hospital and the physicians divide up the basic payment anyway they like. HCFA is expanding the demonstration by going into other heart procedures and are also expanding it to orthopedics. This payment method is having profound effects on the way that anesthesia is practiced in the hospitals. (Of course, private insurers have picked up on the government's lead in this bundled payment arena and negotiated bundled payment arrangements throughout the country.)

- Medicare has debated the adoption of physician diagnostic-related groups (DRG) for at least ten years. HCFA is serious about bringing inpatient physicians under the same Medicare payment incentives that the hospitals have been under for the last ten years. HCFA is setting up a demonstration to test a medical staff DRG payment system where the medical staff, along with the hospital itself, will negotiate a bundled payment for DRGs in the hospital.
- There are Medicare and state reductions in teaching support.
- There has been an aggressive shift toward managed care.

California is a great laboratory for studying arbitrage potential between managed-care and private fee-for-service organizations. The Kaiser Permanente hospitals in southern California have about 0.4 anesthesiologists for every full-time CRNA. The ratio for the rest of California is 2.6 anesthesiologists for every CRNA (Rosenbach et al. 1988). Here is a phenomenal difference in the mix of the two inputs within the same state. If the entire state went the Kaiser way in terms of the mix of the two anesthesia provider inputs, jobs for anesthesiologists in California would decline by roughly 1,200; a similar increase in CRNA jobs in California would also occur.

Occupational Power Struggles

Anesthesiologists are responding to the growing threats to their profession, their incomes, and their practices by expanding practices in order to increase their market power. They have lobbied hard against bundled payment in any kind of hospital arrangement and any kind of DRGs that would force the hospital to internalize its costs of providing anesthesia. They have also shifted strongly to solo practice so they can avoid reduced reimbursement due to concurrent care.

Shifting to solo practice requires limiting CRNA access to hospitals. Anesthesiologists have done this in two primary ways. They have limited CRNA teaching programs. (There were many complaints about anesthesiologists training their competitors.) Then, anesthesiologists around the country presented the hospitals with a "them" or "us" ultimatum. A current lawsuit over CRNA dismissal in Minneapolis-St. Paul symbolizes this occupational warfare between the CRNAs and the anesthesiologists.

Hospitals will be inclined to favor the anesthesiologists over the CRNAs for the simple reason that the hospital right now is not paying for either provider; naturally, the hospital will select the anesthesiologist because of the greater training, and, prestige associated with a physician provider. It is not a cost-effective trend, but it's being forced on hospitals at this point.

Nurse anesthetists, in turn, have not been idle, but have mobilized impressive economic and political power. They've successfully lobbied Congress to not be bundled in the Medicare Part A DRG payment but, instead, to be treated separately and independently. They've lobbied Congress successfully for Medicare direct billing. They've lobbied Congress, HCFA, and the Physician Payment Review Commission for equal reimbursement—not only the ability to bill patients directly, but as independent providers billing at rates roughly comparable to anesthesiologists. They've sued hospitals that have dismissed them. They've also supported the trend toward physician DRGs, that is, internalizing in the hospital the relative costliness of the two providers in order to force the institution to make more cost-effective decisions.

Implications For Training in Anesthesia

Let me summarize five facts that are pertinent to future training decisions in anesthesia. (The first three are also relevant to training in other physician specialties.)

1. Spending in health care will slow dramatically over the next ten years.
2. The government is going to cut back on its teaching support.
3. Meaningful managed care competitive bidding will come to dominate reimbursement over the next five to eight years. A lot of experiments in managed care that have not been effective in terms of cost control in the 1980s are pretty much being weeded out. We now have much more rigorous competitive bidding in managed care.
4. Nurse anesthetists can perform nearly all the anesthesia tasks with minimal supervision and are nearly perfect substitutes for anesthesiologists.
5. Nurse anesthetists are significantly less expensive than anesthesiologists.

From these five facts, I draw four conclusions.

1. CRNAs will be in greater demand over the next ten years, and in significantly greater demand depending on how fast and how hard the public and private payors push.

2. The demand for anesthesiologists will diminish, as already has happened in California and elsewhere.

3. Anesthesiologists are going to find their responsibilities shifting significantly away from hands-on anesthesia towards supervising, concentrating on complex cases and providing other kinds of nonoperating care such as pain-care management.

4. The rate of return to specializing in anesthesia will decline. (It is probably already starting to decline.) The number of applicants will decrease as potential students realize that the future in anesthesiology is not what it was in the 1980s. The reduction in the number of slots will almost inevitably lead to a significant reduction in the number of anesthesia programs around the county.

Works Cited

AANA (American Association of Nurse Anesthetists). 1988. *Membership Survey: Income Supplement Fiscal Year 1988*. Chicago: AANA.

———. 1989. *AANA Survey of Program Directors*. Chicago: AANA.

———. 1994. *AANA Membership Survey: Income Supplement Fiscal Year 1994*. Chicago: AANA.

———. 1995. Unpublished data.

AMA. 1994. *Socioeconomic Characteristics of Medical Practice: 1984–1993*. Chicago: AMA.

ASA (American Society of Anesthesiologists). 1995. Unpublished data.

Cromwell, J. and M.L. Rosenbach. 1988. Reforming anesthesia payment under Medicare. *Health Aff.* 7(5)

———. 1990. The impact of nurse anesthetists on anesthesiologist productivity. *Med. Care* 28(2).

Cromwell, J., M.L. Rosenbach, G.C. Pope, B. Butrica, and J.D. Pitcher. 1991. CRNA manpower forecasts: 1990–2010. *Med. Care* 29(7).

Rosenbach, M.L. and J. Cromwell. 1988. A profile of anesthesia practice patterns. *Health Aff.* 7(4).

Rosenbach, M.L., J. Cromwell, J. Keller, H. Hewes, and G.C. Pope. 1988. Payment Options for Non-Physician Anesthetists under Medicare's Prospective Payment System. Waltham, MA: Center for Health Economics Research. Unpublished paper.

Roles of Educational Institutions

The policies implemented by governments and the marketplace greatly influence policy decisions made by the leaders of the institutions that educate health professionals. The leaders of these institutions also generate internal policies that affect the health workforce. The papers in this section describe the issues that leaders of institutions face as they try to influence health workforce development, either in response to external policies or by creating policies inside their institutions.

New Health Workforce Responsibilities and Dilemmas

NEAL A. VANSELOW

Fueled by concern over cost, quality, and access, our nation's health care system is undergoing massive change. The mere fact that it is changing should not be a surprise. It has been obvious for many years that, sooner or later, rising costs alone would make the traditional delivery system unsustainable. What has been a shock is the source and magnitude of the change.

As recently as 1993, many people assumed that President Clinton's health reform plan would provide solutions to the problems plaguing health care in the United States. One year later it became obvious that comprehensive Federal reform was dead. Although there were predictions then that state governments would take the lead and institute their own health care reform plans, several circumstances have made such reform unlikely. These include opposition by businesses that operate in multiple states and are unwilling to accept 50 different state reform plans; restrictions on the states imposed by the Employee Retirement Income Security Act; and the reality that most states simply do not have the money to fund health care reform.

The vacuum created by the failure of government-initiated reform has been quickly filled by the private sector. Market forces are now shaping the U.S. health care system. The changes are fundamental and profound, and occurring rapidly.

There is a significant difference between government's goals in promoting health care reform and those of the private sector. Whereas the changes advocated by the government were designed to make tradeoffs between cost, access, and quality, the primary goal of the market is to control costs. As a result, relatively little attention is now being paid to the plight of the 40 million Americans who lack health insurance. In addition, it is not clear to what extent the quality of care that health plans deliver will be a factor in determining their financial success. Yet another major difference is the speed at which change is implemented. Major reforms initiated by the government are often phased in over several years. Reforms that result from market forces can occur overnight.

Market-induced changes in the delivery and financing of health care have important implications for both the health care workforce and the academic health centers that serve as the major producers of health professionals. This paper outlines some of the more important workforce issues associated with health care reform, discusses the implications for academic health centers, and suggests some strategies that academic health centers might use to adjust to the dramatic changes taking place.

Health Workforce Issues

Each of the health professions is facing challenges as a result of the change taking place in the delivery system. The issues in dentistry, public health, and allied health are perhaps not quite as threatening as those in medicine, nursing, and pharmacy.

The Physician Workforce

The major issues involving the physician workforce are its size, its composition, and the extent to which current medical education and training programs produce physicians equipped to function in an environment increasingly dominated by managed care.

The U.S. physician workforce is growing at one and one-half times the rate of growth of the general population (COGME 1992). Much of this growth is the result of increases in the number of medical schools and the size of their enrollments during the 1960s and 1970s. Although the combined annual output of U.S. allopathic and osteopathic schools has stabilized in recent years at about 17,500, the number of residents in training has continued to grow at about 4 percent per year (Shine 1995). This growth is due primarily to an ever-increasing number of international medical graduates admitted to graduate medical education programs in this country, and the fact that 75 percent of the international medical graduates who complete their graduate medical education remain here to practice (Mullan, Politzer, and Davis 1995). As a result, the ratio of active physicians to population in the United States has increased from just over 150 per 100,000 in 1970 to well over 250 per 100,000 today (COGME 1992; U.S. Department of Health and Human Services 1993).

Although the output of physicians continues to increase, there is evidence that the demand for physician services is decreasing as the nation moves from a system based on fee-for-service to a managed care system. Studies by the University Hospital Consortium (1995) demonstrate that health maintenance organizations use a lower physician to population ratio than fee-for-service. Recent site visits conducted by the Institute of Medicine Committee on the Future of Primary Care revealed that a number of managed care organizations are using advanced practice nurses, physician assistants, and other nonphysician personnel to perform tasks previously reserved for physicians—a practice known as substitution or offloading.

As a result of the increased supply of physicians and the decreasing demand for physician services, all the major studies of U.S. aggregate physician supply in the last fifteen years conclude that there either is now, or soon will, be a physician surplus (COGME 1992; Graduate Medical Education National Advisory Committee 1981; Weiner 1994). The marketplace evidence of physician oversupply is still mixed, but several recent surveys show that physician incomes are either flat or falling (Borzo 1995). There are also numerous anecdotal accounts of empty office calendars, early physician retirements, and the inability of physicians who complete residency or fellowship training to find employment.

A second issue related to the physician workforce is its composition by specialty. Fifteen years ago, the Graduate Medical Education National Advisory Committee (1981) predicted an oversupply of most specialists, and many subsequent studies have confirmed this conclusion (Weiner 1994). The question of the adequacy of the supply of primary care physicians has been more controversial. For years, most experts believed that a significant shortage existed. More recent studies suggest that if there is a shortage in primary care it is modest in size (COGME 1995), and at least one study of the effect of health care reform on the physician workforce has suggested that the supply of primary care physicians may be in balance with projected requirements of a managed care environment (Weiner 1994).

A persistent problem relating to the composition of the physician workforce has been the underrepresentation of minorities. Despite record enrollments of blacks, Hispanics, and Native Americans in U.S. allopathic and osteopathic medical schools in recent years, the ratio of minority physicians to the minority population is still far below that of white physicians to the white population.

As managed care has grown, complaints have been voiced about the appropriateness of the training that U.S. physicians receive during medical school and residency. During a public hearing and several site visits conducted by the Institute of Medicine Committee on the Future of Primary Care, managed care representatives stated that many of the primary care physicians they hired postresidency required extensive periods of retraining. Specific complaints included the following:

- Too much inpatient tertiary care experience and not enough exposure to ambulatory care.
- Lack of experience with common office problems and procedures in gynecology, orthopedics, and dermatology.
- Poor patient communication skills.
- Inability to function as part of a multidisciplinary patient care team.
- Poor knowledge of public health principles and of health promotion and disease prevention techniques.
- Inadequate referral skills.
- Lack of experience with information systems.

These concerns have caused some managed care organizations to establish their own residency programs and at least one of them to explore the possibility of opening its own medical school.

The Nurse Workforce

The nurse workforce, which numbers over 2.2 million, represents the nation's largest health profession. As is the case for the physician workforce, it has been growing at a rate considerably greater than the growth of the general population. In 1950, there were 246 registered nurses per 100,000 population. By 1992, the ratio had grown to 726 per 100,000 (Aiken and Gwyther 1995). Each year approximately 50,000 nurses are added to the U.S. supply.

There is considerable evidence indicating that the nursing shortage of the late 1980s has now become a surplus, at least for nurses with entry-level credentials (associate degrees, diplomas, or baccalaureate degrees). Two-thirds of U.S. nurses work in hospitals. Their employment has been threatened by the restructuring of nursing service departments caused by decreases in hospital occupancy. Many hospitals are laying off registered nurses and retaining as their replacements the nursing assistants hired during the nursing shortage. The American Nurses Association believes that this practice poses a danger to patients: in March 1995, they organized a protest march in Washington. Nursing layoffs by hospitals appears to be another example of an effort by the health care industry to reduce costs through substitution or offloading.

As inpatient employment opportunities for nurses decrease, the number of nursing positions available in the ambulatory and community and public health sectors of the industry has grown. As Yordy points out in this book, it would require the creation of a large number of new jobs in the outpatient sector to absorb the nurses previously employed by hospitals (see Yordy discussion in this book).

The employment picture is quite different for nurse practitioners and other advanced practice nurses. The growth of managed care, the easing of legal restrictions on advanced nursing practice, and the potential of nurse substitution for resident physicians have created new roles for advanced practice nurses and an increased demand for their services. Nursing education has responded by creating new programs at the master's degree level. Between 1983 and 1994, the number of nursing master's programs increased from 154 to 252. In the single year between 1993 and 1994 alone, the number of master's programs offering a nurse practitioner option increased by over 25 percent (National League for Nursing 1994).

Another workforce issue in nursing education is the entry-level degree. Whereas the number of diploma graduates has been decreasing, there has been considerable growth in associate degree programs, which now produce almost twice as many graduates as baccalaureate and diploma programs combined (U.S. Department of Health and Human Services 1994). This trend concerns many nursing leaders and nurse educators, who believe that the baccalaureate should be the basic nursing credential.

If current trends continue, one can envision a future nursing workforce considerably smaller in size but more highly trained than today's workforce. This situation would imply the need for a reduction in the number of associate degree and diploma programs in nursing and an increase in the number of baccalaureate and graduate programs.

The Pharmacist Workforce

Controversy over the entry-level degree in pharmacy has existed for some time. Leaders of the profession have vigorously promoted the concept of clinical pharmacy and the Doctor of Pharmacy degree as the basic degree for pharmacists. This stance, enunciated by Webb in this book, conflicts with the view of the National Association of Chain Drugstores, which favors the baccalaureate degree and the concept of community pharmacy.

The traditional role of the pharmacist as a dispenser of medication in a community pharmacy is also threatened by increased automation, use of pharmacy technicians, mail order pharmacy, and growth of pharmacy benefit management. In particular, pharmacy benefit management, which is dominated by a few large firms, has raised concerns for community pharmacists and has prompted them to lobby for "any willing provider" and "freedom of choice" legislation.

Faced with uncertainty about the future, pharmacists have been looking for new and expanded roles in the health care delivery system and have attempted to move the focus of pharmacy "from the prescription to the patient" (O'Neil 1993). The concept of pharmaceutical care would appear to assign to pharmacists many of the therapeutic tasks that are now the responsibility of physicians.

Going a step further, some members of the pharmacy profession have discussed changes that would involve pharmacists in the direct provision of primary care services, similar to the involvement of nurse practitioners and physician assistants. One recent article suggests that pharmacies become "health centers with pharmacists providing triage, immunizations, management of chronic disease, and treatment for common problems and injuries" (Rosendahl 1995).

Other Health Professions

Whereas the role of pharmacists is now in a period of adjustment, the changes in the health care delivery system are not as problematic for the dentistry, public health, and allied health professions. Dentistry and dental education have been responding to the changing health care market for over a decade (Capilouto and Ohsfeldt in this book); public health and allied health are just beginning to respond. The size and composition of the workforce in dentistry is probably more closely in line with requirements than is the case for most other health professions. The Institute of Medicine Committee on the Future of Dental Education concluded that the aggregate supply of dentists is approximately in balance with requirements and that the current mix of general dentists (85 percent) and specialists (15 percent) is appropriate (IOM 1995). The committee, however, expressed serious concerns about both dental education today and the credentialing process in dentistry. It recommended major revisions in the undergraduate dental curriculum, creation of additional residency positions in advanced general dentistry, and development of a uniform national clinical examination for licensure to replace existing state and regional exams.

Because public health and allied health workforces are each composed of multiple disciplines, it is difficult to generalize about the current status and future prospects of their different workforces. Both probably stand to gain, however, from the dramatic changes taking place in health care. The role of public health professionals should become more important in the future because of the increasing emphasis on health promotion, disease prevention, community health issues, and health policy. Many of the allied health disciplines will find their responsibilities expanded as the practice of substitution and multiskilling becomes more widespread.

Multidisciplinary Issues

Two additional workforce trends that cut across disciplinary lines deserve mention: increasing use of multidisciplinary health care delivery teams and substitution of personnel.

Health Care Delivery Teams

Teams of physicians, nurse practitioners and/or physician assistants, and registered nurses are often used by health maintenance organizations and group practices in their primary care clinics. Clinical pharmacists, nutritionists, social workers, and other mental health professionals may also be included. Team size and organization vary considerably, as do the team leadership arrangements. Some teams meet formally to discuss assigned patients, but many do not. Teams that are organized more informally generally consist of groups of professionals who work together on a regular basis, share the same panel of patients, and are familiar with each other's capabilities and limitations.

The trend toward team delivery should be of interest to academic health centers for at least two reasons. First, managed care has criticized medical schools and teaching hospitals for failing to expose students and residents to multidisciplinary teams. Curricula should be modified to correct this deficiency. Second, there are a number of research opportunities to be explored. Some questions that deserve investigation are: What is the impact of team delivery on cost, quality, and access to health care? What distinguishes a team that functions well from one that does not? Answering these and other questions related to the use of teams would be a major contribution to the health care delivery system.

Substitution of Personnel

Substitution of personnel, already discussed briefly, is another trend that cuts across disciplinary lines. Clinics and HMOs in highly competitive markets, such as those in Minnesota and southern California, are asking nurse practitioners, physician assistants, and registered nurses to assume responsibilities and perform tasks previously reserved for physicians. Licensed practical nurses and medical assistants, the latter trained on the job, are being assigned duties that were previously the responsibility of registered nurses. In one Minnesota group practice, RNs manage the majority of uncomplicated urinary tract infections in women and also monitor anticoagulant therapy—both over the phone.

Personnel substitution has also changed the role of the primary care physician in significant ways. Routine patients are usually handled by nurse practitioners, physician assistants, or RNs, giving physicians more time to concentrate on more complex cases. As a result, primary care physicians are personally managing many of the patients they previously referred to specialists.

The major force driving personnel substitution is the need to control costs in an increasingly competitive health care marketplace. As emphasized by Schwartz (1994), however, "the marketplace is rapidly implementing new forms of health care delivery with broad workforce substitution without any formal or rigorous evaluation of the safety or effectiveness of such interventions." The practice of substitution represents both an opportunity and a challenge for academic health centers. On the one hand, they have the capability to carry out the research needed to determine if the practice is safe and effective. On the other hand, if substitution becomes widespread there are major implications for the numbers and types of health professionals that academic health centers will be asked to produce.

Implications for Academic Health Centers

As institutions created to serve the public, academic health centers have no choice but to respond to changes taking place in health care, including changes in the delivery system's workforce needs. Most academic health centers have reluctantly accepted the fact that "business as usual" is not a realistic option for their patient care programs and are joining or creating provider networks in order to reduce their costs and thus become more competitive. It is equally important for academic health centers to make changes in their education and training programs to adjust to evolving marketplace requirements for health professionals.

This is not to suggest that every academic health center should be the same. The nation will still need some institutions that are research intensive and specialty oriented, just as it will need some that concentrate on teaching and the production of primary care clinicians. There are, however, some steps that all academic health centers should consider.

1. Review and modify governance structures so that decisions can be made in a timely manner. In the university tradition, academic health center decision-making authority is shared by the administration, faculty, and governing board. Considerable autonomy and power are delegated to individual departments whose leadership sometimes has primary loyalty to its discipline rather than to the institution as a whole. This combination of diffused authority and mixed loyalties has often resulted in an inability to adjust promptly and appropriately to the changes taking place in health care. Effective and timely decision making, especially critical in the patient care area, is equally important for education and training programs.

2. Reduce the physician surplus and stem the relentless increase in the number of residents being trained. At present, there is a state of paralysis in addressing this problem. It is unlikely that the Federal government will take steps to manage the physician supply, other than to reduce Medicare funding for graduate medical education. At the same time, antitrust concerns have restrained residency review committees and specialty boards from acting. Neither of these problems need prevent individual academic health centers and teaching hospitals from reducing the size of their residency programs, however—something they have been reluctant to do so far.

A first step in addressing the physician surplus should be to reduce the number of international medical graduates who are accepted for residency training in the United States. Whitcomb (1995) recently suggested this reasonable way to accomplish reduction.

Until the issue of international medical graduates has been addressed, it would not seem prudent to reduce either the size of U.S. medical school classes or the number of U.S. medical schools. Under present circumstances, such reductions would only result in the recruitment of international medical graduates to replace graduates of U.S. schools in residency training. They would also hamper current efforts to increase opportunities in medicine for U.S. minority students. This is not the time, however, to increase the capacity of either U.S. allopathic or osteopathic schools.*

In view of the physician surplus in most specialties and subspecialties, there should also be a readjustment of the balance between generalist and

---

*In this regard, it should be noted that one new osteopathic school opened recently; another plans to open a second campus; and several are in the planning stages. (See Marker discussion in this book.)

specialist training. Given the growing sense that the U.S. generalist supply may be relatively close to requirements, the best way would be to reduce the number of specialty and subspecialty training slots rather than to increase the number of generalist positions.

3. Reduce the number of entry-level nurses by making cuts in the number accepted for associate degree programs (where the largest increase in capacity has taken place) and diploma programs, rather than in the baccalaureate and graduate nursing programs sponsored by academic health centers.

4. Modify the curriculum content of academic health center programs to better prepare graduates to function in a health care system dominated by managed care. Managed care's criticisms of current education and training programs should be heeded and particular emphasis placed on exposing students to multidisciplinary health care teams. In view of the new emphasis on health promotion, disease prevention, clinical epidemiology, and community health, closer relationships should also be developed between schools of public health and the other components of academic health centers.

5. Devise creative solutions to the problem of financing education and training for the health professions. All major sources of revenue, including state and Federal appropriations, tuition, indirect cost recovery, and funds derived from patient care, either are in danger of being reduced or have been increased to the limit of what the market will bear. There is no simple solution to this problem, and the years ahead will be challenging ones for academic health centers and their parent universities.

In the end, the solution may vary considerably from institution to institution. Tulane University Medical Center, for example, has developed a partnership with Columbia-HCA, an investor-owned health care corporation. Under this arrangement, Columbia-HCA will provide some of the core financial support required by Tulane's School of Medicine and School of Public Health and Tropical Medicine. Other academic health centers are exploring similar arrangements with the for-profit sector. Another approach is the recent merger of Hahnemann University, the Medical College of Pennsylvania, and the Allegheny Health System. Only time will reveal the wisdom of these new partnerships and mergers.

The most logical solution to the funding of graduate medical education would be to move to an all-payor system under which all parties benefiting from residency and fellowship training are required to help support its costs. Although adoption of all-payor legislation at either the Federal or state level seems unlikely in the current environment, academic health centers should continue to work vigorously for such legislation. It should not require the destruction of one of the finest training systems in the world to convince legislators and policy makers of the importance of this national resource.

Conclusion

The revolution in health care is still ongoing. It is impossible to predict what the delivery system will look like when a period of relative stability is reached. What is clear, however, is that the shape and composition of the health care workforce of the future will be considerably different than in the past. This is true no matter whether the outcome is a system based on competition and managed care or, as some predict, a single-payor system. As the major producers of health professionals, academic health centers face new responsibilities and new dilemmas. They are being challenged as never before. Their survival will depend on their willingness and ability to adjust.

Works Cited

Aiken, L.H. and M.E. Gwyther. 1995. Medicare funding of nurse education. *JAMA* 273.

Borzo, G. 1995. Salaries for employed physicians plateau, start to drop. *American Medical News*. March 27.

COGME (Council on Graduate Medical Education). 1992. *Recommendations to Improve Access to Health Care Through Physician Workforce Reform*. Rockville, MD: U.S. Department of Health and Human Services.

———. 1995. *COGME 1995 Physician Workforce Funding Recommendations for Department of Health and Human Services Programs*. Rockville, MD: U.S. Department of Health and Human Services.

Graduate Medical Education National Advisory Committee. 1981. *Summary Report of the GMENAC*. Rockville, MD: U.S. Department of Health and Human Services.

IOM (Institute of Medicine). 1995. *Dental Education at the Crossroads: Challenges and Change*. Washington: National Academy Press.

Mullan, F., R.M. Politzer, and C.H. Davis. 1995. Medical migration and the physician workforce. *JAMA* 273.

National League for Nursing. 1994. *Graduate Education in Nursing: Advanced Practice Nursing*. Vol. 2 of *Nursing Datasource 1994*. New York: National League for Nursing.

O'Neil, E.H. 1993. *Health Professions Education for the Future: Schools in Service to the Nation.* San Francisco: Pew Health Professions Commission.

Rosendahl, I. 1995. Impossible dream? Is the NP-PA model out of reach? *Drug Topics* (March 6).

Schwartz, S. 1994. Matching needs more appropriately to skills and training. *Leonard Davis Institute Health Policy Research Quarterly* 4.

Shine, K.I. 1995. Freeze the number of Medicare-subsidized graduate medical education positions. *JAMA* 273.

University Hospital Consortium. 1995. *Responding to a Dynamic Health Care Marketplace: Implementation Strategies for AHCs.* Oak Brook, IL: University Hospital Consortium.

U.S. Department of Health and Human Services. 1993. *Factbook: Health Personnel, United States.* Rockville, MD: USDHHS.

————. 1994. *The Registered Nurse Population, 1992.* Rockville, MD: USDHHS.

Weiner, J.P. 1994. Forecasting the effects of health reform on U.S. physician workforce requirements. *JAMA* 272.

Whitcomb, M.E. 1995. Correcting the oversupply of specialists by limiting residencies for graduates of foreign medical schools. *N. Engl. J. Med.* 333.

RESPONSE TO NEAL A. VANSELOW

Special Issues for Osteopathic Medicine

DAVID G. MARKER

From the perspective of osteopathic medical education, on the surface, at least, business as usual is what we ought to be pursuing. After all, we have a century-long track record of producing physicians in approximately the right generalist-specialist and geographic mixes. And we do this at significantly less cost than our sister MD-granting institutions.

Of all the practicing MDs, 34 percent are in one of the generalist disciplines; of the DOs, 61 percent are in generalist disciplines. These figures are a bit misleading because they are averages of all active physicians. Moreover, in recent years we have seen an increasing tendency on the part of osteopathic medical students to elect to go into specialties. Nonetheless, we are still producing roughly the proportion of generalists and specialists that seems to be called for in a managed care environment.

One of the main reasons that our educational costs are lower than those of the MD-granting institutions is because a large number of community DOs volunteer their time for community rotations. Osteopathic schools also have significantly less infrastructure and commit less institutional funding to the support of research than most allopathic schools. For example, the annual operating budget of the school of medicine at the University of Iowa is approximately $250 million. The annual operating budget of the University of Osteopathic Medicine and Health Sciences, where we graduate approximately the same number of physicians each year, is $25 million—a tenth the size.

Given that the costs are so much lower, what about the quality of osteopathic medical education? One of the joys I have had as a new president at the University of Osteopathic Medicine is to travel around the country and meet our alumni where they are living, working, and practicing. I like to ask them, especially the younger graduates, "Were you well prepared?" "Can you compete?" "Are you able to do what you need to do?" The overwhelming answer is "yes."

How is it that we have been able to produce what is supposedly, in today's terms, the right mix of physicians and to do it at a lower cost? We say in this profession that we fish for students in a different stream than do our sister MD-granting institutions.

A lot of literature today attempts to analyze who goes into family medicine and the generalist disciplines. Our students, by and large, have the characteristics reported in this literature. They tend to come from small towns or rural areas. Many are over the age of twenty-five and married. Many attended a public college or university. They have a strong motivation for direct, nurturant patient contact, as evidenced by service-related work experience or volunteer work, dissatisfaction with objective-oriented work, and leisure activities involving other people. Finally, they exhibit humanistic over scientific interests, as evidenced by books they read, their hobbies, community involvement, and extracurricular activities while in college (Rezler and Kalishman 1989).

A survey (Singer 1994) found a remarkable fact—virtually a mirror image between hometown size and planned practice location among groups of freshman and senior DO undergraduates. Overall, about half of our current students are going to practice in small towns or areas that are underserved.

In his paper, Neal Vanselow mentions the proposed new colleges of osteopathic medicine. From my perspective, given the projected surplus of physicians, there is no reason to start new schools. I think the majority of people in the osteopathic world feel the same way, but there is a certain amount of opportunism involved here. There is also the historic entrepreneurial tendency that we find everywhere in the academic world. The four new medical schools will enroll a total of 240 to 400 students, resulting in an annual increase in the number of U.S. medical school graduates of about 2 percent. So in some sense, this is a perturbation, but I think building new schools sends the wrong message in these times.

Some people in the osteopathic world say that our institutions are graduating just the kind of physicians that the world of managed care says it needs. Douglas Wood, president of AACOM, has said that osteopathic medicine is ideally suited to serve the managed care community. Primary care concepts are introduced early in the curriculum, and students spend a significant percentage of their time with primary care physicians as role models. We are moving a substantial portion of clinical education into the ambulatory arena and have considerable numbers of faculty members who are primary care practitioners. Osteopathic medical schools emphasize community-based training, which places students where the majority of patients are seen.

So, it may seem that business as usual is where we want to be. This is not true, however. We have a real problem with the decline in osteopathic training sites for undergraduate clerkships and graduate medical education. In large part because of the closing of osteopathic hospitals, we are also seeing intensified competition with allopathic institutions for clerkships and residencies as the MD institutions try to increase the number of family practice graduates.

And the funding equation is starting to cause us trouble, especially in terms of contributed time by volunteer faculty. As I mentioned earlier, one of the reasons we can educate students at such a significantly lower cost is because DOs around the country have been contributing their time to the education of students. As physicians see their incomes decline and as they work harder for what they earn, we are hearing that they are less and less willing to contribute time. This situation will invariably drive up the cost of osteopathic education.

We also do not have a good track record in educating minority students, especially underrepresented minorities. I agree with Neal Vanselow that we need to give special attention to this area; we need to take the high road and resist all the efforts that the managed care environment is likely to press on us to pay little attention to educating minority students.

Another challenge is team education and care. A team approach to patient care seems logical and reasonable. The University of Iowa is developing programs involving physicians, nurses, dentists, and pharmacists. At the University of Osteopathic Medicine in Des Moines, we have a physical therapy program and a physician assistant program. We are looking for ways to do team education. But there is an enormous amount of conservatism on the part of the DO faculty and resistance on the part of the DO physicians on our governing board.

Finally, in a private institution like mine, it takes a lot of courage to think about altering the governance structure in order to streamline the decision-making process. I find it amazing how much my governing board of physicians wants to be involved in the tiniest of decisions and yet sometimes totally ignores decisions of great impact.

So, we know how to produce physicians in approximately the right specialist-generalist mix who distribute themselves appropriately geographically. And we know how to do it at a significantly lower cost than our sister MD-granting institutions. We have the track record for it: We have done it for a century, and we expect to continue to do it. But the evolving environment places significant challenges and problems on us. It won't be business as usual for the osteopathic medical schools, just as it won't for the allopathic schools.

Works Cited

Rezler, A.G. and S.G. Kalishman. 1989. Who goes into family medicine? *J. Fam. Pract.* 29.

Singer, A.M. 1994. *Debts and Career Plans of Osteopathic Medical Students in 1993.* Rockville, MD: American Association of Colleges of Osteopathic Medicine.

RESPONSE TO NEAL A. VANSELOW

The Challenge of Primary Care for Academic Health Centers

VINCENT A. FULGINITI

B ecause I find myself in agreement with most of what Neal Vanselow has described, my response will be mostly supplementary and will apply to the academic health center.

In the 1940s, the academic health center was a simple system. There were physicians in solo practices who rarely sent their patients to the hospital, and the hospital staff was only an inpatient facility. In 1960, physician group practices began to develop, and hospitals started to become the source of ambulatory care because of emergency rooms and outpatient development. But physician solo practices were still the primary source of care.

By 1980, we began to see additional complexity: multispecialty group practices, office buildings for physicians put up by hospitals adjacent to the facility, the development of health maintenance organizations, affiliated hospital systems with complicated interrelationships, and new products produced by the hospital that included satellite clinics and other kinds of home delivery systems. This is the situation today.

Academic health centers have been slow to respond with the necessary educational changes. Why?

First, it is because of what I call the monastery complex. Most of us in academic circles, whether we were in universities or academic health centers, have behaved as if we were monks. We had a wall around our institutions to keep the community out and the monks in. We asked the community, on bended knee and with a beggar's pot, to fund us without assuming any responsibility to respond to that community. We wanted to do our "praying" in cells. (Translate "praying" to research and internal activities.) We really did not care what happened in the community. Obviously, that mentality has to change. It has probably been our single largest impediment to change in the past decade or so.

Institutions, as monasteries, have trouble responding for a number of reasons enumerated in a recent study by the University Hospital Consortium (1995a).* For example, we have an enormous bureaucracy. Faculty, administration, boards of regents, and legislators are all involved in the decision process. We also have internal governance in some of our institutions that is absolutely inhibitory to change. Some of our institutions have twenty-six different internal governance structures, called departments. The faculty practice plan often does not represent a true group practice, but rather a billing and collection agency for the departments.

We are overspecialized. The lack of a primary care mentality is a critical factor. It is not only that we cannot do primary care and that we do not have much primary care, but that we have disdained it. Twenty years ago in the department of pediatrics at the University of Arizona, half of our students were in ambulatory practice, going out into the community to office practice. Other department heads said they were not going to have their students and residents learn about taking care of sore throats and sore knees. They said that was not what training was all about. Our academic megalomania kept our teaching within the monastery. This mentality has persisted and made it very difficult for us to accept the need to go out into the community. Our students in all the health professions and residents need to have experiences that are outside our walls.

We have poor clinical practice procedures. All of us have experienced the failure of faculty to call referring physicians, or send them follow-up letters about patients, and to pay attention to patients' needs as opposed to their own needs. Faculty in all of the institutions I've been in have had patients come at 12:00 Noon because they wanted to be sure that the patients were there at 4:00 P.M. If we run a practice like this we will die on the vine. And we are teaching students the wrong attitude when we do those kinds of things.

We are unable to take and manage risks. A lot of what we must do for our institutions involves risk, including reputational risk. By that term I mean that we fear that the physicians in the community will criticize us for

---

* Now known as the University HealthSystem Consortium.

becoming involved in primary care and for beginning to take care of groups such as our own faculty, state employees, and others. We fear that they will claim that we are competing with them because the state is supporting us. Although most of us know this is a myth, it takes a good deal of effort to dislodge a myth.

Another reason we have difficulty responding is because regents, governors, and trustees do not trust us to take financial risks. We usually must navigate an elaborate system before we can undertake some of the managed care activities that we need to engage in to remain viable.

At our institution, we tried to solve both the governance problem and the risk problem. After educating the regents at retreats and other meetings, we told them that we needed some elbow room, and they have granted it to us. We created a six-person decision-making group comprising the chancellor, the executive vice chancellor, the president and the chief operating officer of the hospital, and the president and the vice president of the faculty practice plan. We also told the faculty and department heads that this group is going to be making decisions, sometimes swiftly—sometimes in twenty-four hours—without necessarily going back to consult with them. All of the noise has not shaken out, but, so far, it is working.

The University Hospital Consortium (1995a) identified some other factors that impede change, including the wrong leaders at some institutions, a disconnect in some of our systems between a hospital and its physician groups, a lack of managed care experience, and a focus on the physician model, which is simply not the model of the future. Those of us who have more than medical schools on our campuses must find ways to represent all of the health-profession disciplines.

One of the challenges that I predict will occur in the next five years is an attack on the disconnect between our traditional values for awarding tenure and those for awarding other academic prizes. We must find a way to reward teaching and clinical care if we are going to make the necessary changes in our institutions.

Our institutions have grown dramatically since World War II. In 1950, there were eighty-six schools of medicine, about 5,200 graduates, and 7,200 full-time faculty. By 1995 there were 126 schools, more than 17,300 graduates, and 83,000 full-time faculty. What are we going to do with our faculty who are now totally mismatched with the educational and clinical imperatives that we face? It is a formidable problem for us because many of these 83,000 are tenured. If you have thirteen tenured cardiologists and you need only four, what do you do?

Dr. Vanselow alluded to the fact that private practice income has been decreasing. The University Hospital Consortium's projections show that a Midwest academic health center could earn $302 million from commercial, Medicare, Medicaid, and other sources under 1995 conditions. However, under a tightly managed care system in that area, there would be a 45 percent decrease in revenue (UHC 1995b). From casual conversations and telephone calls around the country, it is clear to me that many of us have already experienced decreases in clinical revenue of 20 to 30 percent, and in some cases more than that, particularly among specialists.

For the last two years, three of our surgical specialty departments have decided not to increase salaries because they predicted that this decrease in clinical revenues would happen. I think we are going to see more of that. Many of us have moved to a base, supplemental incentive system for paying faculty, where only the base part that comes with tenure is guaranteed. The supplement depends on clinical or research income; the incentive is a bonus and not part of permanent salary. Neither is guaranteed. More and more of us are going to conclude that it is essential to guarantee only the portion of income that we know will be there year after year.

Dr. Vanselow commented that we are not preparing students well for what they encounter in practice. The Pew Health Professions Commission (1991) did a national study in which nurses, dentists, pharmacists, and physicians were asked how well their education had prepared them for practice. When asked about cost as a factor in patient care, only 34 to 50 percent of the survey group believed they were adequately prepared. We do not, and traditionally have not, entertained patient care costs as a factor in education. In fact, we have done the opposite. We have told students, "Oh, sure. You can get daily urinalyses on somebody with Hartnup's disease; you will learn what happens to the red cells." In fact, none of those tests were necessary. But we did the tests because we said they were an educational imperative.

One of the other interesting questions from the study was, "Were you prepared to respond to the scrutiny that the legislature, society, your peers, etc., would have?" Few professionals reported that they were prepared to have people looking over their shoulders at the way they practiced. Pharmacists were the most likely to respond positively (38 percent), with positive responses by physicians and dentists dropping way down to 14 and 11 percent, respectively.

Finally, I would like to make three comments. First, multidisciplinary education is possible. There are many impediments, but I think I have found a simple solution. I told the deans of our four professional schools that their merit increases next year were contingent on their putting together an elective program in multidisciplinary education in geriatrics. They are now planning that curriculum, finding spots in the curriculum, and setting aside time for these small groups.

I feel very much the same way about primary care: It can be done. It requires a change in mentality. It requires support for primary care physicians, who will not necessarily earn their way but are essential as teachers. It requires shifting cost funds from those who can earn more to those who cannot. It means going out into the community. And it means that control is not necessarily vested in the department, department head, or dean of the school of medicine, for example. It means being a guest in a community hospital and living by its rules. Few of us have been willing to do that in the past, but we must do so in the future.

The only issue on which I disagree with Neal Vanselow is the role of schools of public health. I frankly think that much of what is taught in public health belongs in health professions education and should be an integral part of it, not separated by another wall and another monastery. My prediction is that schools of public health will move more and more toward international health, health policy, and the super issues in public health as opposed to the day-to-day preventive medicine issues that should and must be incorporated into our curricula.

Works Cited

Pew Health Professions Commission. 1991. *Healthy America: Practitioners for 2005.* Durham, NC: The Pew Health Professions Commission.

University Hospital Consortium. 1995a. Ownership, Governance, Organization, and Leadership of the Academic Health Center. Oak Brook, IL: UHC.

University Hospital Consortium. 1995b. Sizing the New Marketplace. Presentation at UHC Research Conference. January 5. Oak Brook, IL: UHC.

Measuring the Costs of Primary Care Medical Education

RUTH S. HANFT

I n the last ten to fifteen years, medical schools have begun to make several major shifts in the types and locus of undergraduate and graduate medical education. This has occurred slowly in some specialties and institutions and more rapidly in others.

The shifts result from the exhortations of three groups. Policy experts complained that medical schools and residency programs were not educating physicians for community practice. Health maintenance organizations and other managed care organizations lamented that physicians did not know how to practice in their organizations. And Members of Congress were concerned about the rapidly escalating costs of health care together with a perceived lack of universal access to health care, particularly primary care.

In response to these concerns, a number of studies were conducted on primary care education and the need for ambulatory care training, and numerous conferences were held. A major reason for the slowness in shifting the sites of training has been lack of financing, particularly through Medicare and other third-party payers. However, Congress is reluctant to change the financing of graduate medical education (GME) under Medicare without information on the costs of such training, and such cost information is generally lacking.

A study, funded by The Pew Charitable Trusts, has just begun. It seeks to determine the costs of primary care graduate medical education in the ambulatory care setting. Before discussing the study, it is instructive to review the history of graduate medical education in the United States.

History of Graduate Medical Education

Before Flexner, graduate medical education was rare. If it existed, it consisted of a preceptorship with a practicing physician. There were some teaching hospitals where some medical education took place, but they did not provide the predominant form of clinical education. Until the 1920s, many U.S. medical school graduates went abroad for specialty education, particularly to Germany and Great Britain. However, as internships began to be required for practice, they began moving into the hospital setting as the hospital evolved into the technology center and the physicians' workshop.

The Shift to Specialization

World War II and the period immediately thereafter marked the beginning of a shift from the generalist physician, primarily the general practitioner, to the specialist. A number of factors contributed to the rapid growth in the number, type, and proportion of physicians trained as specialists and to the increasingly large tertiary care hospital as the site of graduate medical education.

First, the United States began an accelerated investment in biomedical research, with ever-increasing support from the National Institutes of Health. Major technological and biological breakthroughs came as a result of these investments. Second, consumers demanded state-of-the-art medical care, and, fueled by the increasing availability of employment-based health insurance (and later by Medicare and Medicaid), access to the latest and the best health care became available to the American public. Adding to these factors was the way providers were paid, namely, cost- or charge-based reimbursement for hospitals and fee-for-service for physicians, with the fees basically set by the physicians themselves.

Until the passage of Medicare and Medicaid and the simultaneous growth of private insurance, interns and residents received meals, uniforms, and small stipends. Except in some publicly supported hospitals and state university medical school hospitals, the majority of teaching physicians were designated "geographic full time." This designation meant that they were full-time medical-school faculty who taught medical students and residents. However, they generated the bulk of their income from physician fees and sometimes received a modest stipend for teaching or supervision. Residencies based in community hospitals relied on part-time attending physicians from the community, who were enticed by the ability to hospitalize patients in a prestigious teaching hospital and a faculty appointment at a medical school. In the mid-60s, medical schools began to shift increasingly to the use of full-time salaried faculty, and this trend accelerated as Medicare payments accelerated.

Graduate medical education is accredited differently and organized differently from undergraduate medical education. It is only in the last thirty years that the majority of residencies have become affiliated with medical schools (osteopathic GME remains a field where many residencies are unaffiliated with an osteopathic school). Residencies are still approved by residency review committees on a program-by-program basis.

Start of Medicare Reimbursement

When the Medicare program was first enacted, the decision was made by Congress and through administrative regulations that education costs in hospitals were allowable costs for Medicare reimbursement. (Blue Cross plans had provided some support for graduate medical education through a similar mechanism by recognizing education costs as allowable hospital costs.) It should be remembered that nurse education programs (the diploma programs) were based in hospitals, and hospital reimbursement was the source of support for those programs.

When the Medicare program decided to recognize hospital-based education costs, the program included the direct costs of salaries and fringe benefits of residents and the teaching and supervision by physicians. It also recognized ancillary costs of space, other personnel, supplies, and so on. The retrospective, reasonable cost-based method of reimbursement under Medicare, the cost-based reimbursement of Blue Cross, and the charge-based reimbursement of commercial insurers were not only inflationary, but have had real consequences for the size and shape of medical and graduate medical education.

The flow of funds to hospitals allowed medical schools to pay for faculty who taught both graduate and undergraduate clinical students. It increased the salaries of residents to a living wage, and because the teaching physician could also bill for a personal and identifiable patient care service, it led to the development of medical school practice plans.

Members of Congress and policy analysts began to recognize some of the problems associated with the change in the character of the medical profession and the growing maldistribution between generalists and specialists more than twenty-five years ago. But the reimbursement system that was in place at least until 1983 impeded both the interest of medical school faculty in primary care and the institution's ability to support the types of training that are more congruent with generalist training.

DRG Method of Payment

In 1983, when the Medicare hospital reimbursement system was changed to payment based on a diagnostic-related group (DRG), there was explicit recognition of graduate medical education costs, and the direct pass-through and indirect medical education adjustments were developed. However, because the legislation requires that the hospital bear the salary costs of residents who provide services in an ambulatory care setting, the reimbursement remains with the hospital only.

It should be noted that reimbursement has followed the form of graduate medical education, since the majority of training takes place in the hospital, with the exception of family medicine and primary care specialty training in osteopathic medicine.

State of Primary Care Training

The DRG method of payment has had unintended consequences. Since hospital payments are fungible, hospitals can still use the funds, particularly surplus funds generated from the indirect medical education adjustment, to subsidize residencies that they believe are revenue-generating, for example, cardiology. Weighting of payment by residency type, therefore, has only a limited effect on the distribution of residencies. Furthermore, the hospital-centered reimbursement base continues to hamper the development of ambulatory care training sites.

Although these problems are well known, only modest efforts have been made to expand ambulatory care training potential. The Federal government, through Title VII, supports a limited amount of primary care training. States have provided funding to their medical schools to encourage an increase in primary care training, and foundations such as the W. K. Kellogg Foundation, The Pew Charitable Trusts, and The Robert Wood Johnson Foundation have launched special programs. However, what has brought the issue to a head is the rapid development of managed care, which despite its heavy emphasis on ambulatory care services has, with a few exceptions, neither participated in nor financed ambulatory care training (not surprising in a highly competitive market).

There is a consensus that an increase in primary care physicians and a decrease in the number of nonprimary care specialists are essential to implementation of health care reform and cost containment. One of the universally recognized barriers to accomplishing this change and to expanding the primary care pool of physicians is the current financing of graduate medical education.

Financing Problems

The problems associated with current financing are fourfold:

- Medicare finances hospital-based education, not ambulatory-based education, with minor exceptions. There is no direct financing of ambulatory-based graduate medical education in any third-party financing mechanism.
- Even with the changes made in Medicare, reimbursement of physicians' fees and the rapid movement toward discounting and capitation, the payment structure rewards primary care faculty less than faculty in other specialties. Fees continue to be skewed in favor of the nonprimary care specialties.
- The majority of medical school role models are research- and clinical specialty-oriented faculty, and this structure is reinforced by the research and patient care financing streams. There is little flexibility to shift funds toward primary care education. Research funds flow to the investigator, department, or division; practice plan funds in most institutions are overwhelmingly departmentally controlled. Nonprimary care departments, because of the fee structure, generate larger revenues than do primary care departments.
- State appropriations to medical schools have not kept up with inflation, further narrowing institutional capability to support primary care programs and ambulatory care education.

One final word about costs. We do not know the real resource costs of graduate medical education, either the hospital-based costs or the ambulatory care costs. The costs that are reimbursed are widely disparate and are distorted by numerous historic factors, such as who pays for supervision and the artifacts of hospital accounting systems. It is also not clear how much of the indirect medical education adjustment payments can actually be attributed to graduate medical education costs.

The Pew Study

Hindering the ability of Congress to change the current methods of payment and to provide Medicare support for ambulatory care training is the paucity of data on the costs of this training. To address this problem, two studies are under way. One is the study funded by The Pew Charitable Trusts, which I am heading and will describe. (The other study is by the U.S. Public Health Service through the Health Resources and Services Administration, which is being conducted by James Boex of Northeastern Ohio University. We are collaborating, although our purposes are slightly different; and our methodologies, while compatible, are not exactly the same.)

The Pew study has several purposes:

- *Explore the different models of ambulatory graduate medical education training.* These models will include HMOs, multispecialty groups that are not wholly capitated; clinics established for teaching purposes; community health centers; and preceptorships. Ten to twelve medical schools, each with several types of graduate medical education training programs in ambulatory settings, were visited in fall of 1995 and from these, five to six were to be selected for full study in early 1996.
- *Identify the costs at these sites.* We are looking at site-specific costs, not the full resource costs of a specific residency, because the purpose of the study is to address financing issues. (The Public Health Service study, by contrast, focuses on resource costs.)
- *Describe the current financing of graduate medical education for ambulatory care training.*
- *Develop models of training based on the current models and construct costs for these models in terms of resources needed to provide the education.*
- *Make recommendations on the financing of graduate medical education ambulatory care education that minimize the effect of change on teaching hospitals.*

Needless to say, this study is a formidable undertaking. There will be two advisory committees. One group will include representatives of the primary care education community, medical school deans and nonprimary care chairs, teaching hospital representatives, and representatives of HMOs and other managed care or multispecialty group practices. The second committee will include representatives from states, policy experts in health workforce issues, and private health insurance representatives.

Conceptual Issues in Identifying Costs

Costs can be looked at in a number of different ways. The 1974 Institute of Medicine methodology (IOM 1974) was a seminal effort to measure the full resource costs of medical education wherever they occurred. The current Medicare methodology measures the costs to a whole institution, of which the hospital is one site. However, if the hospital continues to pay salary costs of its off-campus residents, these costs are included in the hospital cost base. The Pew study will focus on identifying the costs to a specific site or model of graduate medical education in the primary care ambulatory setting.

RESOURCE COSTS VERSUS MARGINAL COSTS

In identifying costs, the mission of a particular institutional setting should be taken into account, particularly when the ultimate purpose of the cost measurement is to recommend financing strategies. Medicare did not focus on the mission of the site of training, but rather on identification of the costs of one of the missions. Some critics believe strongly that this approach has led to overpayment (even double payment) to either the institution, the faculty, or both. When there is a joint product, adding together the costs of each product can lead to an overstatement of total costs.

In the ambulatory care setting, the distinction as to a site's primary and secondary missions is important in determining whether to measure full resource costs at the site or marginal costs. For example, the mission of a special clinic for teaching purposes in most family medicine residencies is primarily educational, as is that of outpatient clinics established in internal medicine and pediatrics departments for teaching purposes. The mission of HMOs and community health centers, by contrast, is to provide patient care services to specific populations. In the first example, education costs are primary and patient care is a byproduct. In the second example, education is an add-on to patient care, and the educational costs are incremental or marginal to the operation.

COSTS FOR JOINT PRODUCTS

Clinical education is a joint product of instruction and patient care. It sometimes also includes a third product—research. One of the most difficult conceptual and methodological problems is separating the joint products in order to calculate their respective costs. This problem is not unique to medical education. In law, graduate education usually takes place in the law firm, where the student is called an associate and learns his or her specialty while practicing law. Pilots receive their graduate training in the cockpit as co-pilots. In the legal and airline industries, these costs are subsumed in the price of the product.

The Concept of Net Expenditures

Although Medicare reimbursement of hospitals does not offset the income generated from the joint product of education and patient care, conceptually, the payor should not pay twice. In the course of the Institute of Medicine's cost of education study, Eli Ginzberg developed the concept of net education expenditures. In a study whose ultimate purpose is to recommend policy on the financing of graduate medical education, the concept of net expenditures is useful. The net expenditures figure is derived by subtracting revenues from costs. It requires determining the revenue generated from the teaching and patient care activity and that generated from the learning and patient care activity. Some observers of graduate medical education assert that first-year residents in primary care generate add-on costs, whereas third-year residents generate more revenue than costs.

The problem with a net expenditures approach is that it will vary with the payor mix of patients. A site in a well-insured community may generate revenue, whereas a community health center site will not generate sufficient revenue without supplementation. Using net revenues as a payment method is therefore fraught with problems. However, how to achieve equity in methods of payment is not a new problem.

Methodological Issues
Measuring the costs of medical education is fraught with methodological challenges. Isolation and attribution of costs is particularly difficult.

FULL RESOURCE COSTS
In any joint product environment, isolating the costs of any one of the joint products requires dividing both human and capital costs into the component activities and products. On the human capital side, this division is usually done through activity analysis or time logs with rules for dividing simultaneous (joint product) activity. Time allocation can be either on-line or retrospective, with the second much less satisfactory and the first limited by point-in-time problems, particularly when the faculty is not teaching on a year-round basis.

Allocation of support costs also requires a parceling among activities and products. Support costs include ancillary personnel such as nurses, laboratory technicians, and secretaries; supplies; telephones; and administrative costs. Allocating indirect costs is perhaps the most difficult. However, standardized rules used in previous cost studies can be used to calculate the cost of such items as space, libraries, and maintenance.

The net expenditures calculation requires allocating revenues to a specific program or product. What revenue did the resident generate in the joint teaching and patient care activity? Is it a substitute for what the faculty would have generated, or is it in addition to what the faculty generates?

MARGINAL COSTS

Marginal costs are the incremental costs associated with adding a product to an existing major function, mission, product, or activity.

There are several ways to assess these costs:

- Compare the productivity of the teaching physician with and without students. Clinic records and time logs that include patients seen and some procedural information can be used to make this comparison. A similar determination can be made for residents.
- Use focus groups to reach a consensus on the extra patient care time needed if students of different types participate in the patient care.
- Collect data on extra costs incurred, such as the amount of time that nurses and other personnel spend on education, classroom space needed, and so on.

Again, net expenditures need to be looked at. The problem with marginal analysis is the difficulty of assigning central program costs, which may or may not be shared by the site at which the training takes place. This is a generic problem in determining site-specific costs rather than full resource costs. For example, every residency program has a program director, a central office, secretarial assistance, faculty who lecture at a central site, a recruitment program, and accounting, accreditation, and other administrative costs. If knowing the full costs is important (and it is) and marginal or site-specific costs are the only costs paid for, there will be a shortfall to the institution, even when each clinical site receives its full or marginal net costs. The policy analysis recommendations must deal with this issue and the methods for covering these costs.

DIFFERENCES IN SPECIALTIES AND YEARS OF TRAINING

Different specialties have different training modalities and residency review requirements. Generalizing from one specialty to another masks important differences in costs. Some specialties require more time in hospital-based education; some have tighter clinical supervision; some use nonphysician faculty such as nurse practitioners, social workers, or clinical pharmacists as educators. Some are physician-only education sites, whereas others educate students from a variety of health professions. Generalizing from a small sample of ambulatory care sites is risky.

Years of training will affect costs. Theoretically, the time spent by faculty declines as residents advance in skills. In addition, more senior residents teach junior residents and medical students. Some sites may teach residents in all three primary care years; others may teach only first-year or third-year residents. These differences must be captured in any study. In addition, revenue generation offsets should increase as productivity increases.

Effect of Organizational Mode

Costs will vary by organizational structure and efficiency. The organizational arrangements for primary care graduate medical education include:

- Traditional outpatient departments of hospitals.
- Primary care clinics within hospital outpatient departments, HMOs and closed group practices.
- Multispecialty group practices (which may be a mix of capitation and fee-for-service payment).
- Medical school faculty group practices used for graduate and undergraduate training.
- Special clinics set up for primary care training.
- Community health centers.
- Urban and rural preceptorships.

There may be distinct cost differences that can be attributed to the organization of a particular practice or clinic.

Conclusion

Capturing the costs of primary care education in ambulatory settings, either the full resource costs or the resource or marginal costs to the institution, is fraught with numerous conceptual, methodological, and data collection and analysis problems. Such studies generally raise as many questions as they answer and create controversy no matter what the findings. Nonetheless, information on costs is an essential first step in devising more appropriate financing mechanisms for primary care education.

Work Cited

IOM (Institute of Medicine). 1974. *Costs of Education in the Health Professions, Parts I and II.* Washington: National Academy of Sciences.

Health Workforce Policy and Planning in a University

A New Approach

LEONARD L. ROSS

T
he issue of workforce planning is one aspect of the metamorphosis of the cost, availability, quality, and delivery of health care in our country today. It is not only a key component of overall policy that must be addressed directly; it is also a part of the larger system that is influenced by and reflective of the policies of other components, such as cost and access, for example. As academic health centers reconsider types of training programs, degree offerings, curricula, numbers of health care professionals produced, and evolving new relationships among the health professions, we find ourselves responding not only to the obvious, stated external mandates, but also to a universe of new internal institutional pressures arising both to support and to challenge them. Our task is to be creative and, while acting thoughtfully and responsibly, to act quickly.

The Medical College of Pennsylvania and Hahnemann University, as part of the Allegheny Health, Education, and Research Foundation (AHERF), believes that change is more likely if a few guiding principles are adhered to:

- Policy decisions must be initiated and executed by senior management with the absolute support of the board.
- Policy adjustments must occur quickly, with faculty and student buy-in sought as an integral part of the implementation phase rather than the decision-making phase.
- Communication is a key to success. Details must be protected during the decision-making phase. Once implementation commences, however, a constant stream of pertinent information helps to reassure students and faculty as events unfold. An exception to this principle ap-

plies to the board, which must, without fail, be informed of all events before they occur.

- Support for change must be sought and gained from key leaders representing the academic constituencies, including faculty, students and alumni. The support of deans and department chairs is especially critical. The board must be unswervingly committed to the academic mission, which will guide the process of change and their perception of it.

Resistance is inevitable, most notably from faculty, who will perceive change and evolution as threatening and nonproductive. Basic science faculty, in particular, will be resistant, because adjustments in programs will necessitate workforce reductions accompanied by requirements for increased productivity. Issues of tenure and academic freedom will arise, stalling progress and sometimes preventing implementation of the best solutions.

Although change is at times difficult, achieving financial stability and a strong competitive position in the marketplace has enabled AHERF to make productive workforce decisions based on community needs.

The AHERF Model

Over the last decade, the fully integrated, multihospital, and multidisciplinary academic health care system known today as AHERF has grown and diversified in response to a variety of internal and external pressures, opportunities, needs, and challenges. AHERF consists of a primary, secondary, and tertiary hospital system situated on both sides of the Commonwealth of Pennsylvania (with more than 2,500 beds); a freestanding research institute; a neuropsychiatric institute; a substantial network of primary care providers; and a health sciences university comprising a medical school, school of health sciences and humanities, school of nursing, graduate school, and a developing school of public health.

AHERF began simply in 1885 with the founding of Allegheny General Hospital (AGH) in Pittsburgh. A tertiary care urban hospital, AGH grew and developed with the city of Pittsburgh, becoming an integral part of the community and a resource for community support and growth. By the mid-1980s, AGH and its affiliated institutes had more than 900 beds and had become a major tertiary care center in the Pittsburgh area. It had also become dangerously dependent on its residency programs, whose accreditation was dependent on an unaffiliated medical school in Pittsburgh with its own system of hospitals to support. Concern grew that the medical residency programs were at risk of being withdrawn. AGH therefore began to seek its own direct affiliation with—or better yet, acquisition of—a medical school.

While AGH was wrestling with the reality of its lack of total independence, the Medical College of Pennsylvania (MCP) was floundering in Philadelphia, a city overpopulated with medical schools. Founded in 1850 as the Female (later Women's) Medical College, MCP was the smallest of the six medical schools in both size and endowment. Although the Philadelphia region was also saturated with clinical facilities (with more than 100 hospitals in the five-county area) and MCP had emphasized development of its clinical programs in an effort to increase revenues, MCP had a marginal referral base and its research programs, particularly clinical research, were not well regarded.

In the mid-1980s, MCP's trustees began to act on the long-festering need to raise money and establish a more firm financial base so that the institution could expand its educational and research programs, thereby elevating its status in the academic community and becoming competitive in the clinical arena. The trustees directed a newly recruited president to secure an organizational affiliation that would provide financial support.

In 1987–88, MCP and AGH signed an affiliation agreement. AGH was a profitable, freestanding, tertiary care hospital seeking to secure its residency programs and provide an intellectual impetus to its research efforts. It was ready, willing, and able to provide the financial underpinning that MCP sought and to which MCP was willing to commit its intellectual capital on both the student and faculty level. Mutual need driven heavily by external forces created a stronger, more stable, unified institution, that benefitted not only MCP and AGH, but also the medical and academic community in general. The decision was initiated by the hospital's leadership, the agreement was executed by the leadership, and it was communicated, or "sold" to the constituencies by the leadership.

As MCP's educational and clinical programs were being reviewed and restructured, two needs became paramount: (1) the need to develop a strong pediatrics program and the potential difficulty of doing so in a region with two well-regarded children's hospitals; and (2) the need to establish an extensive referral base in the Delaware Valley to feed the tertiary programs at MCP.

In 1991, AHERF, then comprising MCP, AGH, and affiliated institutions, acquired a financially ailing, independent hospital system in the region north of Philadelphia. This system included three community hospitals (one subsequently closed by AHERF) and one of the two well-established regional children's hospitals. Although the system's financial structure was in need of substantial repair, the clinical programs and potential for referrals to MCP were in place. AHERF, in blending the system into its own, would provide the financial guidance and organizational skills to effectively cost-out the benefits.

Another major response of the AHERF system to internal and external pressures occurred in 1993. In that year, Hahnemann University merged into MCP, and the new entity became the Medical College of Pennsylvania and Hahnemann University. The merging of two independent medical schools had not occurred in this century. It was driven by the different needs and desires of the two institutions. As MCP expanded its referral base through its association with the acquired community hospitals and the acquisition of primary care practices, it became apparent that it lacked the preferred location, reputation, and specialty programs to fulfill the potential of its affiliates. Concurrently, Hahnemann, although needing a financial partner to shore it up after years of fiscal neglect, was a well-regarded, centrally located clinical facility that boasted, among its other credentials, a nationally recognized heart hospital with a high-volume medical and surgical practice. MCP recognized its limited ability to respond to the market it had captured (specifically, patient needs and demands), and, following the overture by Hahnemann, the two institutions moved quickly to merge. Thus MCP and the AHERF system had one less competitor, both academic and clinical, while gaining an important center-city Philadelphia location, a newer physical plant with uniquely strong clinical programs, and a private, freestanding university with established programs in allied health and nursing.

At each of the three steps, financially ailing institutions were rendered solvent, costs of care and education were reduced, and missions were expanded.

The New Paradigm

The last major step in the development of the AHERF system established the basis for the Medical College of Pennsylvania and Hahnemann University to further develop a broad health professions university encompassing the major, and in some cases, most important, newly emerging or reemerging health professions. With our new, broader structure, we are now able to study and respond to health policy issues from an integrated perspective, including:

• Total MD output.

- Community needs for newly trained or retrained MDs.
- The types and mix of MDs needed regionally and nationwide.
- Community needs for professionals in the nursing and allied health professions.
- Relationships among the health professions.
- Integration of health education with support of, and service to, the community.
- Training for public health professionals.

Although our new, expanded perspective is less than two years old, AHERF has immediately recognized and responded to a number of significant national, regional, and community needs. First, in response to the overproduction of physicians, we have reduced the size of the combined entering medical school class by 15 percent, from 300 matriculants to approximately 250 (subject to ongoing review and adjustment as national health policy and support evolve).

Second, in an effort to meet the national mandate for health care reform—including improved access, cost reduction through increased screening of specialty services, and a team approach to the provision of health care—we initiated a series of significant curriculum changes in 1993 that will expose all entering medical students to primary care as a career choice. These curriculum innovations are based on significant new community-based programs providing primary care role models in established ambulatory care practices, including opportunities for students to experience population-based medicine and health advocacy for patients. Exposure to diverse practices in family medicine, pediatrics, and general internal medicine provides the students with experience in the practical aspects of managing a day-to-day practice and understanding of the cost and care benefits of the team approach to medicine. This effort is supported by a Robert Wood Johnson Foundation Generalist Physician Initiative grant; the goal is to graduate 50 percent of our students in the primary care specialties.

Realizing the growing demand for advanced practice nurses in a variety of professions, we have taken a third step to elevate and strengthen our nursing programs by establishing a separate school of nursing within the university. Nursing had been a programmatic track within our School of Health Sciences and Humanities. We are in the process of downsizing our general nursing baccalaureate and associate degree programs and establishing and expanding programs that meet more primary care needs, specifically, master's-level practitioner programs such as family health services, acute care services, and family planning. These new higher-level degree programs will enhance the career opportunities of our graduates by preparing them to function as mid-level practitioners. They also offer opportunities to further integrate the training of nurse practitioners with that of physicians in the increasing variety of training sites that are developing in both disciplines. Other specialized programs are in development.

Next, following a market analysis focusing on the need, demand for, and competitive issues driving specific allied health fields, we have expanded our physician assistant, physical therapist, and emergency medical technician programs. With less dependence on tuition revenues for educational support, other programs can be added, expanded, or deleted as community needs dictate. We have also examined the workforce needs and opportunities for biomedical scientists and begun to reduce our output of doctoral degrees in the basic sciences.

Finally, we have identified the need within our region for a community-based school of public health. The only established school of public health in the Commonwealth of Pennsylvania is in Pittsburgh, and it is primarily devoted to epidemiological and policy studies. We are establishing a new school of public health in our university that will join the existing twenty-seven schools of public health in the United States. Our new school, unlike some of the established schools, will be firmly based in the community, actively interfacing with existing community health care facilities and community projects, and utilizing these existing resources as integrated educational and research sites (Dual and Paroo 1995).

We plan to utilize an interactive, cooperative community perspective to improve service and make an important contribution to the health and livelihood of our environments.

Deterrents to Progress

As AHERF has evolved, a series of consequences has necessitated adjustments to the initial motive and in some cases, created situations and events that have hampered progress:

- Reducing the size of the entering medical school class resulted in both a financial and a programmatic need to reduce the size of the faculty. Not reappointing faculty and offering early retirement were not warmly accepted by all faculty and resulted in a general environment of distrust toward administration. Imagined challenges to tenure heightened the adversarial climate. As the consolidation process proceeds, the academic environment is restabilizing, although it is recognized that rebuilding trust will take time.

- Merging the two medical schools created the need to consolidate duplicative academic departments under a single department chair. The resultant winners versus losers attitude and merging of two distinct organizational cultures has created professional and emotional conflict that is only gradually dissipating.
- Consolidating two sets of support services (legal, information services, human resources, etc.) has resulted in workforce reduction and the expansion of the winners versus losers environment.
- Downsizing our production of medical scientists has forced us to evaluate all graduate programs, identify the less productive programs, and contract or terminate some programs. Due to ownership and fiscal issues, departments have been resistant to, and less than compatible with, the process.
- Redirecting our nursing program from the School of Health Sciences and Humanities to a separate, independent school and upgrading the degree programs from associate and baccalaureate level to master's level has necessitated hiring better qualified faculty and dismissing those less qualified.

Creating a new, consolidated university and individual school bylaws—and the associated issues of joint faculty personnel policies (including sabbatical and fringe benefits policies)—has fostered internal stress and resistance to the required educational program adjustments. Consolidating two governance boards into a single board and thus reducing representation by the individual constituencies has led to a sense of disenfranchisement among the school of nursing faculty and students. The alumni associations of two previously independent medical schools perceived the consolidation as a "loss of identity" and did not uniformly support the process.

One might argue that many of the impediments appearing during consolidation* could have been avoided, or at least diffused, if strict adherence to a democratic process were followed in all cases. In fact, the speed and initial confidentiality that many decisions required have not allowed the privilege of democratic process. It was understood at the outset, and it continues to be a basic premise of the change process, that many constituencies affected by the change perceive the process as damaging and counterproductive. To adjust to our rapidly changing environment, we have had to

---

* Consolidation refers here not only to the merging of two institutions, but also to the programmatic and service adjustments and consolidations.

make decisions at the top administrative level and then seek consensus largely after the fact.

A prime example of how the democratic process, sadly, can be counterproductive in a time of rapid and dramatic change, was the first attempt at merger in 1991. Discussions were held in an open and democratic forum, but a groundswell of opposition from the constituencies caused leadership to abort the discussions.

The second attempt at merger, in 1993, was engaged in a "surgical" manner, with all discussion and negotiations conducted behind closed doors. Only the required top management representing the institutions was involved. When announced, the consolidation was presented as a fait accompli.

In an effort to respond responsibly to appropriate internal and external influences, the task since the announcement and during continuing adjustments has been to build a strong, financially viable health professions university and supporting clinical services organization capable of meeting the health care needs of our community. As we approach this goal, once-disenchanted constituencies are beginning to realize the personal advantages of the merger. The "what can the merger do for me" phenomenon has won the day, and most faculty, students, and alumni now fully accept the consolidation.

Moving Forward

In responding to external and internal influences, we have made a number of critical organizational and managerial changes. In 1992, to allow for the acquisition of private primary care practices, the school and hospitals were legally separated into independent operational units, and the academic entity became the employer of the physicians.

Each hospital CEO, the university provost, and subsequently each dean and department chair was given full responsibility and authority for the budgets of their operating units. This alignment eliminated the traditional confusion of authority by department chairs relative to academic versus hospital functions. Where there had been two concurrent sources of support, and hence authority, functions were now aligned with the budgeting unit. Clinical practices that were acquired initially became employees of the medical college. More recently, a not-for-profit entity, Allegheny Integrated Health Group, was created under AHERF to employ the primary care practitioners.

A major revision of the academic budgeting process was undertaken to align fiscal responsibility with productivity and provide more accountable measures of results. The university engaged in a lengthy process of analyzing the functions it performs and services it provides for the direct benefit of its students versus those it provides or supports on behalf of the hospitals. Through a number of detailed studies, formulas were devised to calculate the actual cost of undergraduate medical teaching, research, and central services. These calculations led to further considerations relative to teaching and central services. Once the institution's total cost was determined, that total had to be distributed to the appropriate departments. Relative to research, the calculated cost, which resulted in a net deficit of supported activities, led us to determine the extent to which the university wanted and needed to supplement the deficit in support of the ongoing enterprise. An additional question particular to the clinical departments was raised: What are the faculty and support personnel costs associated with providing purely clinical services to the hospitals and their ancillary services (ICU, emergency medicine, resident training)? Analysis of "essential" teaching and research costs led to identification of a third cost category: costs that must be supported or "reimbursed" by the hospitals.

Defining and delineating component costs facilitated compartmentalization of responsibility, which led to an entirely new academic budget template and budget process. The basic premise was that each department should be viewed and managed as a business and, recognizing that some departments can never do so, should break even to the extent possible. Since clinical activity is now accounted for and reimbursed—and since research is supported by the university, as are educational activities—full accountability has become a reality.

With departmental operating accountability came individual professional accountability. In order to respond to external conditions—the shrinking revenue support from clinical reimbursement, government appropriations, and research grant income—and the internal mandate to become more accountable, a vehicle was implemented to help guide the faculty to more productive activity. An annual evaluation of individual goals and objectives was instituted that closely aligns professional activity with mutually agreed-on future accomplishments. Although a minority of faculty members are resistant to this process because they still think it threatens tenure, the process supports the institution's need to increase accountability and productivity. The evaluation also serves as a tool for career guidance and development. This policy model will become increasingly valid as the managed care sector continues to absorb a greater and greater portion of the market-place, replacing fee-for-service with capitated and bundled schemes.

The same shift in the ratio of fee-for-service to capitated revenue also guided us toward the need to reassess the ways we compensate and provide incentives for our faculty. Compensation theory, closely aligned with the goals and objectives process, has resulted in a new formula that will put a larger amount of compensation "at risk," and will increasingly tie a greater and greater proportion of total compensation to measurable results.

Conclusion

In the last decade and with increasing acceleration in recent years, a variety of external and internal influences has necessitated a broad response on the part of the academic health center. In some instances, AHERF's responses have been reactive, as in the case of reducing class sizes and realigning programs as external sources of financial support have shrunk. In other instances, our responses have been preemptive, more reflective of our need to maintain a competitive edge, as when we reorganized our business structure to create new opportunities, or when we redesigned our curriculum and our educational forums to more clearly match the needs of our students and the populations they will serve.

Successful implementation of our responses has been, and will continue to be, dependent on the willingness of senior leadership to make high-risk, difficult, and sometimes unconventional decisions affecting virtually all aspects of our academic lives.

The acceptance of decisions by all constituencies, especially the faculty, is dependent on the ability of leadership to communicate the positive impact of change not only on the academy, but also on each individual. The single most significant individual issue for faculty is professional respect, as exhibited by financial security. The single most significant issue for the alumni and students is the continuation of tradition.

As we go forward, the most resistant constituency will be the faculty as they fight fear of loss of academic freedom (i.e., job security) and the imagined jeopardy of tenure. As we at AHERF have seen, and as we expect to continue to demonstrate, the traditions of academic discovery, combined with a willingness to explore new horizons, will be a key to maintaining calm and a creative perspective through the transition.

The Medical College of Pennsylvania, Hahnemann University, and the entire AHERF system have taken dramatic and unprecedented steps over the last decade to respond productively to repeated waves of both internal and external influences. Our responses have been manifest in new organizational, budgetary, human resource, and programmatic adjustments, all demonstrated in our evolving workforce policies. As we go forward, we anticipate the need to make adjustments to our environment: Our mission (To Learn, To Teach, To Heal the Sick, and To Conserve Health) and our institutional culture mandate that we not only respond effectively, but that we seize every opportunity to create progressive models that we can share with our academic colleagues. In this way we can learn from each other even as we learn from our own experiences.

Work Cited

Dual, P.A. and I.F. Paroo. 1995. Urban health in the twenty-first century: The case for a community-based school of public health. In *The University in the Urban Community: Responsibilities for Public Health*, J.R. Hogness, C.J. McLaughlin, and M. Osterweis, eds. Washington: Association of Academic Health Centers.

Forecasting

Forecasts of health workforce demand, need, and supply have provided the rationales for much of the workforce policy implemented by the Federal and state governments over the last fifty years. The papers in this section explain the difficulties of making such measurements and describe their continued value and importance, despite their shortcomings, in policy decision making.

Health Workforce Modeling

Lessons From Dentistry

ELI CAPILOUTO AND ROBERT OHSFELDT

R ational workforce planning requires some type of forecast of the future supply, demand, or need. In the context of health, "supply" is generally defined in terms of the size of the available workforce, either by type of health personnel, or in terms of the total service capacity for health services. "Demand" is generally defined in terms of the level of employment for different types of personnel or the amount of utilization of various types of health care services. "Need" is generally defined in terms of workforce requirements necessary to meet the health services needs of a population, given the population's patterns of disease and the appropriate treatments for disease.

This paper provides a brief overview and analysis of three traditional methods used to construct forecasts for a health sector workforce.

Although forecasting models for a particular health profession may present some unique challenges, the general issues involved are similar across most of the health professions. We, therefore, focus first on models for dentists and dental services as a representative example. An overview of forecasting methods and how accuracy of forecasts is assessed appears next. The paper concludes with a discussion of issues that should be addressed in future health workforce forecasting models.

Forecasting Models for the Dentist Workforce

During the 1970s, in the midst of an often highly charged debate about dental workforce shortages or surpluses, significant attention was directed to the need for more precise estimates of the future supply of dental person-

---

Note: This chapter is based on a paper by Capilouto, Capilouto, and Ohsfeldt (1995).

nel and the future need and demand for dental care. The Federal government turned to elaborate econometric models. Practitioner and dental school organizations developed supply models. At the state level, where many questions regarding dental education must be decided for public schools, studies using various models were undertaken.

Much controversy has surrounded the forecasts made by these models (Goodman and Weyant 1990; Solomon 1990). At the request of the Institute of Medicine Committee on the Future of Dental Education, we critically examined these models and their forecasts to see how well they predicted the future (Capilouto, Capilouto, and Ohsfeldt 1995). Through hindsight, we assessed past forecasts to evaluate the usefulness of these models as guiding lights for today's policy makers. To our knowledge, this type of retrospective workforce assessment is absent from the policy literature.

We reviewed three categories of models:
- Supply models, which simply forecast the number of practicing dentists without explicit recognition of need, demand, or market forces.
- Workforce requirement models, which base their supply forecasts on the demand or need for dental care.
- Econometric models, which use interdependent mathematical equations to predict performance of many variables in the dental health care sector of the economy.

We confined our review and analysis to models for which forecasts have been generated and published. We did not include forecasts for specialists because the reviewed models did not make estimates for these personnel.

Supply Models

Supply forecasts of the dental workforce are conducted by three organizations: the American Association of Dental Schools (AADS), the American Dental Association (ADA), and the Bureau of Health Professions (BHPr) of the U.S. Department of Health and Human Services. Basically, the models forecast the number of dentists by predicting the number of entrants into and departures from the profession each year.* Transition probabilities determine the likelihood that someone moves from any of the possible states (e.g., student, generalist, specialist, retiree, deceased) in time i to any other

---

* The Bureau of Labor Statistics (BLS) also estimates the current number of jobs for dentists and makes job projections. The BLS uses complex macroeconomic models that generate estimates substantially greater than those generated by the three organizations discussed in this paper.

state in time $i + 1$. These determinations are made, in many cases, according to the projections from related series approach. (See section later in this paper on an overview of forecasting methods.)

For almost a decade, the ADA has utilized its Dental Manpower Model for supply projections. The model was developed by RRC, Incorporated, a consulting firm in Bryan, Texas, that specializes in mathematical modeling. The AADS also uses the RRC model for its forecasts. The BHPr supply model is similar to the RRC model in that it projects the level of dentists by estimating the number of dentists who enter and leave the profession each year (U.S. Department of Health and Human Services 1991). Regardless of the choice of model, each organization uses its own estimates of entering class sizes, dental school attrition, graduation figures, and other parameter probabilities (e.g., retirement, mortality). Periodically, these models are updated with information from the ADA's distribution of dentists census survey (ADA 1993b), which contains information on virtually all dentists in the United States.

Bases of the Supply Models

Supply model forecasts rely on assumptions about current social trends that are expected to influence the supply of both practicing dentists and dental students in future years. These trends are monitored and reflected in the forecasting models.

TRENDS IN THE SUPPLY OF DENTISTS

The unavailability of the mathematical equations and parameter estimates used in the ADA-AADS model makes it difficult to compare them to the BHPr assumptions for items such as professional ascent, retirement, and mortality. The ADA, unlike the BHPr, can use data from its census surveys to generate gender-specific estimates. Presently, about 9 percent of the dentists in the United States are female; however, this percentage should nearly double by 2005 (Iglehart 1986). In view of this trend, gender-specific estimates may become more important in calculating the supply of dentists, or, more accurately, the supply of "full-time-equivalent dentists." Early research does not reveal a significant gender gap in terms of work time. Although women dentists are more likely than their male counterparts to take a leave of absence for illness (13% versus 9%) and child rearing (33.4% versus 1.7%), a significant disparity in working hours does not exist. On average, women reported working about one week less a year and two to four fewer hours a week than their male counterparts (Dolan 1991).

Trends in Enrollees and Graduates

Perhaps of more importance to dental educators who must arrange financial and facility support based on expected numbers of students are the assumptions that supply model forecasts used to predict trends in applicants, enrollees, and graduates. The ADA, AADS, and BHPr forecasts all predicted that declines in dental school applicants and enrollees would persist until the late 1990s. Instead, beginning in 1989, applicant pools began to increase significantly. From 1989 to 1992, the applicant pool increased by 23 percent, from 4,964 applicants to 6,108. Yet over the same period, the number of enrollees increased by a little less than 100 students (ADA 1993a).

On what basis were the assumptions about continual decreases in applicants and enrollees made? On this point, the ADA, AADS, and BHPr forecasts agreed that decreases were predicated on three major factors: demographic, economic, and oral disease trends. At first glance, their assumptions seem plausible. On review, however, we must note that these assumptions were based on generalities that were seldom buttressed with referenced sources. A closer review of each of these factors follows.

Demographic assumptions. The most significant demographic trend noted in the forecasts was the secular decline in college-age students, specifically, the twenty-one to twenty-four age cohort. Although assumptions about the shrinking twenty-one to twenty-four cohort were accurate, this decline did not translate into a decline in the number of college and university students. Enrollment in the nation's institutions of higher learning has increased dramatically over the past two decades (U.S. Department of Education 1991, 1992). Between 1980 and 1990, the number of bachelor's degrees conferred increased by 12 percent (U.S. Department of Education 1991).

Underlying this growth is a dramatic increase in the number of women receiving degrees. In 1970, 43 percent of the recipients of college degrees were women; by 1990, women accounted for 53 percent of graduates (U.S. Department of Education 1991). A parallel trend occurred in the nation's dental school enrollment. From 1983 to 1993, the percentage of female dental school graduates grew from 20 percent to 33 percent (ADA 1993a). It is probably safe to assume that the recent upswing in dental school applicants would not have occurred had it not been for the trend in female college graduates. Moreover, past declines in enrollments in U.S. dental schools would have been much greater if they had not been offset by the continual rise in female enrollees.

Another demographic trend unmentioned in past forecasts and that eventually may be of significance to health professions applicant pools, is an apparent increase in the number of people delaying enrollment in schools of higher education (both undergraduate and graduate education). Growth in the number of older students has far outpaced growth in the number of younger students. Between 1980 and 1990, the enrollment of students twenty-five years of age or less grew by 7 percent, compared with 34 percent for students older than twenty-five (U.S. Department of Education 1991).

The National Center for Education Statistics expects this trend to continue. From 1990 to 1997, the center projects an increase of 16 percent in enrollments of students over twenty-five and an increase of just 5 percent for younger students. The trend in older students is manifesting itself in medical education. Over the past ten years, small but steady increases have been observed in the percentage of applicants and matriculants above age thirty-two. In 1982, 2.9 percent of applicants were older than thirty-two; in 1992, 5.2 percent were older students (AAMC 1992). A similar trend has not been observed in dental schools (AADS 1993a).

Economic assumptions. Even with ever-increasing numbers of college graduates, by 1989 the number of dental applicants had dropped by more than half from the peak levels of 15,000-plus applicants seen in the mid-1970s (AADS 1993a). All the supply forecasts we reviewed agreed that dampened prospects of an adequate return on the investment in dental education would lead to further declines, and there were many signals to support these claims. Anecdotally, it is believed that dentists actively discouraged potential applicants with complaints of declining incomes and a scarcity of jobs. These perceptions of a surplus of dentists were reinforced in the popular press (Green 1984). Stories about dental school closings and negative employment and income prospects in dentistry still appear. In June 1993, a front-page story in the *Wall Street Journal* reported that overcapacity, personal loans, and corporate cuts to dental plans were limiting job opportunities for graduating dentists. Furthermore, the article reported that young dentists were either working part-time or filling in as dental hygienists while looking for full-time jobs.

Although perceptions of potential economic returns and job security likely play a significant role in career choices, it is important to review the health services literature to determine whether such perceptions were consistent with reality, especially when applicant pools for dental school were declining rapidly. From 1972 to 1983, real (adjusted for inflation) net average earnings for dentists declined in all but three years according to the ADA (Nash 1991). In contrast, the twenty years that preceded this period were marked by continual annual increases in incomes. The ADA attributed these declines to U.S. wage-price controls, rapid inflation, and the surge of new dentists following the post-capitation grant periods to U.S. dental schools. Younger and older practitioners typically earn less than their middle-age colleagues (Mennemeyer 1977). This discrepancy is generally expected because new dentists face start-up costs and older dentists have a lighter practice load. The period in which the ADA reported declining incomes was coincident with the surge in younger dental school graduates. Hence, we are unable to tell how much of this decline in real income could be attributed to age distribution.

Moreover, trends in dentist incomes must be viewed in the context of incomes from alternative professions. It is true that dentist incomes failed to keep pace with inflation after 1972, but real incomes for other comparison groups declined as well. From 1972 to 1980, dentist real incomes declined by 1.5 percent, while real incomes for college graduates with a bachelor's degree, lawyers, and physicians declined by 1.4, 1.2, and 0.8 percent, respectively (Burnstein and Cromwell 1985). An economywide phenomenon of high and accelerating inflation rates during this period negatively affected most professions.

Perhaps more revealing than relative changes in income are the relative trends in the economic returns from an investment in education. From an economic perspective, the choice of alternative educational paths can be equated to an investment decision with costs, benefits, and a rate of return. The desirability of an investment can be assessed using the internal rate of return (Phelps 1992). Investors who use this method ask, "If I put the same amount of money into a bank account as in this investment, what rate of interest would the bank have to pay to make me indifferent to the two options?" A 1985 study made such a calculation for dentists, physicians, and lawyers and compared each case with the alternative of going to work directly after college graduation (Burnstein and Cromwell 1985). The study made adjustments for tuition costs, wages received during training, and average hours worked during the years following training. Dentists showed consistent internal rates of return of approximately 75 percent over the thirteen years studied. This rate surpassed returns typically expected from other types of investments. Moreover, when adjustments were made for hours worked, the rate of return for dentists greatly surpassed not only that for lawyers but that for physicians as well. Previous work corroborated the finding of superior returns for dentists compared with physicians (Mennemeyer 1977).

The steady and high economic returns for dentists were not consistent with the notion of a dentist glut as portrayed in the popular press. Economic theory suggests that the superior economic returns would signal new entrants into the market, which in time leads to declining returns. One must ask whether an information gap existed between perceptions about dentist income potential and reality. Did perceptions of a surplus of dentists and diminishing financial rewards falsely signal the market and deter new entrants? Alternatively, on the demand side, did increases in overall dental care utilization help sustain high rates of returns (Capilouto 1991)? Without further study, one can only speculate.

Assumptions about oral disease. Most forecasts mentioned declining oral disease levels as another reason to predict downward trends in enrollees and graduates. However, none of the models attempted to integrate oral health trends into the forecast estimates explicitly and quantitatively. Certainly, translation of epidemiological data into workforce supply or requirements is difficult. Trends in oral health needs have varied. For example, tooth decay has reversed in children (U.S. Department of Health and Human Services, NIDA 1989), but the number of older dentulous adults in need of restorative and periodontal treatment is increasing (Douglass and Gammon 1985; U.S. Department of Health and Human Services, NIDA 1987). Physician workforce studies, notwithstanding the difficulties posed by a greater number of diseases and treatment options than encountered in dentistry, have used needs-based models to project requirements for physicians (Feil, Welch, and Fisher 1993). Needs-based models have been used only at the state level for dental supply forecasts. Further discussion of these forecasts follows later in this paper.

Accuracy of Forecasts of Enrollees and Graduates

The accuracy of the forecasts generated by supply models can only be determined after sufficient time has elapsed to permit comparisons with actual data. These comparisons allow researchers to judge the accuracy of the assumptions used in the models.

We assessed projections that were made for the years beginning in 1987 and continuing through 1992, the last year for which actual comparison data were available (ADA 1993a). We were limited to this period because current models of the three organizations were not used to make projections until approximately 1987.

Tables 1 and 2 illustrate the accuracy of the projections of first-year enrollees (FYE) and graduates made by the AADS, ADA, and BHPr. For nearly a decade, the ADA (1987b, 1988–91) and the BHPr (U.S. Department of Health, Education, and Welfare, BHPr, 1978, 1980b; U.S. Department of Health and Human Services 1982, 1984, 1986, 1988, 1990) have made annual and biennial projections, respectively. The AADS has issued only two reports (Solomon 1988 and AADS 1989). The 1989 AADS report provided revised enrollment projections based on 1987 ADA census data.

First-Year Enrollees

For the entire six-year period represented in table 1, the ADA overestimated the number of FYEs by 1,737, while in its two studies, the AADS underestimated the number by 624 and 2,035, respectively. The BHPr underestimated the number of FYEs by only 15 students.

What is the explanation for these differences? Although all forecasts assumed that the number of first-year enrollees would decline with each succeeding year, the ADA projections assumed larger numbers of first-year enrollees in the 1987 base year than the AADS and BHPr projections. Each forecast assumed a different rate of continuous decline, ranging from 5 percent for the AADS projections to less than 1 percent for the ADA projection. Each forecast also assumed a different rate of dental school attrition. The ADA chose the highest attrition rate, nearly 12 percent, followed by

Table 1. Actual and Predicted First-Year Enrollment in U.S. Dental Schools, 1987–92

Year	Actual Enrollment[a] (A)	First AADS Report[b] Predicted (B)	First AADS Report[b] Difference (B–A)	Second AADS Report[c] Predicted (C)	Second AADS Report[c] Difference (C–A)	ADA Report[d] Predicted (D)	ADA Report[d] Difference (D–A)	BHPr Report[e] Predicted (E)	BHPr Report[e] Difference (E–A)
1987	4,370	4,370[e]	0	–	–	4,487	117	4,300	–70
1988	4,196	4,100	–96	4,198	–2	4,455	259	4,220	24
1989	3,979	3,792	–187	4,055	263	4,413	434	4,140	161
1990	4,001	3,651	–350	3,896	–105	4,380	379	4,070	69
1991	4,047	3,422	–625	3,743	–304	4,350	303	4,000	–47
1992	4,072	3,295	–777	3,596	–476	4,317	245	3,920	–152
Total			–2,035		–624		1,737		–15

[a] AADS 1987–1992.   [b] Solomon, E. 1988.   [c] AADS 1989.   [d] ADA 1987a.
[e] U.S. Department of Health and Human Services 1988.

attrition estimates of 7.5 percent and 5 percent, respectively, in the AADS and BHPr reports.

In reality, all estimations failed to predict the modest upswing in FYEs observed from 1990 through 1992. Because the AADS reports assumed continual annual declines for first-year enrollees of 5 percent and 4 percent, wide differences exist between actual and predicted levels of enrollees in the AADS reports for this three-year period. By 1992, the second AADS report underestimated the actual class size of 4,072 students by nearly 476 (13 percent). By using only a 2.5 percent decline with each successive class and a lower base figure of FYEs in 1987, the BHPr underestimates were a third as large as those in the more recent AADS report. In every year, the ADA overestimated the number of FYEs because it assumed a high base-year figure and a low rate of continual annual declines for first-year enrollments. Even the higher attrition rate used by the ADA failed to offset the higher base-year estimates, as the total overestimate exceeded 20 percent for the five-year period.

Conclusions drawn from the data in table 1 point to a common pitfall of forecasts. Based on trends seen in the previous ten years, all three organizations assumed continual annual declines. In time, mistaken assumptions of continual declines, or even stability, result in growing discrepancies. Another example of large differences between predicted and actual enrollees that occurred when future trends did not mirror past trends can be found in the BHPr estimates of 1978 (U.S. Department of Health, Education, and Welfare, BHPr 1978). Based on a short period of stability in FYEs in the late 1970s and early 1980s, it was assumed that beginning in 1982 the number of FYEs would level off for the remainder of the decade. Instead, a continual decline occurred. As a result, in just eight years the total overestimate of FYEs by the BHPr amounted to nearly 7,500. Consequences of such an overestimate can be severe for dental educators who planned for 7,500 enrollees who never materialized.

DENTAL SCHOOL GRADUATES

The ADA (1987a) and the AADS (1987–92) both underestimated the number of total graduates in 1987–92, in a range from 673 to 1,628 (table 2). The BHPr estimates again were closest to the actual number.

Estimates of graduates are influenced by three factors: estimates of the number of students who enrolled four years earlier, trends in class sizes, and dental school attrition rates. For each of the six years represented in table 2, the differences between the estimates and the actual number of graduates

Table 2. Actual and Predicted Dental School Graduates, 1987–92

Year	Actual Enrollment[a] (A)	First AADS Report[b] Predicted (B)	First AADS Report[b] Difference (B–A)	Second AADS Report[c] Predicted (C)	Second AADS Report[c] Difference (C–A)	ADA Report[d] Predicted (D)	ADA Report[d] Difference (D–A)	BHPr Report[e] Predicted (E)	BHPr Report[e] Difference (E–A)
1987	4,744	4,747	0	–	–	4,599	–145	4,870	126
1988	4,581	4,442	–139	4,473	–108	4,266	–315	4,660	79
1989	4,312	4,099	–213	4,207	–105	4,061	–251	4,470	158
1990	4,233	3,937	–296	4,038	–195	3,694	–539	4,210	–23
1991	3,995	3,690	–305	3,900	–95	3,636	–359	3,970	–25
1992	3,918	3,413	–505	3,748	–170	3,899	–19	3,900	–18
Total			–1,458		–673		–1,628		297

[a] AADS 1987–1992. [b] Solomon, E. 1988. [c] AADS 1989. [d] ADA 1987a.
[e] U.S. Department of Health and Human Services 1988.

were small, but not necessarily because of correct assumptions. For instance, the ADA's high overestimates of enrollees were partially corrected by an incorrect assumption of high dental school attrition. The most surprising finding concerning graduates, although not entirely obvious from the data in table 2, was the influence of a large influx of foreign dental school graduates starting around 1989. These students were admitted with advanced standing into the second, third, and fourth years of dental education (ADA 1993b). From 1990 to 1992, the number of foreign dental school graduates enrolled in U.S. dental schools nearly doubled (ADA 1990, 1993a). As of 1992, nearly 900 foreign dental graduates were enrolled in thirty-five of the nation's fifty-four dental schools.*

The decision to admit graduates of foreign dental schools may be a consequence of previous projections. Dental schools threatened by falling class sizes and predictions of even more severe decreases in applicants may have sought a new pool of students from abroad. Such behavior is difficult to predict. Neither the AADS, ADA, or BHPr anticipated the influx of foreign graduates in their forecasts for 1989–92—nor do they account for foreign graduates in their present-day modeling.

---

* More than half of these students are enrolled at New York University alone, and another 21 percent are enrolled at the University of Southern California, Boston University, and the University of Pennsylvania.

Forecasts of the Supply of Dentists

The AADS, ADA, and BHPr also extend the time line of their supply models to project the number of practicing dentists in the United States (U.S. Department of Health and Human Services 1982; ADA 1987a, 1987b, 1993c). All three groups periodically revise their projections based on the ADA's census, conducted every five years. This information combined with the rather stable output of new graduates over the past ten to fifteen years produced little volatility in the projections of the number of practicing dentists through the year 2020. Projections would be affected by sharp changes in the number of dental school graduates, but even then, the overall impact on supply projections would be small, given the time it takes for these changes to greatly affect the large current stock of practicing dentists.

The AADS, ADA, and BHPr agree that the number of dentists should peak at the turn of the century and then begin to decrease. Thereafter, the impact of the influx of young dentists in the 1970s resulting from the Federally supported expansion of dental school enrollments should begin to diminish. The decline in the number of dentists, coupled with expected declining birth rates in the general population, also will mean that the dentist-population ratio should crest at 1:54 at the end of the 1990s and then decline to 1:48 by 2010 (AADS 1989).

Problems in Making Supply Forecasts

Although many contend that the supply of the health workforce is the easiest dimension to measure, this review has pointed out its difficulties and shortfalls. Even near-term projections of enrollees and graduates are fraught with pitfalls. It has been shown that wide differences between predictions and actual numbers have occurred when past trends have been used to predict future trends. When past is not prologue, these simple supply models cannot predict the future very well.

It has also been shown that certain demographic trends and economic factors may provide more illumination for assumptions about changes in applicant pools and enrollees. However, more rigorous research is needed before the additional secular trends or economic factors can be used to predict enrollees and graduates more precisely.

Even so, antecedents still do not account for the unanticipated, such as emigration of foreign dental graduates. Whether foreign dental graduates remain in the United States after graduation from U.S. dental schools is not known. However, one could safely assume that most do. A major incentive to pursue a U.S. dental degree must be to satisfy the requirement of nearly all states that a dentist graduate from a U.S. dental school before taking the dental licensure exam. Dental school motivations to admit foreign dental graduates are undocumented. Financial concerns in an environment of school closings could be posited. If this practice continues or expands and foreign dental graduates remain in the United States, the supply of U.S. dentists could be affected significantly.

Perhaps more problematic in dentist supply data is the usefulness of the outcome measure. The AADS, ADA, and BHPr models all project dentist counts that are eventually translated into dentist-population ratios. Yet what is the optimal ratio for any given geographic location? Most analysts would agree that it depends on many other factors, including the health of the population, the distribution of specialists and ancillary support, the working hours and productivity of providers, and the mobility of patients (Hemenway 1984). Moreover, it has been demonstrated that equity in provider-population ratios is not necessarily a desirable goal (Hemenway 1982). The ideal level depends on which standard—economic efficiency, health maximization, equal doctor-population ratios, or equal health status across regions—society uses as the criterion to determine workforce supply. Once the standard is agreed on, strategies to produce the desired locational pattern of providers can be determined.

Workforce Requirement Models

Although provider-population ratios can provide general information about trends in supply, their usefulness for workforce planning is limited unless one is willing to simply assume that all providers produce the same amount and mix of services and that all geographically defined populations have similar and stable service requirements. Demand-based and needs-based, demand-weighted workforce planning models have been used to overcome the deficiencies inherent in crude provider-population ratios. However, these models also have limitations.

Unlike the dental workforce supply models just discussed and the econometric models to be described later, the demand/needs models do not generate predictions against which actual data can eventually be compared. Consequently, an analysis of the accuracy of these models is not presented. Instead, focus is given to the potential use of these studies and experiences with their use.

Needs- and demand-based models are normative. They tell what should be done if society desires to guarantee its citizens access to "needed" or "demanded" health services. These approaches have been used in medicine at the national level to determine physician workforce requirements. This methodology was used in the late 1970s by the Graduate Medical Education Advisory Committee for its requirement estimates. More recently, the Bureau of Health Professions worked with the congressionally mandated Council on Graduate Medical Education to update the needs-based projection model for six physician specialties (U.S. Department of Health and Human Services 1981; Katzoff 1991). Similar national studies for dental workforce requirements have not been undertaken. A few state-level studies, however, have been conducted and serve as the basis for discussion.

Demand-Based Models

Pure demand-based models determine the amount of shortage or surplus in the dental care sector by comparing estimates of the volume of dental visits that a given population will demand and the supply of visits available from practitioners. Data for the volume of visits demanded are usually obtained from utilization estimates from national surveys. Extrapolation of these data to state or intrastate areas typically is done by making adjustments for a limited number of determinants (e.g., income, education) of utilization among the targeted population. Data on the supply of visits are based on practitioner opinion surveys that report the current level of visits supplied, the number of additional visits that could be supplied, and practitioner beliefs regarding shortage areas throughout the state. Projections of the future supply of visits combine results of the current practitioner supply capacity with estimates of the future number of dentists.

DeFriese and Barker (1982) reported that three states (Minnesota, Ohio, and Tennessee) have conducted variations of demand-based studies. In Minnesota, shortage-area counties were determined from practitioner opinion surveys. Shortage-area designation was made in two ways. The first method was the frequency-of-mention approach, which designated a region as a shortage area if five or more surveyed dentists, regardless of where they practiced, said it was one.

A major drawback to this approach is that a bias may have existed in those counties where few dentists resided and for which knowledge of the local workforce picture was not widespread. Therefore, a second approach used a ratio criterion to delineate shortage areas. Shortage-area determination was made if the ratio of the total number of shortage-area designations by all respondents to the total number of practitioner respondents in a given county exceeded one. For example, if one dentist from outside a particular county mentioned that county as a shortage area but two dentists from that county responded to the survey, the one-to-two ratio would result in the county not being designated as a shortage area. The frequency-of-mention approach identified seventeen shortage-area counties in Minnesota, whereas the ratio approach identified fourteen counties.

In Tennessee and Ohio, estimates of dentist capacity to supply visits were compared to estimates of the demand for visits (Born 1974; Clemens 1975; Engler 1975, 1979; Tiede and Born 1975a, 1975b). The estimates of demand for dental visits came from national dental care utilization data, which were adjusted for median family income and education characteristics of the respective states. Other considerations such as age and dental insurance coverage were not taken into account. Not surprisingly, the services currently utilized nearly matched the number supplied. Theoretically, this finding is as it should be. Only when the additional capacity (i.e., the number of additional visits dentists believed they could supply) was factored in, was it shown that supply exceeded demand by about 30 percent (Engler 1979).

Needs-Based, Demand-Weighted Models

Needs-based models determine workforce requirements according to the level of oral health needs in the population. According to Schonfeld (1981), four steps are necessary to estimate dental workforce requirements using the health needs approach: (1) assessment of the dental health status of the population; (2) translation of dental conditions into needs for services; (3) estimation of the time required to provide the needed services; and (4) conversion of required time into estimates of the workforce needed. Most health analysts believe that realistic workforce forecasts must be based on effective demand, not need (Reinhardt 1981). Thus, the need estimates are further weighted in consideration of patterns of consumer demand (DeFriese and Konrad 1981).

Assessment of oral health status is based on epidemiological surveys that measure dental conditions such as caries, edentulism, and periodontal disease. Because of the prohibitive costs of longitudinal surveys, cross-sectional prevalence data must be converted into incidence data to estimate the annual amount of disease needing treatment. This conversion has been done by using a synthetic cohort model, which assumes that the conditions observed in one age group will be experienced by the next-younger age group when it ages (Schonfeld 1981). Conversion of dental conditions into annual need involves a professional-consensus judgment about the type and quantity of services required to treat a particular condition within a given year. Normative professional recommendations about maintenance therapy and preventive services also are factored into the annual need estimates. Total needs are converted into treatment time requirements. Final service requirements are estimated by determining the portion of the needed services that will be "effectively demanded" according to utilization studies. Estimates of the requisite workforce to meet the service requirements ideally not only are based on the supply and distribution of dentists but include dental office practice productivity in terms of available auxiliary support.

Execution of these steps presents formidable methodological hurdles. First, it is acknowledged that estimation of treatment needs depends on the extensiveness of the epidemiological data. Although data on caries and periodontal measures usually are collected, data on other measures may not be sufficient to provide treatment estimates for various needed or demanded treatments such as orthodontic care, bridgework, endodontic treatment, cosmetic treatment, and temporomandibular therapy. Second, although national epidemiologic and treatment need surveys have been conducted, this information does not lend itself to use in small-area estimations of dental workforce requirements. Hence, costly area-specific data must be collected. Third, recent epidemiologic data have noted remarkable secular declines in dental conditions that controvert the premise that disease levels do not vary with succeeding cohorts (U.S. Department of Health and Human Services, NIDA 1987, 1989). Fourth, there are many socioeconomic and behavioral factors influencing the relation between "need" for and "utilization" of services. Studies have shown that utilization of dental services varies according to income, insurance coverage, age, and type of service (Manning et al. 1985). Again, small-area requirement estimations necessitate area-specific data on these factors.

A final, and perhaps the most significant, threat to the usefulness of the needs-based approach is the incongruence between normative judgments made by consensus panels and the practicing community over diagnosis and treatment decisions. Nuttall (1983) compared the eventual treatment of 281 patients in Britain's National Health Service with treatment recommendations made in a national dental epidemiologic survey. Within three years of the survey, three-and-a-half times as many surfaces had been filled than had been predicted on the basis of the survey. Even so, 46 percent of the restorative needs identified by the survey criteria remained unmet. Shugars and Bader (1992) showed inconsistencies in restorative treatment decisions among U.S. dentists who examined identical patients. Almost every recommendation for treatment that a patient received was not agreed to by the majority of other dentists making the same examination. Grembowski, Milgrom, and Fiset (1990a, 1990b) detected variations in restorative service rates among 200 general dentists treating homogeneous patient groups. Evidence of variations in care and incongruence with normative judgments is suggested in areas other than restorative care as well. Le Resche, Truelove, and Dworkin (1993) reported wide disagreements between general dentists and an expert panel concerning statements about the etiology, diagnosis, and treatment of temporomandibular disorders.

The North Carolina Dental Manpower Project used a needs-based, demand-weighted model to estimate the level of workforce productivity necessary to meet the need/demand of the state's citizens (DeFriese and Barker 1982). Armed with more than $400,000 in direct support plus much more assistance through in-kind contributions, the study was able to overcome many of the problems mentioned. An extensive and elaborate data collection activity provided critical information on oral disease, treatment needs by type of service, and practice productivity capacity for generalists and some specialists (Bawden and DeFriese 1981). Data from a statewide oral epidemiological survey could be used, along with data from a follow-up survey conducted as part of a workforce project to gain insights about secular changes in disease. The landmark North Carolina study developed service requirements for each of the six health service areas in the state. Service requirement estimates by county or other geographic subdivision could not be made because of limitations in data collection.

Analysts participating in the North Carolina project recommended that the measurement of consumer demand be given additional attention, since demand was not directly addressed. Based on results from other studies that examined the many determinants of dental care utilization and on consideration of the socioeconomic characteristics of population subgroups within the state, estimations of dental workforce requirements were made at several levels of anticipated demand, depending on the category of service in question. Sensitivity analyses were used to produce alternative estimates of service requirements. It was beyond the scope of these models to quantitatively account for the interdependence of socioeconomic determinants of demand and dental care market forces.

Finally, a review of this state-level analysis provided reminders that expectations and interpretation of workforce studies depend on the perspective of the interested parties (DeFriese and Barker 1983). The large unmet periodontal need prompted the North Carolina Dental Society to acknowledge to the state's citizens that a serious public health problem existed (White and Settle 1983). Proposals for public education programs stressing the need for treatment were supported by academic institutions, professional organizations, and public health departments. Even so, shortly after completion of the study, the North Carolina Dental Society approached the University of North Carolina School of Dentistry about reducing its entering class size.

Pros and Cons of the Two Models

The chief appeal of demand-based models rests in their analytical simplicity and low costs. However, they have many drawbacks (DeFriese and Barker 1982). Chief among these is the underlying assumption that the level of services being used can be equated with services needed. Recognition is not given to the oral health needs of the population. The current market, with whatever barriers to care it may hold, essentially is used to define the demand for care.

These studies reported use of simple straight-line simulations to predict changes in demand. At most, a couple of covariates of utilization were factored into the simulations. Other significant socioeconomic, behavioral, and market determinants were disregarded. Practitioner productivity also was assumed to be static. Allowances were not made for increases in office productivity as a result of technology or increased use of auxiliary personnel. Use of a "visit" as a crude measure of demand and supply did not differentiate the quantity and type of services delivered. Neither were these studies able to verify estimates of underutilized capacity from provider opinion surveys. Finally, shortage-area designations were made according to geopolitical county boundaries, which may not accurately reflect service catchment areas (Morrisey, Sloan, and Valvona 1988).

The needs-based, demand-weighted model certainly advances workforce planning beyond the facile assumptions inherent in the workforce-population ratios and the inherent limitations of the pure demand-based approach. Synthesis of the vast information collected in the North Carolina study clearly led to increasingly precise approximations of the gap between the available supply of services and the supply necessary to meet the need/demand. Even with modest assumptions about the portion of needed services that would be demanded, it was shown that present utilization of preventive and periodontal disease therapies was much lower than anticipated according to standards of care used in the study. In light of previously mentioned findings of variations in care, one could posit that the gap between the services needed and those supplied could be rooted partially in discrepancies in dentist treatment decisions.

Econometric Models

The workforce supply forecasts reviewed earlier in this paper assume that historical trends in workforce supply will prevail. Explicit recognition is not given to the effect of new factors such as population growth, changes in levels of dental insurance coverage, and fluctuations in income—all of which have been shown to effect the demand, price, and costs for dental services. Needs-based and needs-based, demand-weighted models go a step further than the basic workforce supply models by factoring in disease levels and utilization rates of the recipient population, but these models still rely heavily on historical data and do not assess the interdependent relations of the multiple factors that affect the market for dental care.

Econometric models use a system of interactive mathematical equations to represent the interrelations of various factors and to predict behavior within the market. Take, for instance, the following example of the effects of a rapid increase in the demand for dental care (Feldstein and Roehrig 1980). In the absence of a corresponding increase in the supply of dental care (e.g., training of more dentists or time-saving technological improvements), there would be an increase in the backlog of patients awaiting appointments. Prices would likely increase because dentists could increase their incomes while maintaining a desirable workload. As prices rise, dental care services would become less affordable and demand would eventually decline. Dentists could then increase productivity by employing more personnel (as long as production exceeds costs) and working longer hours. Prices should continue to increase until supply and demand equalize, at which point the incentive to change price would no longer exist and the system would reach equilibrium with stable prices. In econometric models, economic theory and empirical evidence are used to predict the consequences of this illustration.

The EMODS Model

The BHPr econometric model of the dental sector (EMODS) takes into account these relationships between supply and demand to predict such future variables as the price of dental care, utilization of services, and employment levels of auxiliaries. Interrelationships in the model factor in the demand and supply factors that influence the market for dental services.

These factors, known as exogenous variables, include the size of the population, income, and the supply of dentists. Endogenous variables are determined by the model and include price, consumption, and employment. (A discussion of econometric models, including endogenous and exogenous variables, appears separately in this paper.)

The model can be used in two ways (Feldstein and Roehrig 1980; U.S. Department of Health and Human Services 1982). The exogenous variables can be set and the endogenous variables determined. For example, based on the projections of the supply of dentists (through the BHPr supply model) and expected trends in other exogenous variables, EMODS forecasts the inflation rate for dental prices. Alternatively, EMODS has been used to determine the required number of dentists necessary to maintain a long-run, inflation-free trend in dental prices. In the latter case, the endogenous variables are set according to some desirable policy (e.g., stable prices), and the exogenous variable level necessary to meet the stated policy is determined. Examination of the model's predictive capabilities in both of these cases follows.

The validity of EMODS was tested using a historical simulation method, and the model was found to behave quite accurately for the period 1971 through 1977 (Feldstein and Roehrig 1980). However, this assessment was not made without some uncertainty. Ideally, the data used in the simulations should be separate from the actual comparison data, thereby providing a completely independent test of validity. A paucity of reliable data precluded researchers from following this approach.

Another opportunity to assess the model's validity is through retrospective examination of its forecasts. We examined the accuracy of the EMODS forecast published in the *Fifth Report to the President and Congress on the Status of Health Personnel in the United States* by comparing the forecasted estimates of dental prices and expenditures for the years 1985 through 1991 to actual data (U.S. Department of Health and Human Services 1986). We also developed a simple, single-equation "Trend" model to generate a forecast for the same period. Predictions for the "Trend" analysis were made by respective linear regressions of independent variables (dental prices and expenditures) on a variable representing the number of years since the first year of the time series. We used data from the 1974–84 time series in these regressions. We also used coefficient estimates from these regressions to estimate dental prices and expenditures for the 1986–91 *ex post* forecast period. We then compared the results of the "Trend" model analysis with the EMODS forecast and the actual data for 1985–91.

Table 3. Forecasts of Economic Activity in the Dental Sector and Actual Prices and Expenditures, 1985–91

Year	Real Price[a] (1974=100)			Real Expenditures[b] 1974=100)		
	(Y_t) EMODS Forecast	(Y_t) Trend Model Forecast	(Y_t) Actual[c]	(Y_t) EMODS Forecast	(Y_t) Trend Model Forecast	(Y_t) Actual[d]
1985	99.9	101.5	108.8	163	139	145
1986	101.0	101.6	112.8	170	143	151
1987	102.0	101.7	116.2	178	146	159
1988	103.0	101.8	119.1	187	150	166
1989	105.0	101.9	120.7	195	153	167
1990	106.0	102.0	122.2	203	156	174
1991	107.0	102.1	126.0	211	160	180
U (inequality coefficient)	0.07	0.08		0.07	0.05	
U^M bias proportion	0.95	0.89		0.95	0.87	
U^V variance proportion	0.05	0.11		0.04	0.12	
U^C covariance proportion	0.00	0.00		0.01	0.01	

Note: "Real" indicates that data are adjusted for inflation.
[a] Real price is defined as a relative real price or the ratio of the dental component of the consumer price index (CPI) to the overall level of the CPI.
[b] Real expenditures in 1974 were $7.4 billion.
[c] Consumer price index is from U.S. Department of Labor, Bureau of Labor Statistics.
[d] Data are from U.S. Health Care Financing Administration, Office of the Actuary.

Both the EMODS and the "Trend" model forecasts consistently under-estimated real prices for the 1985–91 period (table 3). The disparity with actual prices increased with time, more so for the "Trend" model forecast than for the EMODS predictions. Regarding real expenditures, EMODS forecasts for each year were always high, whereas the "Trend" forecasts were low compared with actual data. The degree of departure from actual data was slightly greater for the EMODS forecast than for the "Trend" forecast.

Statistical evaluation of the forecasts in table 3 showed that the two models performed similarly. Thiel's inequality coefficient (U) scores were in the 0.05 to 0.08 range for both prices and expenditures. These low inequality coefficient (U) scores indicate that both models simulated positive values in concert with the positive values in the actual data.

Of additional significance, however, are the statistical scores derived from disaggregating Thiel's inequality coefficient (U) into proportions of inequality.

Overview of Forecasting Methods

Quantitative methods of developing projections use models that vary from very simple models to extremely complex, multiple-equation models. It is useful to identify three general categories of models: (1) univariate techniques, (2) projections from a related series or series, and (3) econometric models.

Univariate Techniques

A univariate model projects future values of a variable based on past values of the variable. The term "univariate" emphasizes that no other variables are used. The trend in the past values of the variable is simply extrapolated to future periods. The nature of the time trend, however, may take many different forms; a particular form must be specified in the model. In some cases, the nature of the time trend may be specified by assumption to be a simple linear time trend. In other cases, a more complex, nonlinear trend may be specified in an attempt to account for patterns of change in the past values of the variable.

The key advantage of univariate methods is obvious: simplicity. Only past values of the variable of interest are needed. The principal disadvantage is the lack of behavioral content in the model. In other words, univariate models do not attempt to uncover the underlying sources of change in the variable of interest. As a result, univariate models will tend to perform poorly if there is any change in underlying factors. The lack of behavioral content in the model also limits the usefulness of univariate models for policy simulations.

Projections From a Related Series

A relatively simple alternative to a univariate model uses both past values and assumed future values of a related time series to project the future values of the variable of interest. For example, a projection of the number of active patient care physicians in the United States in any particular year (N_t) might be obtained by a mapping from related series:

$$N_t = N_{t-1} - (r + m)N_{t-1} + i\,l_{t-1} + aA_t,$$

where N_{t-1} is the number of physicians in the prior year, $(r + m)N_{t-1}$ is the number of physicians active in the prior year who retire or die, iI_{t-1} is the number of inactive or non–patient care physicians from the prior year who enter patient care, and aA_t is the number of newly licensed physicians selecting patient care. Of course, the values of I_t, A_t, r, m, i, and a must be specified in the model. In some cases, these values are obtained through estimates from past data; in other cases, they may simply be specified as an assumption of the model.

The key advantage of this method is that it may be used to illustrate the implications of changes in model components rather easily. For example, determining the quantitative impact of an increase in the rate of retirement (r) or the proclivity of new physicians to enter patient care (a) on the projected numbers of patient care physicians over time is a simple matter. This type of projection model also is much less complex and requires less data than econometric models do. However, as with the univariate model, the principal disadvantage of this type of model is its limited behavioral content. For example, while it is easy to project the impact of a change in the rate of retirement, the model does not attempt to account for any underlying behavioral causes for the change.

Econometric Models

Econometric models consist of a series of equations that define the assumed nature of interrelationships between model variables. The model's variables can be categorized as endogenous or exogenous variables. All of the dependent variables in the model's equations are endogenous variables, in that their values are determined within the model through the solution of the system of equations. An endogenous variable also may serve as an explanatory independent variable in one or more of the other equations in the model. Exogenous variables are the independent variables in the model's equations that are not endogenous (e.g., per capita income in the population). The values of the exogenous variables are not determined by the model and thus must be supplied to the model from an external source.

The parameters of the model's equations generally are obtained using econometric methods applied to existing cross-sectional or time-series data, or both. Projected future values of the exogenous variables and the estimated values of the parameters of the model's equations are used to solve the system of equations. The solution provides the predicted future values of the endogenous variables.

As with the projection method, a key issue is the determination of the future values of the exogenous variables. In some cases, univariate methods are used to extrapolate future values of an exogenous variable from its past values; in other cases, future values are simply specified as an assumption of the model. The objective in econometric models is to limit the use of nonbehavioral projection methods to projections of variables external to the health care sector (exogenous variables).

The main advantage of an econometric model is that it provides a systematic approach for taking into account interrelationships among variables when forecasting the future values of particular variables of interest, rather than examining each variable in isolation. The detailed behavioral content of econometric models also allows policy simulations to focus on the impact of changes in variables that can be directly influenced by policies.

Both the advantages and the disadvantage of econometric models relate to the level of detail they contain. It is not uncommon for econometric models to contain hundreds of equations with thousands of parameters. Extensive quantities of high-quality data are needed to estimate model parameters accurately. Because such data often are absent, econometric models often employ dubious simplifying assumptions to reduce the number of equations. In many cases, the values of some model parameters are simply specified as assumptions of the model because adequate data to estimate the parameters are lacking. The systems-of-equations approach also creates the potential for transference of errors from one equation to other equations in the model. In other words, due to the interrelationships among model variables, an error in any one of the equations in the model may affect the resulting forecasts of many endogenous variables.

The bias proportion (U^M), the variance proportion (U^S), and the covariance proportion (U^C) total 1 regardless of the value of U. For both model forecasts, the consistently large values for U^M are an indication of systematic error because (U^M) measures the extent to which the average values of the simulated and actual series deviate from each other. A U^M greater than 0.1 or 0.2 signifies a high degree of systematic error and indicates that revision of the model should be considered to determine if the systematic bias can be reduced.

The relatively low values (0.04 to 0.12) for the variance proportion (U^S) from both models are desirable and indicate little systematic difference in variance in the actual series and the simulated series. Conversely, the extremely low covariance measures (U^C) in table 3 are worrisome: They indicate that the model forecasts have little unsystematic error (the error remaining after accounting for deviations in average values and average variabilities). The low values of U^C in this case result from high values of U^M (most of the error is systematic).

Earlier, we noted that EMODS has also been used to answer relevant public policy questions. In particular, EMODS has generated estimates of the number of dentists required to prevent inflation in the dental sector. EMODS estimates of the number of dentists required to prevent inflation are similar to the actual number of U.S. dentists identified in the ADA census surveys (table 4). Nonetheless, from 1980 to 1990, real dental prices nearly doubled. Even when dental prices are standardized according to the

Table 4. EMODS Estimates of the Number of Dentists Required to Prevent Inflation in the Dental Sector and Real Prices for Selected Years, 1980–2000

Year	EMODS Estimates		Real Dental Prices[c] (1974=100)	Real Price[d] (1974=100)
	1982 Study[a]	1984 Study[b]		
1980	126,240	–	163.6	98.1
1985	138,914	142,363	237.0	108.8
1990	148,593	154,300	323.2	122.2
1995	158,946			
2000	170,021	162,200		

Note: ADA data for 1987 (ADA 1987b) show 137,914 dentists and for 1990 (ADA 1988–1991) show 150,762 dentists.

[a] U.S. Department of Health and Human Services 1982.
[b] U.S Department of Health and Human Services 1984.
[c] Real dental are prices are adjusted for inflation and presented as an index of the dental component of the consumer price index.
[d] Real price is defined as the ratio of the dental component of the consumer price index to the overall level of the consumer price index.

overall consumer price index, the last column in table 4 shows that real dental prices increased by nearly 25 percent relative to overall prices from 1980 to 1990.

Accuracy of EMODS Forecasts

The fifth report to the President and Congress states that the EMODS "forecasts should be viewed in terms of predicted trends and turning points of important variables over the forecast period, rather than a prediction of the actual values that will be realized for that year" (p. 5–14). The analysis undertaken in this paper reinforces that caveat. EMODS did accurately predict the positive direction in dental expenditures and prices; however, it underestimated prices and overestimated expenditures. Statistical evaluation of EMODS pointed to the possibility of systematic error in the model. Hence, the inverse relation of the price expenditure predictions may be attributed to the high price elasticity of –1.5 used in the model (i.e., demand for services will decrease 1.5% when price increases 1%). This price elasticity represents the upper bound of studies that have derived demand elasticities for dental care prices (Manning et al. 1985; Grembowski et al. 1988) and ADA census data on the actual number of dentists. Nonetheless, it is difficult to confirm any conjecture about EMODS forecasts because the complete list of parameter estimates and structural equations in its "black box" are not readily available.

Although EMODS did not precisely determine actual values, it revealed valuable information about performance within the market. The EMODS forecast revealed explanations for the predicted positive trends in prices. The fifth report stated that the predicted rise in prices following an actual period of flat prices would be largely attributable to a greater growth in demand relative to slower growth in supply and productivity. This explanation illustrates the model's value in providing insights about price behavior. However, EMODS inaccuracies in predicting the precise supply "requirements" necessary to maintain stable dental prices underscore its limitations as a definitive policy guide.

A major factor in EMODS deviations from actual trends must be attributed to a lack of available data. Creators and users of EMODS have long acknowledged that creativity and ingenuity are required to overcome the deficiencies in the quality and quantity of data necessary to develop sound models (Feldstein and Roehrig 1980; Hixson 1981; U.S. Department of Health, Education, and Welfare, BHPr 1980a). It is probable that the 195 interactive mathematical equations embedded in EMODS represent dental sector activity, but without supporting data the model faces constraints.

The simple, and less costly, one-equation "Trend" model performed similarly to EMODS. We do not mean to suggest that historical trends are a substitute for econometric models. Historical trends may serve as adequate predictors when there is little fluctuation in the dental care sector. Under different circumstances, such as an expansion of dental insurance coverage or a government policy of price controls, econometric models may provide greater insights.

The EMODS predictions reviewed here were made by the model as specified in the 1980s. In 1990, EMODS underwent major revisions to incorporate clinical and epidemiological developments, such as the decline in dental caries among children and the decline in edentulism among adults (U.S. Department of Health and Human Services 1992). The revision includes a new series of updated exogenous variables as well as new parameter estimates. For instance, a much lower price elasticity of –0.81 is incorporated into the model. Decisions about whether these modifications have improved EMODS forecasting ability must await enough elapsed time to permit another *ex post* forecast evaluation.

Assessing the Accuracy of Forecasts

In any particular year, past forecasts for future values of a variable appear inaccurate when compared to the actual values of the variable observed in that year—particularly as time passes and true values become known. This phenomenon is the result of at least two of the realities of forecasting. First, the forecasts themselves may influence change in the actual values of the variable in question. For example, a prominent and credible forecast of a severe shortage of a particular health professional is likely to induce entry into the profession, thereby mitigating the shortage anticipated by the forecast. Second, forecasting the future is an inherently difficult task. Since perfect foresight is not attainable, retroactive analysis can be used to compare the forecasting accuracy of one particular model to other feasible models.

The performance of an econometric forecasting model is assessed over time bounds. The value T_1 corresponds to the earliest time period, and T_2 to the most recent time period, for which data are available to be used in the econometric model (the estimation period). The model can be used to forecast the values of the endogenous variables from the last year of available data (T_2) to the present (T_3) or beyond.

To conduct an *ex post* or historical simulation, historical values of the endogenous variables in year T_1 are supplied to the model as initial conditions, and historical time-series data for the exogenous variables beginning in T_1 and ending in T_2 are used to determine values of the endogenous variables after year T_1 through T_2. Simulation of the model over a period of time for which historical data are available provides an opportunity to assess model validity by comparing simulated estimates of the endogenous variables with actual data. Ideally, the data used in the simulations should be separate from the actual comparison data, thereby providing a completely independent test of validity.

Another opportunity to assess model validity comes through retrospective examination of its forecasts. An econometric forecast is simply a simulation of the model to a time beyond the end of the estimation period (T_2). To make such a forecast, one must have estimates of all the exogenous variables for the entire forecast period. An *ex post* forecast is often used to assess the forecasting accuracy of a model. Short-term forecasts of endogenous variables are compared with actual values as new data for past time periods become available. Finally, an *ex ante* forecast extends the forecast beyond the current year. Recall, however, that the forecast itself may affect the behavior observed after T_3.

A useful statistic for the evaluation of *ex post* forecasts is Thiel's inequality coefficient (U), defined as follows (Maddala 1977):

$$U = [(1/T) \ \Sigma(Y^*_t - Y_t)^2]^{(1/2)} / \{[(1/T) \ \Sigma Y^*_t)^2]^{(1/2)} + [(1/T) \ \Sigma(Y_t)^2]^{(1/2)}\},$$

where Y^*_t is the predicted value of the endogenous variable from the econometric model, Y_t is the actual value in each period t, and T is the number of time periods. Note that $0 \le U \le 1$. If $U = 0$, the model predicts perfectly $(Y^*_t = Y_t)$, whereas $U = 1$ indicates a "perfectly bad" prediction. Further, U can be decomposed into proportions U^M, U^S, and U^C:

$$U^M = \{[(\text{mean } Y^*_t - \text{mean } Y_t)^2]/[(1/T) \ \Sigma(Y^*_t - Y_t)^2]\},$$

$$U^S = \{(\sigma^* - \sigma)^2/[(1/T) \ \Sigma \ (Y^*_t - Y_t)^2]\}, \text{ and}$$

$$U^C = \{[2(1 - \rho)\sigma^*\sigma]/[(1/T) \ \Sigma \ (Y^*_t - Y_t)^2]\},$$

where σ^* and σ are the standard deviations of Y^*_t and Y_t, respectively, and ρ is the correlation between Y^*_t and Y_t. Note that $U^M + U^S + U^C = 1$. The statistic U^M is the "bias proportion" of U and indicates systematic error in the model. Ideally, U^M should be close to zero (a U^M greater than 0.1 or 0.2 should be considered troubling). U^S is the "variance proportion" and indicates the ability of the model to replicate the variance in the actual data; it too should be small, ideally. U^C is the "covariance proportion" and indicates nonsystematic error. Ideally, most of U should be attributable to U^C (that is, U^M, $U^S \approx 0$ but $U^C \approx 1$). If either U^M or U^S is "large," the model should be examined for possible revisions that would reduce systematic errors.

Conclusion

Certain observations should be made about the reviewed literature, unanswered questions, and the art of forecasting itself.

- Many of the model results or forecasts reviewed in this paper did not undergo the scrutiny of peer review because they were published by government agencies or trade organizations. The use of proprietary models also hampered closer examination of these forecasts. We did not rigorously examine many assumptions about demographic trends and the economic attractiveness of the dental profession.

- A substantial number of foreign-born students are entering U.S. dental schools either with advanced standing or as first-year students. The effect of this phenomenon on the supply of dentists in the United States has not been evaluated.

- Although much attention has been given to the supply of dentists, this review has raised questions about *what* dentists supply. Even when the need for treatment can be firmly documented, it is difficult to estimate requisite workforce requirements realistically if variations in diagnosis and treatment decisions are widespread in the practicing community.

- This review has presented data on positive trends in dentist incomes relative to other professions and relative to overall inflation. Nonetheless, during this same period there was some evidence that the lay press painted a contrary view of a dentist glut and falling incomes. Perceptions conveyed in the popular media may be significant signals to potential applicants to dental schools. Closer and more recent examinations of the basis of the incongruence in the findings of health services research and reports by the popular media are needed.

- The reviewed forecasts gave little attention to the consequences of potential advances in technology. What promise do bacterial replacement therapy or chemotherapy hold for controlling dental diseases? How will subtraction radiography, guided tissue regeneration, and osseointegrated implants affect the utilization of dental services?

- Tension naturally exists between the practicing community and dental schools about the size of enrollments. However, the literature sheds little light on how these relationships affect decisions by dental school administrators to expand or reduce enrollments. It has been observed that enrollments of foreign dental graduates have been confined largely to private institutions. Financial exigencies likely play a role in these decisions, but one must question whether these institutions are inclined to make such decisions because they are more insulated from political pressures than state-supported institutions. These questions and relationships will become more relevant if the number of applicants continues to rise as it has since 1989.

- Regardless of the model's precision, determination of the appropriate numbers, types, and distribution of providers inherently requires value judgments that vary depending on one's perspective. For example, a government policy to train an adequate number of providers to sustain affordable health care for its citizens will invariably run contrary to the interests of the practicing community.

- These models do not lend themselves to providing answers for today's pressing policy questions regarding health care reform. For instance, what would be the effect on the demand for dental care if tax exemptions for employer-provided dental benefits were removed? What are the distributional costs for employers, employees, and government of an employer-mandated program of universal coverage for dental benefits? Econometric models permit simulations in accord with these or other policy questions. However, this review casts doubts on the reliability of the only existing econometric model that addresses the dental market.

Rational workforce planning requires the development of some mechanism for assessing the future, either by entities formally charged with a responsibility for workforce planning or by the individuals and entities involved in decentralized (market-based) planning. In this context, forecasting models are most useful if they permit simulations of the effects of policy changes and assessments of the sensitivity of model forecasts to changes in model assumptions. Ideally, the models should be constructed to give the ultimate users of the forecasts the flexibility to conduct their own policy simulations and sensitivity analyses. However, it must emphasized that there exists an unavoidable trade-off between the behavioral completeness of the model and its complexity and data requirements.

Works Cited

AADS (American Association of Dental Schools). 1987–92. Unpublished enrollment data. Washington: AADS.

———. 1989. *Manpower Project Report No. 2*. Washington: AADS Manpower Committee.

———. *Applicant Analysis—1992 Entering Class*. 1993a. Washington: AADS.

AAMC (American Association of Medical Colleges). 1992. *Trends in Medical School Applicants and Matriculants 1982-1991*. Washington: AAMC, Section for Educational Research.

ADA (American Dental Association). 1987a. *Annual Report to the American Dental Association House of Delegates—Bureau of Economic and Behavioral Research*. Chicago: ADA.

———. 1987b. *Distribution of Dentists in the United States by Region and State 1987*. Chicago: ADA.

———. 1988–1991. *Annual Reports to the ADA House of Delegates—Bureau of Economic and Behavioral Research*. 1988–1991. Chicago: ADA.

———. 1990. Supplement—*Dental School Trend Analysis*. Chicago: ADA.

———. 1993a. Supplement—*Dental School Trend Analysis 1992/93*. Chicago: ADA.

———. 1993b. Supplement—*Dental Schools Admissions 1992/93*. Chicago: ADA.

———. 1993c. *Distribution of Dentists in the United States by Region and State 1991*. Chicago: ADA.

Bawden, J.W. and G.H. DeFriese. 1981. *Planning for Dental Care on a Statewide Basis—The North Carolina Dental Manpower Project*. Chapel Hill: Dental Foundation of North Carolina.

Born, D.O. 1974. Dental manpower research in Minnesota. *Northwest Dentistry* 53.

Burnstein, P.L. and J. Cromwell. 1985. Relative incomes and rates of return for U.S. physicians. *J. Health Economics* 4.

Capilouto, E. 1991. Access to appropriate dental care. *Cur. Opin. Dent.* 1.

———, M.L. Capilouto, and R. Ohsfeldt. 1995. A review of methods used to project the future supply of dental personnel and the future demand and need for dental services. *J. Dent. Educ.* 59(1).

Clemens K.M. 1975. Dental manpower. *Ohio Dent. J.* 49(9).

DeFriese, G.H. and B.D. Barker. 1982. *Assessing Dental Manpower Requirements—Alternative Approaches for State and Local Planning* Cambridge, MA: Ballinger.

———. 1983. The status of dental manpower research. *J. Dent. Educ.* 47(11).

DeFriese, G.H. and T.R. Konrad. 1981. Estimating dental manpower requirements on a statewide basis. *J. Pub. Health Dentistry* 41(1).

Dolan, T.A. 1991. Gender trends in dental practice patterns. *J. Am. Coll. Dent.* 58(3).

Douglass, C.W. and M.D. Gammon. 1985. Implications of oral disease trends for the treatment needs of older adults. *Gerodontics* 1.

Engler, D. 1975. Dental manpower in Ohio: A question of supply and demand. *Ohio Dent. J.* 49(7).

———. 1979. The supply and demand of a dental care in Tennessee. *J. Tenn. Dent. Assoc.* 59(4).

Feil, E.C., G. Welch, and E.S. Fisher. 1993. Why estimates of physician supply and requirements disagree? *JAMA* 269.

Feldstein, P.J. and C.S. Roehrig. 1980. A national econometric forecasting model of the dental sector. *Health Serv. Res.* 15(4).

Goodman, H.S. and R.J. Weyant. 1990. Dental health personnel planning: a review of the literature. *J. Dent. Educ.* 50(1).

Green, R. 1984. What's good for America isn't necessarily good for the dentists. *Forbes* (August 13).

Grembowski, D., D. Conrad, M. Weaver, and P. Milgrom. 1988. The structure and function of dental-care markets. A review and agenda for research. *Med. Care* 26.

Grembowski, D., P. Milgrom, and L. Fiset. 1990a. Variation in dentist service rates in a homogenous population. *J. Pub. Health Dent.* 50.

———. 1990b. Factors influencing variation in dentist service rates. *J. Pub. Health Dent.* 50.

Hemenway, D. 1982. The optimal location of doctors. *N. Engl. J. Med.* 306(7).

———. 1984. *Prices and Choices.* Cambridge, MA: Ballinger.

Hixson, J.S. 1981. Long-term forecasts of economic activity in the dental sector. *J. Am. Coll. Dent.* 48(2).

Iglehart, J.K. 1986. Datawatch: Trends in health personnel. *Health Aff.* 5(4).

Katzoff, J. 1991. The needs-based approach for estimating physician specialty personnel requirements. In *Federal Forecasters Conference 1990: Proceedings*, K.S. Hamrick, ed. Report No. AGES 9109. Washington: U.S. Department of Agriculture.

Le Resche, L., E.L. Truelove, and S.F. Dworkin. 1993. Temporomandibular disorders: A survey of dentists' knowledge and beliefs. *J. Am. Dent. Assoc.* 124.

Maddala, G. 1977. *Econometrics.* New York: McGraw-Hill.

Manning, W.G., H.L. Bailit, B. Benjamin, and J.P. Newhouse. 1985. The demand for dental care: Evidence from a randomized trial in health insurance. *J. Am. Dent. Assoc.* 110.

Mennemeyer, S.T. 1977. Really great returns to medical education? *J. Human Resources* 13.

Morrisey, M.A., F.A. Sloan, and J. Valvona. 1988. Defining geographic markets for hospital care. *Law and Contemporary Problems* 51(2).

Nash, K. 1991. Will earnings continue to rise? *J. Am. Dent. Assoc.* 122.

Nuttall, N.M. 1983. Capability of a national epidemiological survey to predict general dental service treatment. *Community Dent. Oral Epidemiol.* 11.

Phelps, C. 1992. *Health Economics.* New York: Harper-Collins.

Reinhardt, U.E. 1981. The GMENAC forecast: An alternative view. *Am. J. Pub. Health* 71(10).

Schonfeld, W.H. 1981. Estimating dental treatment needs from epidemiological data. *J. Pub. Health Dent.* 41(1).

Shugars, D.A. and J.D. Bader. 1992. Appropriateness of care. *J. Am. Coll. Dent* 59(3).

Solomon, E. 1988. *Manpower Project Report No. 1.* Washington: American Association of Dental Schools.

Solomon, E.S. 1990. Errors in federal report on dental health personnel resent problems. *J. Dent. Educ.* 54(8).

Tiede, J.W. and D.O. Born. 1975a. Professional opinions in the identification of dental manpower shortage areas. *J. Am. Dent. Assoc.* 91.

———. 1975b. The dental manpower shortage area study in Minnesota. *Northwest Dentistry* 54.

U.S. Department of Education. 1991. *Digest of Education Statistics 1991.* Washington: USDOE, National Center for Education Statistics.

———. 1992. *The Condition of Education, 1992.* Washington: USDOE, National Center for Education Statistics.

U.S. Department of Health, Education, and Welfare, BHPr (Bureau of Health Professions). 1978. *Report to the President and Congress on the Status of Health Personnel in the United States.* Washington: USDHEW.

————. 1980a. *The Econometric Model of the Dental Sector: Purpose, Scope and Uses.* OMA Report No. 80-44. Washington: USDHEW.

————. 1980b. *Report to the President and Congress on the Status of Health Personnel in the United States.* Washington: USDHEW.

U.S. Department of Health and Human Services. 1981. *Report of the Graduate Medical Education National Advisory Committee to the Secretary.* Vol. 1. Hyattsville, MD: USDHHS.

————. 1982. *Third Report to the President and Congress on the Status of Health Personnel in the United States.* Washington: USDHHS.

————. 1984. *Report to the President and Congress on the Status of Health Personnel in the United States.* Vol. 2. Washington: USDHHS.

————. 1986. *Fifth Report to the President and Congress on the Status of Health Personnel in the United States.* Washington: USDHHS.

————. 1988. *Sixth Report to the President and Congress on the Status of Health Personnel in the United States.* Washington: USDHHS.

————. 1990. *Seventh Report to the President and Congress on the Status of Health Personnel in the United States.* Washington: USDHHS.

————. 1991. *Eighth Report to the President and Congress on the Status of Health Personnel in the United States.* Washington: USDHHS.

U.S. Department of Health and Human Services, Health Resources and Services Administration. 1992. *Econometric Model of the Dental Sector (EMODS): Summary of Work Performed.* Washington: USDHHS.

U.S. Department of Health and Human Services, NIDA (National Institute of Dental Research). 1987. *Oral Health of United States Adults.* Washington: USDHHS.

————. 1989. *Oral Health of United States Children.* Washington: USDHHS.

Wall Street Journal. 1993. Here's the Drill: With jobs scarce, dentists head for existing practices. (June 29) p. 1.

White, R.P. and M.B. Settle. 1983. Discussion summary: The status of dental manpower research. *J. Dent. Educ.* 47.

Extrapolating HMO Staffing to the Population at Large

Jonathan P. Weiner, Christopher J. McLaughlin, and Sandy Gamliel

Even before managed care moved into the mainstream of health care delivery in the United States, health maintenance organizations were of great interest to health workforce planners. Group- and staff-model HMOs have historically represented self-contained microcosms of the larger delivery system, with a provider network contractually committed to serving a defined consumer population. For many years, the staffing patterns in these organizations have been recognized as one of several standards on which physician requirements within the health system at large could be based (U.S. Department of Health and Human Services 1994, Wennberg et al. 1993, Weiner 1993). Similarly, workforce requirement forecasts derived from HMO staffing patterns have often been used for comparisons to workforce forecasts derived from demand-based and needs-based models.

However, the use of HMO staffing ratios to determine national requirements has been controversial. Although most analysts accept the premise that HMO staffing ratios provide a reasonable theoretical reference point, many are concerned that without a series of adjustments, these ratios may not be appropriate for extrapolation.

This paper describes an analysis that attempts to determine the adjustments needed to extrapolate current and future workforce requirements for the nation from HMO staffing requirements (Weiner 1995). The paper also compares these extrapolations with current and forecasted supply figures to determine if workforce requirements meet supply in a U.S. health system that is predominantly managed care. The paper closes by discussing some implications of this comparison and the need for further research to improve the reliability of HMO staffing extrapolations as forecasting tools.

HMO Staffing Requirements

Researchers and analysts interested in extrapolating national workforce re-quirements from HMO staffing patterns rely on published HMO provider to enrollee ratios from select sites, as well as a limited survey (n=10) done in 1992 by the Group Health Association of America (GHAA). However, a more comprehensive survey was fielded in 1994 by the GHAA (Dial et al. 1995). This later survey was mailed to all 106 GHAA staff or group model HMOs. The response rate was 55 percent.

Based on the 1994 survey, table 1 presents the staffing rates broken down separately for medium-size plans (with 45,000–100,000 enrollees) and large plans (with greater than 100,000); the median "full-time equiva-lent direct patient care" physician and nonphysician provider (NPP) ratios are those reported by the medical directors of twenty-eight plans.

In addition to surveying almost triple the number of plans reporting in the 1992 survey, the 1994 survey provides for the first time a benchmark for the NPP ratios of nurse practitioners, physician assistants, and other ad-vanced practice nurses, including nurse midwives and clinical nurse special-ists with direct patient-care roles. The staffing ratios in table 1 measure full-time equivalents (as defined by the plan) either on salary or under contract anywhere within the provider network.

Table 1 indicates that the median number of physician providers for medium-size plans is about 119 per 100,000 enrollees; the median for larger

---

Table 1. Provider to Enrollee Ratios in Staff- and Group-Model HMOs, 1994

(median FTEs per 100,000 enrollees)

	Number of Enrollees	
Physicians	**45-100,000 (12 plans)**	**> 100,000 (16 plans)**
Total MD-DOs	118.7	122.6
Primary care MD-DO	68.8	59.1
Specialty care MD-DO	49.9	63.5
Nonphysician Providers		
Nurse practitioners (NP)	15.0	14.6
Other advanced practice nurses (APN)	6.3	2.3
Physician assistants (PA)	10.6	11.2
Total APNs + PAs	31.9	28.1

Source: Dial et al. 1995.

plans is about 123 per 100,000. The smaller plans report a higher proportion of primary care physicians relative to specialists (58 percent) than the larger plans (48 percent). One interpretation is that these growing plans are in the process of staffing and have hired more primary care physicians in anticipation of new members. In addition, a possible area for undercounting in this and similar surveys are subspecialists loosely affiliated with the plan who may work on an as-needed basis; this type of undercounting might be more common in smaller plans that do not yet have a large enough enrollee base to hire or formally contract with a full complement of subspecialties. For the purpose of the modeling discussed in this paper, the staffing ratios of the larger, more established plans are used.*

The NPP provider to enrollee ratios reported by the 1994 GHAA survey represent the first time that such ratios have been reliably reported by a large cohort of group staff or plans. The reported NPP staffing ratios of about 30 per 100,000 must be taken into consideration when physician ratios are extrapolated as national requirements. In the United States overall, the NPP to population ratio is currently about one-third lower than that reported by these group and staff plans; thus, it is likely that the nonphysician provider ratios in these HMOs are more than double the ratios in the U.S. fee-for-service sector.

Improved Extrapolation Adjustments

Current HMO staffing ratios are based on systems of care that serve populations that are demographically different from the general U.S. population and thus may utilize a different mix of services. To extrapolate staffing requirements for the nation as a whole from current HMO staffing ratios, adjustments to the HMO ratios have to be made to account for demographic differences in utilization. The demographic adjustments that follow were funded by the Bureau of Health Professions and extend the work of Weiner (1994) for the Council on Graduate Medical Education in this area.

The basic methodology used to determine these adjustments was direct standardization, where HMO age- and gender-specific utilization data were applied to a population with age and gender characteristics of the entire U.S. in the three target years 1991, 2000, and 2020. Estimates of adjustments for differing use of specialty care for each age-gender category were

---

* The reader is referred to previous discussions by Weiner (1994) regarding the limitation of HMO staffing data.

extrapolated by applying 1989 U.S. specialty-specific utilization rates as reported by the U.S. National Ambulatory Medical Care Survey (U.S. Department of Health and Human Services 1992a). The methodology is described below.

Age-Gender Adjustments

Table 2 is a summary of the 1991 age-gender distribution of persons enrolled in HMOs vs. the U.S. population at large. The HMO population distribution is derived from a 1992 GHAA survey (GHAA 1993) with 157 plans responding. The U.S. data are from the U.S. Census as reported in U.S. Department of Health and Human Services (1992b).

The HMO survey reported the proportion of enrollees over the age of 65, but it did not identify the proportion over the age of 75. Because it is believed that the HMO population of elderly includes a disproportionately low percentage of persons over 75, an attempt was made to account for this expected difference. Assuming that the over-75 proportion was two-thirds of the proportion in the United States as a whole, the "known" proportion of elderly in HMOs was split into two subgroups. Since nationally about 39 percent of elderly (65+) are part of this older group, it was assumed that about 26 percent of all elderly enrolled in HMOs were 75 or over.

To determine standardized utilization rates for the HMO population,

Table 2. Age-Gender Distribution: HMO Populations and U.S. Population, 1991

| | | Percentage of Population | |
Gender	Age	HMO	U.S.
Female	<15	12.9	10.7
	15-44	27.2	23.4
	45-64	9.2	9.6
	65-74	2.6	4.4
	75 +*	1.0	3.1
Male	<15	13.4	11.2
	15-44	22.4	23.6
	45-64	8.5	8.9
	65-74	2.1	3.3
	75 +*	.7	1.8

Source: GHAA 1993; U.S Department of Health and Human Services (1992b).
*In the HMOs, the proportion of the elderly cohort (65+) assumed to be in the 75+ category is estimated to be two-thirds of the proportion among the U.S. elderly. GHAA data did not identify the 75+ category.

Table 3. Age-Gender Specific Utilization Rates in HMOs, 1991

Gender	Age	HMO Use Rates[a]	
		Ambulatory Visits[b]	Hospital Discharges[c]
Female	<15	4.4	48.7
	15-44	5.5	116.0
	45-64	7.0	97.3
	64-74	9.0	208.2
	75 +[d]	11.9	276.9
Male	<15	4.7	54.8
	15-44	3.2	42.4
	45-64	5.2	106.0
	65-74	8.6	243.8
	75 +[d]	11.4	324.3

[a] HMO utilization data are from GHAA 1992 Survey of U.S. HMOs (GHAA 1993). The hospital utilization is based on the responses from 82 plans; the ambulatory visits are based on 157 plan responses.
[b] Total ambulatory contacts per enrollee per year.
[c] Acute hospital discharges per 1,000 enrollees per year.
[d] In the HMOs, the proportion of the elderly cohort (65+) assumed to be in the 75+ category is estimated to be two-thirds of the proportion among the U.S. elderly. GHAA data did not identify the 75+ category.

the HMO 1991 use rate for total ambulatory visits (based on 1992 survey responses of 157 plans) and hospital discharges (based on the responses of 82 plans) was used. Utilization rates for the over-75 group were estimated to be 33 percent higher than those of the 65–74 group (U.S. Department of Health and Human Services 1992a). The utilization rates for each age-gender category are presented in table 3.

Based on the data in tables 2 and 3, the estimated average utilization rates for the 1991 HMO enrollees and the 1991 United States at large is presented in table 4. The data suggest that if the U.S. population, with its

Table 4. Resource Utilization Estimates: HMO Enrollees and U.S. Population, 1991

Type of Utilization	Average Utilization[a]		% Difference in Utilization
	HMO	U.S.	
Ambulatory visits (person/yr)[b]	5.11	5.43	+ 6.3
Hospital discharges (1,000 persons/yr)[b]	88.20	98.90	+12.1

[a] Calculated by a direct standardization methodology where the 1991 actual HMO utilization rates are applied to (1) the actual age-gender distribution of all 1991 HMO enrollees, and (2) the actual 1991 age-gender distribution of the U.S. population.
[b] In the HMOs, the proportion of the elderly cohort (65+) assumed to be in the 75+ category, is estimated to be two-thirds of the proportion among the U.S. elderly. GHAA data did not identify the 75+ category.

Table 5. Age-Gender Adjusted Utilization Rates in HMOs with Estimated Specialty-Specific Breakdowns, 1991

		Ambulatory Visits[a]			
		Primary	Other		
Gender[b]	Age	Care[c]	Ob-Gyn	Specialties	Total
Female	<15	3.72	.01	.67	4.40
	15-44	2.16	1.61	1.73	5.50
	45-64	3.35	.91	2.74	7.00
	65-74	4.36	.23	4.41	9.00
	75+	6.10	.12	5.68	11.90
Male	<15	3.98	0	.72	4.70
	15-44	1.92	0	1.28	3.20
	45-64	2.59	0	2.61	5.20
	65-74	4.21	0	4.39	8.60
	75+	5.90	0	5.50	11.40

[a] Physician and nonphysician ambulatory contacts per enrollee per year. Total based on GHAA 1992 Survey of U.S. HMOs, 157 plans responding (GHAA 1993). Estimated specialty distribution based on actual 1989 National Ambulatory Medical Care Survey breakdown by age-gender category.
[b] In the HMOs, the proportion of the elderly cohort (65+) assumed to be in the 75+ category is estimated to be two-thirds of the proportion among the U.S. elderly at large. GHAA data did not identify the 75+ category.
[c] Family practice-general practice, internal medicine, pediatrics.

particular age-gender distribution, used visits at the same rate as did persons enrolled in HMOs, the U.S. visit rate would be 6.3 percent higher than the use rate of 1991 HMO enrollees, and the U.S. hospitalization rate would be 12.1 percent higher. This is because HMO populations are substantially younger than the U.S. population at large.

Specialty-Specific Adjustments

To assess whether a different adjustment factor should be calculated for each specialty class, estimates were made separately for three specialty categories. This was done by starting with the overall 1991 age-gender specific visit rates reported by the HMO survey, and then applying specialty breakdowns on an age-gender, specialty-specific basis as derived from the 1989 National Ambulatory Medical Care Survey.* For each age and gender group, the percentage of all U.S. office-based visits that were to one of the three primary care specialties, ob-gyns, and all other specialists was applied to the

---

* These national specialty-specific visit ratios are based on encounters made to a random sample of U.S. office-based physicians (U.S. Department of Health and Human Services 1992a).

Table 6. Specialty-Specific Utilization by HMO Enrollees and the U.S. Population, 1991

Ambulatory Visit (person/yr)	Average Utilization[a]		% Difference in Utilization
	HMO	U.S.	
Total, Primary Care and Specialty	5.11	5.43	+ 6.3
Primary care[b]	2.86	2.98	+ 4.2
Specialty	2.25	2.45	+ 8.9
Ob-gyn	0.53	0.48	− 9.4
Other specialties	1.72	1.97	+14.5

[a] Calculated by a direct standardization methodology where the 1991 actual HMO utilization rates are applied to (1) the actual age-gender distribution of all 1991 HMO enrollees, and (2) the actual 1991 age-gender distribution of the US population. Estimated specialty distribution by age-gender based on 1989 US office-based distribution reported in the National Ambulatory Medical Care Survey. In the HMOs, the proportion of the elderly cohort (65+) assumed to be in the 75+ category is estimated to be two-thirds of the proportion among the U.S. elderly at large. GHAA data did not identify the 75+ category.
[b] Internal medicine-pediatrics, general practice-family practice.

total visit rate reported in the GHAA survey. The utilization rates that resulted from this imputation are in table 5.

Based on the imputed rates in table 5, specialty-specific visit rates were calculated for a population with age and gender characteristics of the United States at large in 1991 and for a population with the demographic characteristics of 1991 HMO enrollees (table 3). The two rates are then compared. The results in table 6 suggest that because of the demographic differences of the HMO population relative to the U.S. population, the adjustment factor for non-OB specialists is significantly higher than for primary care physicians (14.5 percent vs. 6.3 percent). This is due to the fact that elderly people make proportionately greater use of specialists vs. generalists than younger persons. And because HMO enrollees include a higher proportion of women in their childbearing years, the use of ob-gyn specialists is lower in the general population by a factor of about 9 percent. This suggests that before applying HMO staffing ratios for the ob-gyn to the nation, a downward adjustment of about 9 percent is needed.

Extrapolating to the Future
Adjustments were also developed that would be appropriate if current HMO staffing ratios were used to extrapolate requirement to the United States in the years 2000 and 2200 given the expected demographic makeup of the population in those years. Table 7 presents a breakdown of the current U.S. enrollees age-gender distribution and the forecast for the future years based

on Census Bureau predictions. To assess the effect of shifting age-gender trends, standardized adjustments were made based on current HMO use rates. Table 8 presents these adjusted rates. Applying the current HMO use rates to the year 2000 population suggests that ambulatory services would be 8 percent higher and hospital use would increase by 14.4 percent. If HMO enrollees had the demographic characteristics of the year 2020 popu-

Table 7. Age-Gender Distribution of 1991 HMO Population and U.S. Populations, 2000 and 2020

| | | | Percentage of Population | |
| | | HMO | U.S.[a] | |
Gender	Age	1991	2000	2020
Female	<15	12.9	10.6	9.7
	15-44	27.2	21.9	19.4
	45-64	9.2	11.1	12.8
	65-74	2.6	3.7	5.0
	75+[b]	1.0	3.8	4.1
Male	<15	13.4	11.1	10.2
	15-44	22.4	22.0	19.5
	45-64	8.5	10.5	12.1
	65-74	2.1	3.0	4.5
	75+[b]	0.7	2.3	2.8

Source: GHAA 1993, U.S. Bureau of Census 1993.

[a] Year 2000 population = 276,241,000; year 2020 population = 325,942,000.
[b] In the HMOs, the proportion of the elderly cohort (65+) assumed to be in the 75+ category is estimated to be two- thirds of the proportion among the U.S. elderly. GHAA data did not identify the 75+ category.

Table 8. Utilization Differences Between 1991 HMO Enrollees and U.S. Population, 2000 and 2020

| | Average Utilization[a] | | | % Difference in Utilization | |
| | HMO | U.S. | | | |
Type of Utilization	1991	2000	2020	2000	2020
Ambulatory visits (person/yr)[b]	5.11	5.52	5.77	+ 8.0	+12.9
Hospital discharges (1,000 persons/yr)[b]	88.20	100.91	108.20	+14.4	+22.7

[a] Calculated by a direct standardization methodology where the 1991 actual HMO utilization rates are applied to (1) the actual age-gender distribution of all 1991 HMO enrollees, and (2) the projected year 2000 and 2020 age-gender distributions of the U.S. population.
[b] In the HMOs, the proportion of the elderly cohort (65+) assumed to be in the 75+ category is estimated to be two-thirds of the proportion among the U.S. elderly. GHAA data did not identify the 75+ category.

lation, visit rates would increase still further to 12.9 percent and hospital discharges to 22.7 percent due to demographic changes only.

Table 9 extends the specialty specific standardization described in table 6 to the populations in the years 2000 and 2020. If HMOs enrolled populations with demographic distributions comparable to the expected U.S. distributions in each year, the primary care and specialty visit rates increase over current rates and the ob-gyn rates decrease. (The "other specialty" use rate is considerably higher than the primary care adjustment by a factor of about 3.)

Overall Demographic Adjustments

To estimate an overall demographic adjustment factor to apply to the HMO staffing ratio base, the standardized visit and discharge rates must be combined to develop an overall adjustment factor. To do this, the 1993 AMA productivity statistics were used, wherein 77 percent of U.S. office-based physician time is reported to have been spent delivering ambulatory care vs. 23 percent inpatient care (AMA 1994). Table 10 presents the final adjustment factors after the two types of service-use were combined. The final overall adjustment rates range from +7.6 percent in 1991 to +9.5 percent and +15.2 percent, respectively, in the years 2000 and 2020. This means that HMO staffing ratios per 100,000 population in each year would have to be increased by these percentages to create the U.S. ratio of required providers per 100,000 population.

Table 9. Specilaty-Specific Utilization Differences Between 1991 HMO Enrollees and U.S. Population in 2000 and 2020

	Average Utilization[a]			% Difference in Utilization	
	HMO	**U.S.**			
Ambulatory Visit (person/yr)	**1991**	**2000**	**2020**	**2000**	**2020**
Total	5.11	5.52	5.77	+ 8.0	+12.9
Primary care[b]	2.86	3.03	3.13	+ 5.9	+ 9.4
Specialty	2.25	2.49	2.64	+10.7	+17.3
Ob-gyn	.53	.46	.45	-13.2	-15.1
Other specialties	1.72	2.03	2.19	+18.0	+27.3

[a] Calculated by a direct standardization methodology where the 1991 actual HMO utilization rates are applied to (1) the actual age-gender distribution of all 1991 HMO enrollees, and (2) the projected year 2000 and 2020 age-gender distribution of the U.S. population. Estimated specialty distribution by age-gender category based on 1989 U.S. office-based distribution reported in National Ambulatory Medical Care Survey. In the HMOs, the proportion of the elderly cohort (65+) assumed to be in the 75+ category is estimated to be two-thirds of the proportion among the U.S. elderly. GHAA data did not identify the 75+ category.
[b] Internal medicine, pediatrics, general practice-family practice.

Table 10. Adjustment Rates to be Applied to HMO Staffing Ratios for Extrapolation to U.S. Population, 1991, 2000, and 2020

Specialty	1991 (%)	Year 2000 (%)	2020 (%)
Total	+7.6	+9.5	+15.2
Primary care	+6.0	+7.9	+12.5
Specialty care	+9.6	+11.5	+18.5
Ob-gyn	−4.3	−6.7	−6.2
Other specialties	+13.9	+17.1	+26.2

Note: Estimates derived from the ambulatory and hospital utilization data in tables 4, 6, and 8. All estimates assume 23% of physician time in hospital and 77% ambulatory time. All adjusters include the overall (not specialty-specific) hospital utilization adjuster and the appropriate specialty-specific ambulatory utilization adjuster.

Comparison of HMO-Based Requirement to Supply

Now that we have determined the provider requirement, assuming current HMO staffing levels and the expected demographic make-up of the U.S. population, we can compare this number to both the 1992 and forecasted (2000, 2020) supply of providers. The goal is to assess the adequacy of the available physician supply if the demographically adjusted HMO ratios are used as an overall national standard for physician requirement.

The Model

The starting point of the comparison model is the base (unadjusted) HMO staffing ratios for the sixteen large HMOs who participated in the 1994 GHAA survey (Dial et al. 1995). The adjustment factors described in this paper are used to compensate for the fact that the 1992 HMO enrollee age-gender distribution is different than the overall U.S. population in the three target years in the model.

In addition, a series of nondemographic adjustment factors with "low" and "high" range estimates are necessary (Weiner 1994, 1995). These include adjustments for out-of-plan use (both covered and uncovered) for specialists (+10 to +15%) and generalists (+5 to +10%), recognizing that out-of-plan use is more common for specialists. A selection bias/uninsured adjustment (+4 to +8%) is needed because HMO members are known to include no uninsured persons and proportionately fewer Medicaid patients. Finally, a range of productivity adjustments (-15 to - 10%)* is incorporated

---

* See Weiner (1995) for a further discussion of these adjustments.

into the model because the physicians in staff- and group-model plans see fewer patients per year than those in fee-for-service settings or IPA-model HMOs.

The base HMO staffing ratios were multiplied by both the low- and high-range nondemographic adjusters, as well as the year and specialty-specific demographic adjusters to develop estimated "high" and "low" requirement standards for generalists and specialists in each target year.

Results of the Comparison

The resulting requirements were then compared to the supply of direct patient-care, nontrainee physicians available in 1992 and the supply forecasted by the U.S. Department of Health and Human Services, Bureau of Health Professions (1994) to be available in 2000 and 2020 under three training scenarios. The scenarios differ in the number of residency slots available relative to the number of U.S. medical graduates (i.e., 140% or 110%) and the proportion of generalist trainees relative to specialists (i.e., 30:70 or 50:50).*

Figures 1 and 2 present the results of the comparison of the adjusted HMO-based physician requirements to the available supply of specialists and generalists for each of the three years under low- and high-adjustment assumptions and different training scenarios. The data suggest the following:

1. Using the adjusted HMO staffing levels as a national standard for requirement for a fully insured population for 1992 under any set of adjustment assumptions, there is a significant surplus of specialists. The supply of generalists is in approximate balance although, depending on the adjustment assumptions, there could be a 12 percent surplus or a shortage of about the same magnitude.

2. In the year 2000, there will be a surplus of specialists under any set of adjustment assumptions or training scenario. This surplus could range from a low of 142,000 specialists if training programs were to be cut back and if high adjustments were used, to an estimated surplus of 202,000 specialists, if the low adjustments were assumed and if training patterns do not change. The situation for generalists is similar to the situation modeled for the year 1992, ranging from a modest shortage to modest surplus depending on the assumptions.

3. In the year 2020, the forecast suggests that the surplus of specialists

---

* See U.S. Department of Health and Human Services (1994) for further discussion.

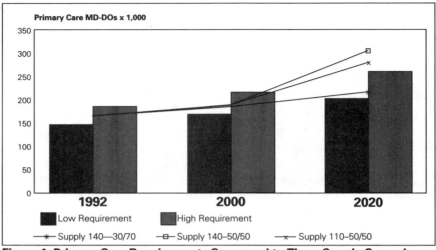

Figure 1. Primary Care Requirements Compared to Three Supply Scenarios, 1992–2020

will increase if no changes in training are put in place, and will decrease significantly under either alternative training scenario that involves an increased proportion of generalists, a downsizing of residency programs, or both. This analysis suggests that if either of the latter training scenarios occur by the year 2020, there will be an adequate supply of generalists, or possibly even a surplus. If the current 140/30:70 scenario is used, there could be a shortage of generalists equaling as much as 18 percent of the current generalist stock.

4. For all years and under any assumptions, when the generalist and specialist numbers are combined, the physician requirement for the nation based on adjusted HMO staffing ratios shows a significant overall surplus of physicians. This analysis provides further evidence that, particularly for the year 2020, the 110/50:50 training scenario will lead to the most appropriate balance of physicians. However, even this training scenario would likely lead to an overall surplus of physicians that ranges from 32 percent to 13 percent of the entire direct patient-care physician stock in that year.

IMPLICATIONS FOR PRIMARY CARE

These data do not support predictions of wholesale shortages of primary care generalist physicians in the workforce at large, although there may be

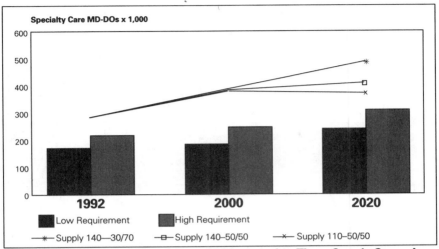

Figure 2. Specialty Care Requirements Compared to Three Supply Secnarios, 1992–2020

specific urban and rural geographic areas in tremendous need of primary care physicians. These numbers also assume that nurse practitioners and physician assistants participate in the workforce at large in rates roughly equivalent to those seen in the HMOs. But this is not the case. The participation rates are different, and shortages of nonphysician providers exist in certain markets (see the Cooney discussion in this book).

IMPLICATIONS FOR SPECIALTY SUPPLY

According to these data, even the conservative 110/50:50 scenario recommended by the Council on Graduate Medical Education (Kindig in this book) results in a significant surplus of specialists. The potential waste of human and social resources signified by this workforce composition is great. In human terms, large numbers of highly trained specialists will be unemployed or underemployed. In social terms, the public capital that went into educating these providers could have been used to improve the overall health system. For these reasons, some analysts believe it may be necessary to introduce another workforce policy lever into the training scenario. A lever recently suggested by the Pew Health Professions Commission (1995) is a reduction in the total output of American medical schools, perhaps as large as 20 percent.

The Need for Further Research

There are many unanswered questions regarding the future health system that need to be kept in mind when HMO staffing extrapolations are used for planning purposes. The resolution of two questions will be particularly important: What effect will changes in managed care organizations have on staffing patterns, both in HMOs and the system at large? Will growth of managed care and increased competition result in an economic equilibrium among the various providers of primary care?

The Changing Face of Managed Care

As mentioned earlier, most of the research on HMO staffing has taken place in a select number of large group- and staff-model HMOs such as Kaiser Permanente or the Group Health Cooperative of Puget Sound. Although they are excellent organizations, they represent only about 10 percent of the managed care market and have recently been losing some market share to more loosely structured managed care organizations. Open-panel HMOs, physician-hospital organizations, and point-of-service plans may represent a more likely trajectory for health plan growth in the future. Health-service researchers know little about staffing in these types of organizations, and it is difficult to equate numbers of providers to numbers of enrollees in plans where enrollees can seek care almost anywhere. Over time, the "escape hatch" offered by these plans may result in a different mix and ratio of providers to enrollees within plans and may also influence the composition of the fee-for-service workforce outside of managed care.

The Future of Primary Care

As competition increases in the cost-effective provision of primary care, there may be a change in the mix of primary care providers used by HMOs to meet what they deem to be the primary care requirements of their enrollees. The equilibrium that develops between nonphysician providers and allopathic and osteopathic physicians in primary care will influence workforce requirements for all of these providers.

As noted above, the current supply and participation rate of nonphysician primary care providers in HMOs is greater than in the system at large. As managed care increases its market penetration, the demand for these nonphysician providers has been increasing (see the Cooney discussion in this book). Educational programs have responded by increasing the numbers of students in training (see the Bednash and Cawley discussions in this book). At the same time, there is an increasing supply of osteopathic physicians in training (see the Marker discussion in this book) and a potential oversupply of specialty physicians that may be retrained to occupy primary care positions. Given a limited number of primary care positions, the professional makeup of the managed care primary care workforce and the processes by which HMOs and other managed care organizations determine this makeup may change.

Conclusion

The HMO-based forecasting methodology and the adjustments described in this paper provides a reasonable, rational planning model for making comparisons of the future supply of physicians with managed care-based requirements. Ignoring these projections entirely is risky. On the other hand, given our lack of certainty regarding the future, we must be careful not to follow these and other similar forecasts blindly. HMO requirement forecasts should represent one of many inputs into a multifaceted decision-making process on health workforce policy.

Works Cited

AMA (American Medical Association). 1994. Socioeconomic Characteristics of Medical Practice 1993. Chicago. AMA.

Dial, T.H., S.E. Palsbo, C. Bergsten, J.R. Gabel, and J.P. Weiner. 1995. Clinical staffing in staff and group model HMOs. Health Aff. (summer): 168-180.

GHAA (Group Health Association of America). 1993. HMO Industry Profile—1993 Edition. Washington: GHAA.

Pew Health Professions Commission. 1995. Critical Challenges: Revitalizing the Health Professions for the Twenty-first Century. San Francisco: UCSF Center for the Health Professions.

U.S. Bureau of Census. 1993. Population projections 1993 to 2050. Current Population Reports. P25-11-4. Washington: Government Printing Office.

U.S. Department of Health and Human Services. 1992a. National Ambulatory Medical Care Survey: 1989 Summary. Series 13, No. 110. Hyattsville, MD: USDHHS.

———. 1992b. Current Estimates From the National Health Interview Survey, 1991. Series 10, No. 184. Hyattsville, MD: USDHHS.

U.S. Department of Health and Human Services, Bureau of Health Professions. 1994. Patient Care Physician Supply/Requirement: Testing COGME Recommendations. Working Paper. Washington: Council on Graduate Medical Education.

Weiner, J.P. 1993. The demand for physician services in a changing health care system: A synthesis. *Med Care Rev.* 50.

———. 1994. Forecasting the effects of health reform on US physician workforce requirement: Evidence from HMO staffing patterns. *JAMA* 272.

———. 1995. Assessing Current and Future U.S. Physician Requirements Based on HMO Staffing Ratios: A Synthesis of New Sources of Data and Forecasts for the Years 2000 and 2020. Final Report. Washington: U.S. Department of Health and Human Services, Bureau of Health Professions.

Wennberg, J., D. Goodman, R. Nease, and R. Kelso. 1993. Finding equilibrium in US physician supply. *Health Aff.* 12.

Changing Values, Changing Policies

The concluding paper develops an analytical framework for examining the processes of health workforce policymaking. Using this framework, the authors make recommendations for improving and coordinating the policy processes and for moving toward a new consensus on our nation's health workforce.

A Framework for Improving the Health Workforce Policy Process

MARIAN OSTERWEIS AND CHRISTOPHER J. MCLAUGHLIN

> Make up your mind how many doctors the community needs to keep it well. Do not register more or less than this number; and let registration constitute the doctor a civil servant with a dignified living wage paid out of public funds.
>
> —George Bernard Shaw, *The Doctor's Dilemma* [1911], preface

As the papers in this volume attest, this advice from Shaw is not so easy to heed. The models for determining workforce need and demand are imperfect, and the politics surrounding health workforce issues are rampant. The health workforce policy consensus of "more of everything is better" that developed following World War II and resulted in extensive direct Federal workforce policy involvement in the 1960s and 1970s has broken down. As a result, over the last two decades, health workforce policy in the United States has been characterized by a patchwork of uncoordinated, overlapping, and often indirect policies enacted by the multiple policy makers that are responsible for workforce policy.

As we approach the twenty-first century, the desire to constrain health care costs has become the dominant factor in health workforce policy design. It overshadows the other traditional values, namely access and quality, that have guided and, we believe, should continue to guide workforce policy. We propose that the overarching health workforce policy question facing the United States should be: How do we ensure an adequate supply of health care professionals with the requisite mix of skills to provide necessary health services to all Americans in a timely, competent, and cost-effective manner?

When we talk about policy we refer to formal and informal, explicit and implicit, plans and courses of actions that influence decisions and determine actions. In health workforce policy, as in other policy arenas in America, there is a traditional separation of powers and sharing of decision-making authority among the various levels of government.

In the health workforce arena, in addition to the laws and regulations enacted by the Federal, state, and local governments, policies also emanate from a variety of other social institutions, including the health professions, educational institutions, insurers, employers, and providers in the market-place. Specific initiatives and commissions supported by private foundations, as well as demands made by labor unions and the public, also influence workforce policies dramatically. The interactions among these players have created a complex web of direct and indirect policies regarding the health workforce. In this paper, we propose a framework to help guide the development of a more rational and coherent set of workforce policies that takes account of changing values and movement toward a new consensus about health care in America.

A Framework for Health Workforce Policy

Health workforce issues are diverse and complex. Embedded in them are myriad questions about whether there is a need for more or different policies, about the rationale for particular policy actions, and about the appropriate locus of policy decision making.

Workforce issues essentially fall into three broad categories: (1) the supply, distribution, and mix of health professionals; (2) the need and demand for health services; and (3) the roles of health professionals. We recognize that any given workforce issue will transcend these three categories, but, for analytical purposes, it is helpful to clarify the questions raised and the players responsible for policymaking. For each category—supply, demand, and roles—there are many players making policy decisions based on implicit or articulated rationales or criteria, with or without valid data to justify their actions.

Therefore, we propose the following matrix (table 1) as a heuristic device to sort out the issues and players. We go on to assign key workforce issues to one of our three categories and answer the questions posed by the sections of the matrix. We then use these findings to suggest recommendations that may improve the policymaking process for the health workforce.

Table 1. Health Workforce Policy Matrix

	Who makes workforce policy?	What workforce policies are made?	What rationales or criteria are are used?	Are the supporting data adequate?
Supply and Distribution of Health Professionals				
Need and Demand for Health Services				
Roles of the Health Professions				

Policies Affecting Supply and Distribution

The most obvious health workforce policies are those that affect the supply and distribution of health professionals. Federal and state governments, the health professions, the marketplace that employs health professionals, and educational institutions are all actively involved.

Federal Government

In the period after World War II, the Federal government entered the workforce policy arena by becoming a major generator of policies influencing the supply and distribution of health professionals. Federal policies generally have fallen into three categories:

1. Indirect supply policies linked to service reimbursement policies that substantially increased the demand for health services and, hence, health professionals (such as Medicare payments for graduate medical and nursing education).

2. Direct supply policy interventions such as student assistance, construction grants, and other institutional support (codified, for example, in Titles VII and VIII of the Public Health Service Act).

3. Workforce geographic distribution programs (such as the National Health Service Corps).

In all three areas, the rationale driving Federal supply policymaking was the desire to increase access to health services.

Expenditures on direct Federal supply interventions have dwindled in the last fifteen years as concerns about workforce oversupply were voiced and as growth in the supply of health professionals came to be seen as a primary source of escalating health care costs. During this same period, Federal expenditures for the indirect supply policies linked to reimbursement programs have grown tremendously, concomitant with the growth in Federal reimbursement of health care services. As a result, most Federal workforce policy discussions are focused on these indirect supply policies. Because the largest is Medicare financing of graduate medical education, most Federal workforce interest revolves around physician supply.

Indirect supply policies are interesting examples of policies whose original rationale—namely, increasing access to services by increasing the supply of professionals—has come into question, given the cost justification required in today's political environment. There is no doubt that Medicare support of graduate medical education (and graduate nursing education) increased access to services by fueling a tremendous growth in the supply of hospital-based health providers. But critics now believe that increasing the numbers of these providers is not the best way to increase access in today's health care environment. Access can be better achieved and at a lower cost by nonhospital-based providers (see the Davidson discussion in this book). Thus these policies are being reevaluated through a different lens.

Data collection is undertaken by the Federal government to support the development, implementation, and perpetuation of all three categories of supply policies. The Bureau of Health Professions in the Health Resources and Services Administration maintains ongoing data collection processes and produces supply forecasts for each of the health professions. Data collected for the Health Professional Shortage Area (HPSA) and the Index of Medical Underservice Area (MUA) designations continue to show substantial populations without access to health services. These Federal data collection efforts have been criticized and their validity questioned for various reasons, including the fact that HPSA and MUA designations measure only physician supply and do not take into account the supply of other health professionals.

State Governments

State policymakers are active participants in supply policy through their financial support of universities, community colleges, area health education centers, research facilities, and teaching hospitals. Policies to improve the statewide geographic distribution of health professionals and to encourage practice location in underserved rural and urban areas are also common. Increasing access for their citizens, as well as spurring economic development and human capital development, are among the rationales used. As was the case with the Federal government, the states undertake data collection to assess the adequacy of the supply of health professionals and to make recommendations regarding the sizes and characteristics of educational programs.

As cost concerns loom larger in both the health and education policy arenas, state policy makers are increasingly using the state budget process to encourage changes in health workforce supply policies at the level of the educational institution; they offer incentives to change, or not to change, educational processes and production. For example, several states have recently made support for medical schools contingent on the increased production of primary care physicians (see the Combs, Horan, and Morse discussions in this book).

Roles of the Marketplace

The market for health professionals plays a critical role in workforce supply policy. Staffing decisions made by hospitals and other health service delivery sites influence the production of workforce supply, reflect the market demand for health professionals, and either support or reject the professional roles adopted by the various health professions. Thus, market-based staffing decisions cross over all three types of workforce issues and both affect and reflect the decisions made by all workforce policy makers.

For example, alterations in staffing patterns for hospital-based nurses caused by changes in the health care delivery market are having a tremendous effect on the nursing supply. Fueled by new reimbursement policies, decreased patient lengths of stay have led to dramatic reductions in the numbers of entry-level nurses employed in hospitals (see the Yordy discussion in this book). Recent data showing a reduction in baccalaureate degree nursing program enrollment may be a result of this marketplace policy shift (AACN 1996). At the same time that the demand for hospital-based nurses has been dramatically reduced, the use of advanced practice nurses in expanded primary care roles in outpatient settings has dramatically increased (see the Bednash and Yordy discussions in this book). These shifts in staffing, and hence demand for nurses, are exerting profound effects on the production and supply of nurses.

Staffing policies are traditionally based on agreed-on ratios of health care providers to numbers of population served. Cost, quality, and access have all been invoked as the criteria that justify these ratios. However, as the marketplace seeks to control costs, the natural response of provider organizations is to deviate from these accepted ratios and employ the least number of people, at the lowest level of professional training, who can still provide adequate care. Managed care organizations are reducing their provider to population ratios and changing their mix of physician and nonphysician providers. The rationale is usually not justified by outcomes data: Rather, the changes are put in place to meet or beat the competition through the process of benchmarking staffing patterns with those of comparable health plans in the area (see the Cooney discussion in this book).

Health professions education is another area where managed care organizations have proposed or initiated policies to ensure an adequate supply of appropriately trained health professionals for their organizations. Concerned that health professionals, especially physicians, being educated at academic health centers are ill-prepared to practice in managed care settings and that too few primary care doctors are being trained, some firms are creating their own educational programs. These programs include residency programs in family medicine at such nonprofit HMOs as Kaiser Permanente and the Group Health Cooperative of Puget Sound, and, most recently, at the for-profit health maintenance organization FHP International in Utah. FHP International has considered starting residency programs in disciplines other than family medicine and has even considered opening its own medical school to increase the supply of generalist physicians in southern California. Ultimately, it could not justify the costs to its board of directors (Firshein 1995). In each case, the rationale behind these education initiatives is cost control, and data for these assertions lie in managed care organization experience with the current supply in their region.

Roles of the Health Professions

The health professions, primarily through professional associations, are also significant players in workforce supply policymaking. By virtue of their financial resources and the limited knowledge that many legislators, particularly at the state level, have about health professional workforce issues, the health professions gain substantial political power in supply policy decisions.

The most important way that the health professions create direct supply policies is through their influence in state credentialing processes. In the case of dentistry, state and national associations have successfully encouraged or perpetuated licensure legislation that indirectly limits the state supply of their profession and constrains the roles and numbers of competing health professionals (such as dental hygienists) in practice (IOM 1995). The declared rationale for this activity is to maintain quality in the dental workforce, but critics, particularly economists, also see the collective self-interest of the profession at work.

Some of the health professions, again perhaps most notably dentistry, have a history of mobilizing their political power to oppose HPSA designations and convince state legislators that publicly funded dental schools should limit the sizes of their entering classes. This sort of supply policy influence has been attempted even in states where credible data were available to document unmet need and demand for dental services (see the Capilouto discussion in this book).

Self-regulation of educational programs provides the professions with an indirect method of making supply policy.* In graduate medical education, for example, residency review committee program requirements not only ensure quality in the medical specialties but also indirectly make supply policy by creating educational and institutional provisions that implicitly limit the numbers of students trained.

Professional organizations undertake quality assurance data collection and often maintain proprietary supply forecasting methodologies that provide them with the data to support their supply policymaking activities.

Roles of Educational Institutions

Colleges and universities create supply policy through their institutional authority to determine the type, character, and size of their health professional programs and schools. Private schools have more authority than state-supported institutions, but both retain some control over the production, and hence the supply, of health professionals. The recent history of dental education provides us with an important example. In the last decade, six private dental schools have closed, and virtually all schools have decreased enrollments to the point where the overall reduction in the number of students is equivalent to the closure of twenty-two schools (IOM 1995). These institutional policy decisions will affect the supply of dentists after the turn of the century—whether appropriately or inappropriately is a matter of debate.

Although dental schools have been reducing their numbers in recent years, medical schools have educated a fairly constant number of MDs. Some osteopathic schools are augmenting their number of DOs, and several

---

* The health professions are prohibited by antitrust measures from making direct policies to limit their supply. The measures described here control professional quality, but nonetheless, they limit the supply of the profession.

new schools of osteopathic medicine are planned. In spite of the general consensus that the nation has too many physicians, osteopathic medical schools justify expansion with data showing that most DOs elect careers in primary care, thereby filling an unmet need within the physician community (see the Marker discussion in this book).

All of these policies raise questions about the ethical responsibilities of educational institutions to ensure appropriate and adequate supplies of health professionals and about the differences, if any, between the obligations of public and private institutions in this regard.

Institutional supply policies are not made in a vacuum. Federal and state policies, in addition to market pressures, influence the institutional policies of academic health centers and their constituent health professional schools. For example, Federal and state direct-supply policies and third-party and Federal service reimbursement policies have encouraged growth in the production of specialized health professionals and promoted research and the development of high-technology specialty care. Driven by these incentives, academic health centers implemented internal policies that created an atmosphere where these activities prospered. Now that Federal and state legislators are proposing and implementing incentives to produce greater numbers of primary care providers, that atmosphere may no longer be appropriate.

Policies Influencing Need or Demand for Health Services

Need and demand are two different measures of the health service requirements of a given population. Need is an epidemiologically based measure of the amount of services necessary to keep a given population healthy. Demand measures a population's willingness to utilize (and often to pay) for health care services. There is no commonly agreed-on definition or definitive methodology for determining either of these measures, yet the desire for health services that these measures represent is the foundation of the demand or need for health professionals.

At the most basic and altruistic level, the purpose of all health policies, including workforce policy, is to improve health status, and hence, ultimately to reduce the need for health services. Policies designed to influence demand typically provide access to health services and provide incentives for their use. Two major categories of health policy instituted in the United States over the last forty years, reimbursement and research, have influenced the demand for health care services and thus the demand for health care professionals.

Reimbursement

By far, the most important policies influencing demand are those related to health insurance reimbursement. In recent years, the reimbursement policies once designed to improve access to care and increase demand for health services have been transformed by utilization management into policies designed to control costs by reducing and otherwise orchestrating demand. The policy makers and the policies that fit into this category are discussed below.

- At the Federal level, Medicare, Medicaid, and other social insurance policies provide increased access to third-party coverage for health services. Any changes in these Federal policies influence demand.
- At the state level, Medicaid policies and health reforms are designed to increase access to insurance coverage.
- Insurance companies and other third-party payors have greatly influenced the type and character of health professions educated in the last several decades by focusing on reimbursement of procedural care and diagnostic testing and by their unwillingness to provide coverage for evaluation and maintenance visits (primary care or preventive care).

The cost-conscious environment in the health sector has nurtured the growth of managed care and brought about substantial changes in reimbursement policies. Third-party payors have now implemented policies that explicitly try to control or manage the demand for, or utilization of, health care services by their insured populations. There is a wealth of financial data to support these policy decisions, at least in the short term; it remains to be seen how controlled utilization in the present will affect subsequent health status and hence the need for health services in the future. Consumer and provider concern over utilization management policies has forced state governments into a greater regulatory role in this area, as we saw in 1995 with state-mandated increases in postpartum hospitalization reimbursement periods in New Jersey and Maryland.

Another way that managed care organizations control workforce demand is by circumscribing the roles of physicians and simultaneously expanding the roles of other health professionals. The use of gatekeepers to control access to specialists and the use of advanced practice nurses and physician assistants for much primary care and chronic disease management are some examples.

Research

Federal and market sector biomedical research policies are primary among policies to influence demand for health services. Research leading to new pharmaceuticals, devices, and procedures can fuel demand for new products and services and lead to the creation of new types of specialty health providers, including numerous allied health personnel such as cytologists, x-ray technologists, perfusionists, and genetic counselors.

Research also has the potential to both reduce the need and demand for health services and, ultimately, for health professionals. Outpatient surgery that obviates the need for hospitalization, vaccines that prevent life-threatening diseases, and water fluoridation policies that control dental caries are some notable examples.

Policies Determining the Roles of Health Professionals

The policies that determine the roles of health professionals lie at the root of all other workforce policies. These limiting factors determine the character of the workforce supply and influence the demand for health services. The process of determining the roles of health professionals is highly political and largely controlled by the professions, but recently there has been increasing marketplace involvement in this sphere.

Federal Roles

Historically, the Federal government has played a minor role in direct policymaking related to professional roles. Although it does not specify roles and scope of practice, the Federal government does set eligibility standards for accrediting agencies, provides training grants, and legitimizes professional roles through reimbursement policies. The threat of a more explicit Federal role as was proposed in the Clinton Health Security Act, was enough to cause professional organizations to lobby against such Federal involvement.

State Roles

The regulatory policy process at the state level is the major political battleground where professional roles are determined. State laws controlling professional credentialing (licensure, certification, and registration) and scope of practice are at the heart of professional regulatory policy. The stated purpose of credentialing, scope-of-practice laws, and professional disciplinary authority is the protection of the common good—ensuring a basic level of quality in the health professional workforce. As Reinhardt points out in this book, some economists see the reason as one of self-interested supply control. Regulation ensures that the supply of health professionals is smaller than it might be otherwise, thereby ensuring demand for health services and a healthy income for health professionals.

Elsewhere in this book, Weissert describes the politics of health professional regulation as "client politics." It is an area of decision making where the benefits are concentrated on a few people or groups, and the costs are distributed widely among the population. Usually these decisions do not attract much public attention and are an opportunity for powerful interest groups to achieve highly profitable changes in law or to maintain their profitable positions without substantial opposition or public debate.

Physicians have maintained their dominant role in the health system and have been afforded the most responsibility of the health professions through their current scope-of-practice laws. As other professional interest groups have gained strength and other policy rationales, such as concerns for increased access and low-cost providers, have started to influence scope-of-practice decision making, the political process has afforded some increased roles for nonphysician providers in many states. However, this role expansion, as reflected in revised scope-of-practice acts, has not been consistent among the states or even within states. For example, nurse practitioners with identical training are sometimes granted greater prescribing and diagnostic privileges in rural underserved areas than in urban areas where they are in more direct competition with physicians (Safriet 1992).

Roles of the Marketplace

Given the largely political nature of the state regulatory policy process, it is not surprising that, as the political strength of market players in the health sector grows, the professions may lose some ground. The professions have had near total control over the role-definition process, so this reaction would bring a substantial change.

Using their political influence in the state regulatory policy process is only one way that market players are influencing the roles of the health professions. As Webb describes in this book, the power and involvement of for-profit market interests such as chain drugstores and HMOs have grown— not only at the level of collaboration and discussion but also in attempts to become involved in policymaking regarding curricula, accreditation, and other aspects of professional role definition.

Roles of Educational Institutions

Finally, educational institutions have significant influence in determining the roles of the health professionals that they train. Through the general socialization process to the profession, the types of educational programs offered, and curricular design, institutional policies can instill ethical values and encourage or discourage acceptance of new or different professional roles (see the Brock discussion in this book). In this domain, market players, particularly managed care organizations, are also trying to influence educational institutions in their curricular design.

Findings

The above examples, the papers in this collection, and other sources cited lead to a number of important findings about the current health workforce policy process.

1. The post–World War II policy consensus that "more of everything is better" has been replaced by a patchwork of policies emphasizing cost control.

2. There are many players, each making policy based on rationales designed to achieve individual goals. Not only has this led to conflicting policies, but the justifications for the same policy on the same issue sometimes vary.

3. The three traditional values underlying health policy are out of balance. Despite rhetoric to the contrary, cost concerns overshadow access and quality considerations.

4. The traditional balance among policy players has shifted. In the absence of comprehensive Federal and state policies, marketplace policies based primarily on cost concerns have dictated changes that are unprecedented in scope and speed and have influenced policymaking at all other levels.

4. Policies are typically designed to address issues related to supply, demand, or professional roles. Because the three are so interdependent, however, policies implemented in one area usually influence the others.

6. Policy decisions about each health profession are made in isolation, as if each profession exists in a vacuum. Instead, policy makers should consider how policy related to one profession affects other professions with overlapping functions and substitutable skills.*

---

* Nowhere is this more apparent than in the emerging policies to increase the supply of primary care physicians without simultaneously considering the roles and supplies of advanced practice nurses and physician assistants.

7. The clash of market values and professional values raises unprecedented questions about the appropriate locus of policy decision making, the traditional preeminence of the professions in role definition, and the wisdom of a laissez-faire marketplace.

8. Most policy is based on incomplete and often questionable data. The models for measuring need and demand, as well as those for forecasting supply, need to be strengthened. Moreover, policy is sometimes made in the absence of data. The converse also is true; sometimes the data exist without the obvious policies flowing from them.

Recommendations

From these findings flow some perhaps obvious, though difficult to achieve, recommendations about how the policy processes for the health workforce might be improved.

1. Because the workforce issues of supply, demand, and professional roles are so intertwined, the policy formulation process should explicitly consider those interactions.

2. Because the roles of health professionals have implications for both demand and supply, policy should start from knowledge and broad agreement about roles, rather than from actions designed to affect the supply of professionals.

3. Policies should take into account the substitutable and complementary roles of multiple professions to make the best and most efficient use of the available workforce and to simultaneously promote cost control, quality, and access.

4. Recognizing that there are and always will be multiple, legitimate policy players, we suggest that a decision-making hierarchy be developed.

5. Ideally, policy decisions should be guided by broad societal principles and values (such as access, quality, and cost) about which there is general societal consensus and that would be applied as consistently as possible to the full range of workforce issues. In this way, policies would not conflict with and undermine each other.

6. Data collection and analysis regarding supply, demand, and need are sorely needed, as are studies on the effects of new staffing patterns and roles. Ideally, such activities should be done on the state and local levels because need and access vary by geographic area. Often good infrastructure for this study exists at the state level.

Academic health centers, through their schools of public health, health policy centers, epidemiology departments, and other venues, should be seen as a resource for data collection, analysis, and evaluation. They, in turn, should seek out opportunities to become more involved in statewide and regional planning for the health care workforce.

7. Because workforce needs are determined locally, the state or regional level should be the primary locus for health workforce policy regarding the supply, distribution, and mix of health professionals.

8. Uniform national standards and role definitions for health professionals are needed to promote consistent quality of care, more efficient use of national resources, and more equality among the professions, and to depoliticize the professional entanglements at the state level.

9. In light of the rapid changes in health care delivery and the interests of the nation, a national policy board that represents all the competing interests is needed to sort out the policymaking boundaries and other basic issues and to ensure that quality and access do not suffer in the interest of cost containment. Among the responsibilities of such a board could be the promotion of more uniform state laws regarding the roles of health professionals, coordination of data collection and analysis to justify supply policies, analysis of both the intended and unintended consequences of workforce policies, and other planning and advisory functions involving all the relevant stakeholders.

The creation of such a board would undoubtedly be controversial. Among the most sensitive issues would be determining who would decide on the composition of the board and whether the board would have policymaking authority or simply serve in an advisory capacity to Federal and state governments.

Taken together, this set of recommendations encompasses the key elements of health workforce planning and can, we believe, foster more rational workforce policy development at all levels.

Works Cited

American Association of Colleges of Nursing (AACN). 1996. 1995-1996 Enrollment and Graduations in Baccalaureate and Graduate Programs in Nursing. Washington: AACN.

Firshein, J. 1995. Health plans, teaching centers seek strategic alliances. *Medicine & Health Perspectives* (September 11).

Institute of Medicine (IOM). 1995. *Dental Education at the Crossroads: Challenges and Change.* Washington: National Academy Press.

Safriet, B. 1992. Health care dollars and regulatory sense: The role of advanced practice nursing. *Yale Journal of Regulation.* 9.